50 HIKES

IN OHIO

OTHER BOOKS IN THE 50 HIKES SERIES

50 HIKES

IN OHIO

FOURTH EDITION

Ralph Ramey

THE COUNTRYMAN PRESS

A division of W. W. Norton & Company

Independent Publishers Since 1923

To my wife, Jean, and sons, John and Jim, without whose writing, editing, computer skills, and patience I could not have completed this new edition of 50 Hikes in Ohio.

50 Hikes in Ohio at a Glance

Hike Number/Name	Town/Mountain	Distance (in miles)	Difficulty
1. Battelle Darby Creek Metro Park	West Jefferson	4.5	Low
2. Blackhand Gorge State Nature Preserve	Newark	2.5	Low
3. Clear Creek Metro Park	Rockbridge	4.5	Moderate
4. Conkle's Hollow State Nature Preserve	South Bloomingville	3.5	Low
5. Green Lawn Cemetery and Arboretum	Columbus	3.75	Low
6. Highbanks Metro Park	Worthington	4.75	Low
7. Hocking Hills State Park	South Bloomingville	6	Moderate
8. Malabar Farm State Park	Lucas	5	Moderate
9. Slate Run Metro Park	Canal Winchester	3.5	Low
10. Tar Hollow State Park and Forest	Adelphi	12	High
11. Cedar Bog Nature Preserve	Urbana	1.5	Low
12. Charleston Falls Preserve	Tipp City	2	Low
13. Goll Woods State Nature Preserve	Archbold	3	Low
14. Kelleys Island State Park	Marblehead	7.5	Low
15. Kendrick Woods State Nature Preserve	Findlay	3	Low
16. Kiser Lake State Park and State Nature Preserve	St. Paris	2.5	Low
17. Lake La Su An Wildlife Area	Pioneer	5	Low
18. Lockington Reserve	Piqua	3.5 to 6.5	Low to Moderate
19. Maumee Bay State Park	Oregon	2.25	Low

Rise (in feet)	Views	Waterfalls	Good for Families/Kids	Notes
90	√		√	Shaded stream, Prairie plants, bison, nature center
23	√		√	A trip through histrory via canoe, canal boat, train, and interurban
300	√		√	Clear creek, sandstone outcrops, wildflowers, and hemlock shade
230	√	√		Great scenery, fine flora, a hiker's must!
25			√	Birders old and young find their way here eventually
110	√		√	Prehistoric peoples and pioneers chose this setting for living, Nature center
183	√	√	√	Follow the route of the Central Ohio Glacier meltwater, Nature center, camping
260	√		√	Make a visitor's center stop before walking Bromfield's woods
110	√		√	Farm setting 100 years ago, barn, covered bridge, waterfowl
498	√		√	CCC legacy with buildings and fire tower, camping
6	√		√	Woods, wetlands, prairie plots, peat bogs, unique flora and fauna
65		√	√	High waterfall, woodland and prairie flora
10	√		√	NW Ohio's "Blackswamp" with ancient trees worth hugging
40	√		√	Rock-solid experience: lake, beach, hiking, camping, boating
20			√	Undrained "Blackswamp" in ditch and tile drained country
80			√	Quiet lake setting next to perched wetland, camping, canoeing, boating
60	√		√	Man-made multi-laked area with fishing. A keen pursuit
70			√	*A River Runs Through It* except in high water stage
5	√		√	Boardwalk, nature center, butterfly house, lake, lodge, visitor center, camping

Hike Number/Name	Town/Mountain	Distance (in miles)	Difficulty
20. Oak Openings Preserve Metro Park	Swanton	16.6	Moderate to High
21. Atwood Lake Park	Mineral City	3.75	Moderate
22. Beaver Creek State Park	East Liverpool	5	Moderate
23. Brecksville Reservation Metro Park	Brecksville	4	Low
24. Cuyahoga Valley National Park–Ledges Trail	Peninsula	2.5	Low
25. Cuyahoga Valley National Park–Ohio & Erie Canal Towpath Trail	Boston	9.5	High
26. Eagle Creek State Nature Preserve	Garrettsville	4.75	Low
27. Findley State Park	Wellington	3	Low
28. French Creek Reservation	Sheffield Lake	2.5	Low
29. Hinckley Reservation Metro Park	Hinckley	5	Moderate
30. Mohican State Park	Loudonville	3.5	Moderate
31. AEP ReCreation Land	McConnelsville	8	High
32. Cooper Hollow Wildlife Area	Oak Hill	9	High
33. Dysart Woods	Belmont	2	Low
34. Great Seal State Park	Chillicothe	4.75	Moderate
35. Lake Hope State Park	Zaleski	1 to 4.2	Low to Moderate
36. Lake Katharine State Nature Preserve	Jackson	4.5	Moderate
37. Wayne National Forest–Archers Fork Trail	New Matamoras	9.5	High
38. Wayne National Forest–Vesuvius Recreation Area, Lakeshore Trail	Oak Hill	8	Moderate
39. Wayne National Forest–Lamping Homestead Trail	Graysville	5	Moderate
40. Wayne National Forest–Wildcat Hollow Trail	Glouster	5 or 15	Moderate to High
41. Caesar Creek Gorge State Nature Preserve	Oregonia	2.5	Low

Rise (in feet)	Views	Waterfalls	Good for Families/Kids	Notes
50	√			Windblown dunes, great flora, well-marked long trail, visitor center
175			√	Resort lodge, visitor's center, lake-centered activities
140	√		√	Great woodland trail, gristmill, canal locks, camping
20			√	Nature center, rock shelter, planted prairie, Buckeye Trail
100	√	√	√	Spectacular scenery
200	√		√	Ohio and Erie Canal corridor, visitor's center
20	√		√	Ponds, woods, wetlands, and waterfowl
25	√		√	Forrested park, lake activities, camping
43	√	√	√	Waterfalls, nature center, cultural programs
304	√		√	Buzzards return in the spring, nature center, lake activities
265	√	√	√	Hemlocks, cliffs, swift water, covered bridge, camping
363	√		√	The land bounces back. Camp sites, fishing, Buckeye Trail, Visitor permit required
186	√		√	Iron furnace, wildlife, swamp, rugged country, hunting allowed
180	√		√	Huge trees to hug, no amenities
170	√		√	Statehood country, old and new trails, Scioto Valley views, camping
195	√		√	In the footsteps of early settlers, cemeteries and all
170	√		√	Gorgeous ravines, spectacular flowers, visitor's center
375	√			Long difficult trail, stone arch and shelters, deep woods, wildlife
104	√		√	Historic furnace, lake, campsites with a view, rugged country
290	√		√	Hike to site of early Ohio settlement
250	√		√	Regrowth forest, nice workout, no wildcats!
140	√		√	Splendid place to learn Ohio's spring flora

Hike Number/Name	Town/Mountain	Distance (in miles)	Difficulty
42. Clifton Gorge State Nature Preserve and John Bryan State Park	Clifton	5	Moderate
43. East Fork State Park	Bethel	14	Moderate to High
44. Edge of Appalachia Preserve–Buzzardroost Rock Trail	Lynx	4.4	Moderate
45. Edge of Appalachia Preserve–Lynx Prairie Preserve	Lynx	1.3	Moderate
46. Edge of Appalachia Preserve–The Wilderness Trail	Lynx	2.5	Moderate
47. Fort Hill Earthworks and Nature Preserve—Fort and Gorge Trails	Hillsboro	1.4 to 3.1	Moderate to High
48. Glen Helen Nature Preserve	Yellow Springs	3 to 10	Low to Moderate
49. Miami Whitewater Forest	Harrison	3.6	Moderate
50. Shawnee State Forest	West Portsmouth	6.5	High

POMPEY'S PILLAR, GLEN HELEN NATURE PRESERVE

Rise (in feet)	Views	Waterfalls	Good for Families/Kids	Notes
150	√	√	√	Florid limestone/dolomite gorge, camping, nature center
125	√		√	Woodland and meadowland trails, camping, lake-centered activities
400	√		√	A hike with a view "above it all"!
250	√		√	A pristine preserve in three seasons
235	√		√	Rare forst and plairie flora
470	√		√	Hilltop prehistoric site, incredible flora, cliffs, museum
133	√	√	√	Waterfalls, pillars, spring raptor center, visitor's center
215	√			Almost out of Ohio on stomping grounds of President Harrison, visitor's center
512	√			Rugged trail in Ohio's largest state forest, camping, lodge, cabins

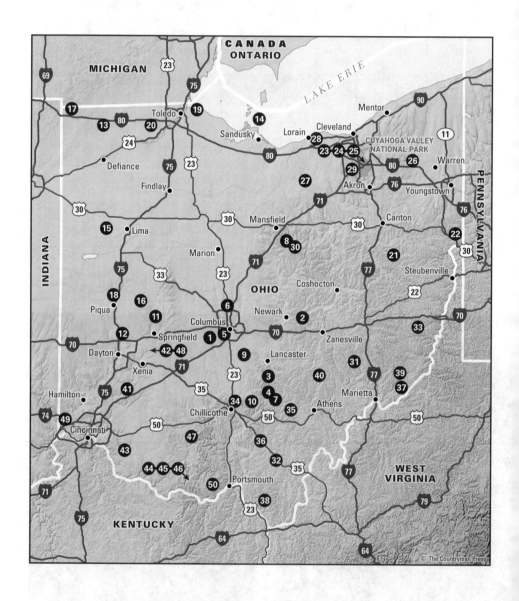

CONTENTS

IV. SOUTHEASTERN OHIO | 217

V. SOUTHWESTERN OHIO | 279

Acknowledgments

My special thanks to the personnel of the Ohio Department of Natural Resources, both in the Columbus office and in the field, for sharing their knowledge and providing maps and literature. Also, thanks to the folks at the metropolitan parks, the federal facilities, the conservancy districts, the Ohio History Connection, The Nature Conservancy, and the Buckeye Trail Association, who all readily shared their knowledge.

I will forever be indebted to the late Bill Cohn and the late Mac Henney, who, as the Scoutmasters of my youth, in Troop 3, in Bexley, started me hiking Ohio's trails; and to the Scouts and Scouters of Troop 417 in Upper Arlington, who, when I became a Scoutmaster, shared with me the joy of exploring the Ohio countryside on foot. Thanks to the staff and volunteers at Antioch University's Glen Helen Nature Preserve, where I was employed when I wrote the first edition of this book, for graciously accepting weekend program duties in my stead while I trekked Ohio's trails. Likewise, my gratitude goes to friends throughout the state who offered advice and encouragement.

A special thank you to Lisa Wood at the Ohio History Connection for her tireless service in ferreting out and formatting suitable photos for this edition from my slides archived there. Finally, I appreciate the professional and persistent guidance and prodding from Dan Crissman, senior editor, to guide this edition to completion.

MARSH MARIGOLDS IN BLOOM, CEDAR BOG NATURE PRESERVE

Introduction

Hiking has been an important part of my life since I was in grade school. It was in the fields, woods, and river valleys east of my Bexley home that I developed my love of all things natural; where I first found monarchs sipping the nectar of milkweeds; where I found trilliums, wild blue phlox, and Virginia bluebells, garter snakes, click beetles, and much more. Yearning to be able put names to these, and to the birds I found around my yard, I rode the streetcar to downtown Columbus and, at McClelland's Book Store, began buying the *Putnam Field Books of Nature*. Boy Scouts and summers at YMCA Camp Willson hardened my desire to spend my life out-of-doors as a naturalist.

The rest is the story of my life: a degree in wildlife conservation from OSU, a hitch in the army where I served as hike master for the Forth Army Chemical Defense School. Back in civilian life, I landed a job as specialist for the Ohio Division of Parks and Recreation. Since then, with a hand lens in my pocket and binoculars over my shoulder, I have explored every corner of the Buckeye State on foot and occasionally by bicycle or canoe. I spent 4 years with regional park districts, 17 years as director of Antioch College's wonderful Glen Helen Nature Preserve, and ended my working years as Chief of Ohio's Division of Natural Areas and Preserves. I would like to think that many of my readers have been among the groups that accompanied me on my explorations of the "land between the river and the lake." If you were, you know that I have a strong penchant for human history and that there wasn't a towpath that I wouldn't hike nor a mound, pioneer graveyard, iron furnace, covered bridge, barn, or dam site that I wouldn't take time to explore. I spent many happy years walking the woods and fields of the Buckeye State with groups of fellow outdoor enthusiasts.

When I began scouting trails for inclusion in my books, I became a devoted solo hiker. My only companion most trips was a microcassette tape recorder. In preparing this edition, I spent many hours listening to these old tapes. Don't get me wrong, I am not recommending hiking alone as a general practice; but I do love it. As with all of life's actions, you weigh the risks and make your own decision.

No longer able to hike, for this edition I have depended on those tapes, my memories from years of hiking trails throughout Ohio, websites, up-to-date agency literature, and long phone conversations with hiking friends and workers at the sites. There have been many changes to the trails over the more than 25 years I have been writing 50 Hikes books—some big, many small. First of all, nearly all trails, short and long, now have names. Some, like "rim" or "lakeside," are descriptive. Others, such as "red" and "blue," don't describe the trail but simply tell you what color paint blaze to look for. Effort has been made to include such name changes; however, undoubtedly some have been

A HEAD WATER STREAM, DYSART WOODS

missed or even changed very recently. In a number of cases the managing agency or the name of the area where the hike is located have changed. New bridges and steps have been built. New visitor centers and nature centers have arisen and in at least three cases, locations of parking areas have changed. But the years have enhanced the natural beauty to behold, and outdoor Ohio is as gorgeous as ever. I also believe that the stewardship of the resources by public and private organizations is better than ever.

Hiking Trails in Ohio

Though Ohio ranks 36th in size among the 50 states, it is 7th in population. A major agricultural state, it is also heavily industrialized, with most of its 11 million people living in one of six urban areas. Shortly after World War I, civic leaders recognized a need for large, publicly owned natural places for outdoor recreation near the cities. Thus was born the state's system of local park districts, one of the nation's finest. There are now metropolitan park systems in all of Ohio's urban areas and in many rural counties as well. Most operate on a philosophy that calls for retaining 80 percent of the land in a natural state. They have many miles of trails and are great places to hike. This book includes a selection of hikes in parks with especially nice natural features from several districts.

In 1918, Ohio began to systematically acquire state forest land. Though originally established to preserve (or perhaps restore) the timber resources of the state, the 173,415-acre system now includes an area designated as wilderness where no timber-management activities occur.

The federally operated Civilian Conservation Corps (CCC) of the 1930s built many recreation facilities, including trails in the state forests, and many of these still provide great pleasure to hikers. New trails, including two backpacking trails, have been added in recent years.

In 1949, a unified Ohio Department of Natural Resources (ODNR) was created, establishing for the first time a state park system. Publicly owned lands that were being used as parks or that had the potential to be developed into parks were put under the control of the ODNR, and they became the nucleus for the present 200,884-acre state park system. Nineteenth-century canal feeder lakes, scenic areas of state forests, and lakes created for fishing, flood control, stream-flow augmentation, or water supply were among the diverse areas brought into the system. As major flood-control projects were built in the 1950s and 1960s, they joined the fledgling park system. Today, virtually all of the 72 state parks have some foot trails.

A direct descendant of the earlier Division of Conservation and Natural Resources of the Department of Agriculture, the Division of Wildlife manages areas large and small across the state that provide places for the public to hunt and fish. Though paid for with fees and taxes collected from sportsmen, state wildlife areas are now being managed for overall biological diversity as well as for fish and game production. Some offer good opportunities for hiking, and two such areas have been included in this book, although hikers will want to explore these areas outside hunting season. A complete list can be obtained from the ODNR.

The newest agency within the ODNR with land holdings attractive to hikers is the Division of Natural Areas and Preserves. Since 1971 it has acquired 110 parcels totaling more than 20,000 acres

WETLANDS AT LAKE HOPE STATE PARK

in all corners of the state. These areas preserve habitat for threatened and endangered plant and animal species and are examples of the wide variety of ecosystems that made up Ohio prior to settlement. Hemlock-filled sandstone ravines, fern-lined limestone gorges, fens, bogs, mature upland woods, swamp forests, and prairie are but a few of the special places now under public ownership. Hikes in a few of these areas that have good trail systems have been included here. A directory of natural areas and preserves can be purchased

from the division. A list of natural areas and preserves—and, often, brochures describing individual areas—is available free from the same source.

The Ohio Historical Society, now called Ohio History Connection (OHC), has long been guardian of the state's treasury of old forts, battlefields, historic homes, and prehistoric mounds and earthworks. Explore the two state memorials included here, then seek out others on your own. Some include small, on-site museums (often with restricted months and hours of operation) and developed trail systems. The state tourism office will send you a free list of the properties operated by the OHC, with information about the Connection.

The federal government also plays a role in providing hiking opportunities in Ohio. The United States Army Corps of Engineers (USACE)—responsible for flood control of the nation's navigable streams—has built dozens of reservoirs in all parts of the state. These are managed by a variety of agencies, including the Corps itself, local park districts, and the Department of Natural Resources. In eastern Ohio, the Muskingum Watershed Conservancy District (MWCD), a local political subdivision of the state organized to control flooding, owns and manages the land behind the dams the Corps built there. A hike in one MWCD park is included here, but there are trails in others. Information about this agency's other facilities is available from the MWCD office.

The National Park Service (NPS) operates several areas in Ohio, including the Cuyahoga Valley National Recreation Area (CVNRA), which preserves the pastoral beauty of that northeastern Ohio River corridor. The CVNRA is already a good place to hike and new facilities continue to open. The North Country National Recreational Trail is also a responsibility of the NPS, but development of the trail is up to local jurisdictions. A section of this congressionally authorized trail uses one of the Wayne National Forest trails included in this book.

The U.S. Forest Service (USFS) has been present in Ohio in a quiet way for many decades. In recent years, it has consolidated landholdings and aggressively pursued the development of recreational trails. It offers some of the best wilderness hiking in the state in its Wayne National Forest. Four trails suitable for backpacking or day hiking in the Wayne are included here.

Two university-owned nature preserves have been included, and there are many privately owned nonprofit nature centers around the state, all with good trail systems aimed at helping visitors learn more about the natural world. Self-guided, interpretive trail guides are available for many.

The American Discovery Trail, a footpath across the nation, passes through Ohio. For the most part, it uses existing trails on federal or state land or rural roads. When hiking some of the trails in this book, you may see symbols indicating that the trail is part of this system.

The Nature Conservancy (TNC) has been active in protecting natural areas in Ohio for nearly four decades. It owns and manages more than 13,000 acres of good wild land in all parts of the state, operating some in conjunction with other agencies and organizations such as the Museum of Natural History & Science of the Cincinnati Museum Center. A call to TNC's Ohio office will get you a list of its areas and information about visiting them.

With the continuing consolidation of the country's railways, many miles of rights-of-way have been abandoned. The Rails-to-Trails Conservancy (RTTC) has worked closely with many local and state organizations to convert these corridors to recreational use. To date, nearly 250 miles of such trails have been developed in Ohio. Since all of them allow bicycles and in-line skates, they are more congested than most hikers prefer. Information about such facilities in the Buckeye State is available from the Ohio office of the RTTC.

No discussion of trails in Ohio would be complete without mention of two organizations: the Buckeye Trail Association (BTA) and the Boy Scouts of America (BSA). The BTA was established in 1959, originally to complete a trail from the Ohio River to Lake Erie. The trail now links the four corners of the state and is more than 1,200 miles in length. It crosses public and private land and, when an off-road route cannot be found, uses lesser-traveled rural roads. Maintained almost entirely by volunteers, the Buckeye Trail takes the hiker through some of Ohio's most spectacular countryside. Though there are many loop trail opportunities along its circuitous route, it is essentially a linear path. Many of the hikes in this guide are partly or totally on the Buckeye Trail.

Over the years, a number of active Boy Scout troops around the state have established officially sanctioned Scout hiking trails. Often these are 10 miles in length, with 5-mile options to allow Scouts to complete requirements for the hiking merit badge. Unfortunately, because of their locales, many of these trails are on paved roads and city streets. Two long-established and well-maintained off-road Scout hiking trails are included.

ABOUT THIS BOOK

For purposes of making order out of heart-shaped Ohio for this guide, I have divided the state into five sections, starting with Central Ohio. This is where I grew up and spent most of my working life. I include in Central Ohio the counties whose commerce flows to and from the Columbus area. Then I divided the remainder of the state into quarters. I used US Route 40 to separate north from south, and US Route 23 (from Portsmouth to Marion) and Ohio Route 4 (from Marion to Sandusky) to divide

east from west. I have selected ten hikes from each of the five areas. I hope you enjoy them all.

MAPS

The maps that accompany the trail descriptions in this book are all based on U.S. Geological Survey (USGS) 7.5-foot quadrangles, which are available for the entire state. These "topos" have all been prepared since World War II, but changes that have occurred since they were prepared mean that they don't always exactly match man-made features. You can gain insight into the early character of an area by studying the old 15-foot quadrangles, most prepared around the turn of the last century. Though these can no longer be purchased from state or federal map agencies, many can be found in the federal document repositories and map rooms of libraries, colleges, and universities. They can often be copied to carry on the trail and are a great help in identifying old trolley and railroad lines, long-gone home sites, industrial complexes, cemeteries, roads, bridges, and even entire communities. Clues to early human activity are the presence of fruit trees, plantings of ornamental bulbs and shrubs, and fallen-down buildings and dumps. Other guides for the curious hiker are the inexpensive folders sold by the OHS that show the locations of early canals, covered bridges, and iron furnaces.

Many of the managing agencies have trail maps available for their areas. These can be good supplements to the maps in this book as they sometimes reflect changes made during the current season. Nearly all can be downloaded from managing agencies' websites. They can also usually be obtained at no charge by writing or calling the appropriate agency. In some places they are available at the trailhead, but don't depend on it. Buckeye Trail section maps can be purchased from the BTA, which will send you information and a list of available maps upon request.

HIKE STATISTICS

The hiking times shown for suggested routes are based on my experiences surveying the trails, and on an average of 45 minutes of hiking time per mile. Always allow ample time for road and trail travel. In both cases, expect and be prepared for the unexpected. The vertical rise calculation is the difference between the highest and the lowest points on the trail; there will never be a single climb of that amount. The mileage figures are from measurements made on the topographic maps and/or from figures provided by the managing agencies.

EQUIPMENT

There are many good books on the subject of hiking and backpacking, so there is no point in covering that material here. In my opinion, no hiker should be on the trail without at least a copy of the map as presented in this book (if not the USGS quadrangles), a compass and knowledge of how to use it, a Swiss army knife, a thunder whistle, sunscreen and insect repellent if needed, and a pocket first-aid kit. A good pair of broken-in hiking shoes and socks of a weight and material appropriate for the season are a must. Though many people hike in sneakers, I prefer an ankle-high boot of leather or nylon. A twisted ankle can ruin a hike. Dressing in layers makes the most sense for hiking, since clothing can be adjusted for the temperature during the course of the day. A day pack or fanny pack with a poncho and a water bottle of adequate size are always in order. On most of the scouting trips for this edition, I carried a hydration pack that held 2 liters of water and had room for many small items I formerly carried in my fanny pack. The weather was in the '90s on many of the days that I was on the trail, so having sufficient water was vital to my well-being. No surface water is safe to drink anywhere in the state.

Pocket-size tree, flower, berry, animal track, and fern identification books, such as the Finder series published by the Nature Study Guild, can help you learn more about the things you'll encounter along the trail. A pocket magnifying glass and a pair of lightweight binoculars allow a closer look at plants and animals large and small. Pentax and Eagle Optics offer close-focusing glasses that allow you to observe things like butterflies, damselflies, and dragonflies as near as the tip of your toes. Most hikers now carry digital cameras that allow them to capture incredible images under all sorts of environmental conditions. Seek advice at a camera store in choosing one for your treks. A walking staff will serve as a third leg when crossing creeks or climbing hills and as a monopod (really the third leg of a tripod when added to your two legs) to stabilize a camera in the low-light situations often found on woodland trails. I walked most trails using a pair of trekking poles. Mine were from Leki, but there are several good brands on the market.

Some folks carry a cell phone. My experience has been that on most trails very far removed from an urban setting it is difficult to get a connection, but coverage is improving by leaps and bounds. My practice is to find a place where I can get service before arriving at the trail. It may be at the top of a nearby hill or somewhere that I can make visual contact with a cell tower. From there I call home to tell my wife where I'm about to begin walking, when I expect to be off the trail, and whom to call in the event that I don't report back by a specific time. I allow enough extra time to create the least apprehension on the home front, then I leave the phone in my car. Leaving an unoccupied car at a trailhead always makes me a bit nervous, but in a half century of doing so I've never had a problem. It goes without saying that precautions are in order. Put everything of value out of sight. If you have more than one car, use the older model. A steering wheel lock that is visible through the window is a good idea, and I put a sun screen in the front window to keep the inside temperature down.

ACCOMMODATIONS

Ten of the trails in this book can accommodate backpackers, and 17 hikes are located in or near public recreation areas where there are family campgrounds.

Many of these areas offer boating, fishing, swimming, and interpretive programs. Most are near other suggested hikes or close to recreational or tourism resources such as amusement parks, museums, festivals, or crafts shops. Call 1-800-BUCKEYE for information on places and events in the area you are planning to visit. Local convention and visitors bureaus (CVBs) can also supply useful information on local attractions. The official "Ohio Tour and Highway Map," available from the same source, lists the names, addresses, and phone numbers of all Ohio CVBs.

Much has been written about the desecration of outdoor recreation resources by careless users. The special places along the trails in this book deserve the best possible stewardship. Practice minimal-impact hiking and camping as described in many books and periodicals: Pack it in; haul it out. As I used to tell the Boy Scouts of Troop 417 in Columbus, "Let no one say unto your shame, all was beauty here until you came." Go home with good pictures and wonderful memories and leave behind only light footprints. Happy hiking!

LAKE KATHARINE NATURE PRESERVE

Information Resources

Acorn Naturalists
155 El Camino Real
Tustin, CA 92780-3601
1-800-422-8886
emailacorn@aol.com
www.acornnaturalists.com
Catalog of resources—books, etc.—for
    the trail and classroom

AEP ReCreation Lands
AEP Service Center
4991 N. SR 66
McConnellsville, OH 43256
(740) 945–3543 (Camping permits)
www.aep.com/environment/
    conservation/recland

American Discovery Trail
P.O. Box 20155
Washington, DC 20041-2155
1-800-663-2387 or 703-753-0149
info@discoverytrail.org
www.discoverytrail.org

Arc of Appalachia
7660 Cave Road
Bainbridge, OH 45612
(937) 365-1935
arcofappalachia.org

Buckeye Trail Association
P.O. Box 254
Worthington, OH 43085-0254
www.buckeyetrail.org
Enclose a stamped, self-addressed,
    business-size envelope

Cedar Bog Association
980 Woodburn Rd.
Urbana, OH 43078
800-860-0147
www.cedarbognp.org

Cincinnati Museum Center at Union
    Terminal
1301 Western Avenue
Cincinnati, OH 45203-1130
513-287-7000 or 1-800-733-2077
www.cincymuseum.org

Cleveland Metro Parks
4101 Fulton Parkway
Cleveland, OH 44144-1923
216-635-3200
generalinfo@clevelandmetroparks.com
www.clemetparks.com

Columbus Metro Parks
1069 West Main Street
Westerville, OH 43081-1181
614-891-0700
info@metroparks.net
www.metroparks.net

Cuyahoga Valley National Park
15610 Vaughn Road
Brecksville, OH 44141-3018
1-800-445-9667 or 216-524-1497
www.nps.gov/cuva or
    www.dayinthevalley.com

Glen Helen Association
405 Cory St.
Yellow Springs, OH 45387
(937) 769-1902
www.glenhelen.org

Glen Helen Ecology Institute
405 Corry Street
Yellow Springs, OH 45387-1843
937-769-1902
annshaw@antioch-college.edu
www.glenhelen.org

Great Parks of Hamilton County
(formerly Hamilton County Park
District)
10245 Winton Rd.
Cincinnati, OH 45231
(513) 531-7275
www.greatparks.org

Green Lawn Cemetery and Arboretum
1000 Greenlawn Ave.
Columbus, OH 43223
(614) 444-9815
www.greenlawncemetery.org

Hancock County Park District
1424 East Main Cross St.
(419) 476–7275
www.hancockparks.com

Kelleys Island Chamber of Commerce
P.O. Box 783F
Kelleys Island, OH 43438-0783
419-746-2360
www.kelleysislandchamber.com

Metropark District of the Toledo Area
5100 West Central Avenue
Toledo, OH 43615-2106
419-407-9700
www.metroparkstoledo.com

Miami County Park District
2645 East State Route 41
Troy, OH 45373-9692
937-335-6273
protectingnature@miamiparks.com
www.miamicountyparks.com

Muskingum Watershed Conservancy
District
P.O. Box 349,
1319 Third Street NW
New Philadelphia, OH 44663-0349
330-343-6647
info@mwcdlakes.com
www.mwcdlakes.com

The Nature Conservancy
Edge of Appalachia Preserve
3223 Waggoner Riffle Road
West Union, OH 45693-9784
937-544-2880
eoa@bright.net
www.nature.org/wherewework/
northamerica/states/ohio/preserves

North Country National Scenic Trail
700 Rayovac Drive, Suite 100
Madison, WI 53711-2468
608-441-5610
www.nps.gov/noco

North Country Trail Association
229 East Main Street
Lowell, MI 49331-1711
www.northcountrytrail.org

Ohio Biological Survey
P.O. Box 21370
Columbus, OH 43221-0370
614-457-8787
ohiobiosurvey@rrohio.com
www.ohiobiologicalsurvey.org
Catalog of available publications on
Ohio flora, fauna, and biodiversity

Ohio Department of Development
Division of Travel and Tourism
P.O. Box 1001
Columbus 43216-1001
1-800-BUCKEYE
www.discoverohio.com

Ohio Department of Natural
  Resources
Division of Forestry
2045 Morse Road, Building H-1
Columbus, OH 43229-6693
614-265-6694
www.ohiodnr.com/forestry

Ohio Department of Natural Resources
Division of Geological Survey
2045 Morse Road, Building C-1
Columbus, OH 43229-6693
614-265-6576
geo.survey@dnr.state.oh.us
www.ohiodnr.com/geosurvey
Catalog of maps and other resources
  on Ohio geology

Ohio Department of Natural
  Resources
Division of Natural Areas and
  Preserves
2045 Morse Road, Building F-1
Columbus, OH 43229-6693
614-265-6453
dnap@dnr.state.oh.us
www.ohiodnr.com/dnap

Ohio Department of Natural
  Resources
Division of Parks and Recreation
2045 Morse Road, Building C
Columbus, OH 43229-6693
614-265-6561
www.ohiodnr.com/parks

Ohio History Connection
800 East 17th Ave.
Columbus, OH 43211-2474
(614) 297-2300
www.ohiohistory.com

Shelby County Park District
9871 Fessler Buxton Road
Piqua, OH 45356-9602
937-773-4818
shelbycoparks@voyager.net
www.shelbycopark.org

Wayne National Forest
Ironton Ranger District
6518 State Route 93
Pedro, OH 45659-8912
740-534-6500

Wayne National Forest
Marietta Unit
27750 State Route 7
Marietta, OH 45750-5147
740-373-9055

Wayne National Forest
Supervisor's Office and Athens Ranger
  District
13700 U.S. Highway 33
Nelsonville, OH 45764-9552
740-753-0101
r9_wayne_website@fs.fed.us
www.fs.fed.us/r9/wayne

Wayne National Forest Headquarters
13000 US Highway 33
Nelsonville, OH 45764
(740) 753-0101
www.waynenationalforest.com
www.fs.usda.gov/wayne

I.

CENTRAL
OHIO

Battelle Darby Creek Metro Park

TOTAL DISTANCE: 4.5 miles (6.7 km)	
HIKING TIME: 2.5 hours	
MAXIMUM ELEVATION: 920 feet	
VERTICAL RISE: 90 feet	
MAPS: USGS 7.5' Galloway; MPDCFC Battelle Darby Creek Metro Park map	

The Darby Creeks are considered to be among the finest of Ohio's streams. The Nature Conservancy designated them and their riverine environment as one of the nation's Last Great Places. They receive virtually no industrial effluent, and very little municipal, as they flow from the Darby Plains area of Madison and Union Counties to their confluence with the Scioto River just north of Circleville. Designated as a State Scenic River for many years, in the early 1990s the (Big and Little) Darby Creeks were added to the National Scenic River System. The Big Darby is a stream of pristine beauty, and passes below the high bluffs in Battelle Darby Creek Metro Park in southwestern Franklin County.

A facility of the Metropolitan Park District of Columbus and Franklin County, this 27,495-acre metro park takes its name from the streams that flow through it and from the locally based Battelle Foundation, which provided the funds for a major expansion in the 1970s. It includes more than 11 miles of trails, public and reservable picnic areas, and a winterized meeting lodge. There is a year-round program of nature interpretation conducted by park naturalists. Large areas of restored tallgrass prairie within the park are now open to the public, adding a new dimension to a summer or fall visit to Battelle Darby.

GETTING THERE

To reach Battelle Darby Creek Metro Park, travel 14 miles west of downtown Columbus on I-70 to Exit 75. Travel 2.5 miles south on OH 142 to US 40, then 1.5 miles east (left) to Darby Creek Drive. About 1.5 miles after you leave Route 40, you will see a sign on the west (right) side of the road directing you to enter

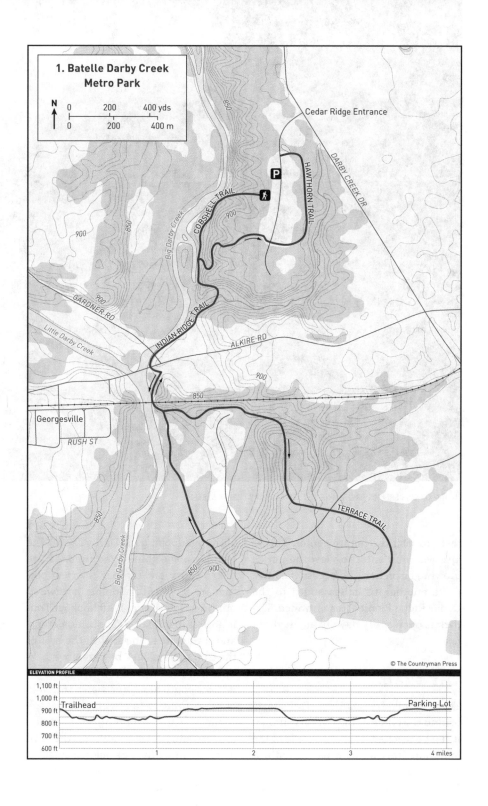

1. Batelle Darby Creek Metro Park

N
| 0 | 200 | 400 yds |
| 0 | 200 | 400 m |

Cedar Ridge Entrance

850

DARBY CREEK DR

P

HAWTHORN TRAIL

COBSHELL TRAIL

900

Big Darby Creek

900

GARDNER RD

INDIAN RIDGE TRAIL

Little Darby Creek

850

ALKIRE RD

900

850

Georgesville

RUSH ST

850

Big Darby Creek

TERRACE TRAIL

850

900

© The Countryman Press

ELEVATION PROFILE

Trailhead · · · · · · · · Parking Lot

1,100 ft
1,000 ft
900 ft
800 ft
700 ft
600 ft

1   2   3   4 miles

EIGHTY-SIX FISH SPECIES HAVE BEEN FOUND IN THE DARBY CREEK SYSTEM

there to visit the nature center. This is also where to enter to view the park's growing bison herd. To access the hike, drive another 1.5 miles south to the Cedar Ridge Picnic Area entrance. The park is open every day during daylight hours.

THE TRAIL

The 4.25-mile Indian Ridge Trail starts behind the office of the park naturalist. It can be reached from either side of the building. Starting as a paved path, it becomes a gravel trail when it leaves the picnic area, heading due west toward the bluffs overlooking Big Darby Creek. The woods on the thin-soiled uplands are oak/hickory, and those in the river bottom are a typical floodplain hardwood mixture. Note: Cedar Bluff Lookout Trail is now a separate trail. The bridge, steps, and trail connecting it with the rest of the trail system have been removed.

When Indian Trail reaches the river, it turns south along the water with lots of opportunities to stop and enjoy the scenery. After dropping to a ravine and crossing a small stream, the trail emerges onto a hillside below a meadow fast filling with young trees. It then follows the contour of the land close to the

Chapel. One hundred yards beyond the bridge a sign—"begin loop"—points left for a 2-mile round trip. Turn left and go upslope on what appears to be an old road. There is a picnic area through the trees to the right with drinking water and restrooms. Old concrete fenceposts mark the edge of the railroad right-of-way. Staying left at an intersection, the trail heads uphill to cross a bridge before swinging right, all the time in young oak/hickory woods. At one spot the present trail deserts the old road, leaving the water-filled ruts as good spawning areas for frogs and toads. Continuing through more woods, the trail finally reaches the mowed parkway. After entering a wet forest beyond the road, it crosses a number of obviously man-made ditches, early attempts to make this poorly drained land productive. Here grow pin oaks, good indicators of the acidity of the soil in this part of the park. Some stretches of the trail are covered with wood chips, others with gravel. There are a few places where the trail is soggy a good bit of the year. Not far off the trail lie the rusting bodies of a 1950s–era Chevy truck and some farm equipment. As the trail turns west parallel to a ravine, some great, old, open-grown trees can be seen.

The trail now descends toward the river bottom, where for several hundred feet it runs on a boardwalk made necessary by the constant drainage of water across the area from the hills to the east. A side trail to the right leads to play and picnic areas, but Indian Ridge Trail completes its loop back to the intersection via a riverside path.

Return to the northern part of the park over the same trail, but take the first trail to the right after entering the woods past Alkire Road. This trail goes up another set of steps to an overlook, then to

river before passing beneath two new concrete bridges.

Once south of Alkire Road, it is called Terrace Trail and passes paths to the nearby parking lot and to the canoe-launching area at stream's edge, then returns to the riverbank. A large catalpa tree at this trail junction reminds me of one that stood beside my home when I was a small child. The trail now heads south to pass under a high railroad bridge coming into Columbus from the southwest. It was once a main line but now carries a largely grain-hauling, short-line railroad that serves a grain elevator at nearby Lilly

RED DARTER AT RIVER'S EDGE

another picnic area. As it passes through a wooden fence into the picnic area, the trail is paved once more. To return to the trailhead, cross the road and follow Hawthorn Trail as it loops east, then north, through young woods and shrubland. It emerges from the woods opposite the parking lot where it began.

WHAT IS A METRO PARK?

Ohio's metropolitan parks are the result of legislation passed at the close of World War I that allowed the establishment of special districts for the conservation of the state's natural resources. The Cleveland Metropolitan Park District was the first, and it set the standard for the others that followed. Most important was the determination to keep 80 percent of the land within the park in a wild, undeveloped state; no more than 20 percent could be used for playgrounds, picnic areas, ball fields, parking lots, and reservoirs.

Park districts have been leaders in environmental interpretation and education, many building nature centers and hiring staff naturalists, even in the late 1930s. In more recent years, they have led the way in restoration management, using controlled burning, alien plant eradication, and other techniques to reestablish original ecosystems. They have also led the way in creating facilities for "under your own power" outdoor recreation opportunities, providing hundreds of miles of footpaths through field and forest, beside lakes and streams, and along old railroad and canal towpath rights-of-way.

There are metro parks within an hour's drive of virtually every Ohioan, providing places for many quick walks on short notice. For a brochure with the names and addresses of 67 park districts around the state, write to the Ohio Parks and Recreation Association, 1069 West Main Street, Westerville, OH 43081, or call 614-895-2222.

Blackhand Gorge State Nature Preserve

TOTAL DISTANCE: 2.5 miles (4 km)

HIKING TIME: 1.5 hours

MAXIMUM ELEVATION: 803 feet

VERTICAL RISE: 23 feet

MAP: USGS 7112' Tobosa ODNR Blackhand Gorge Nature Preserve map

On July 4, 1825, at a site near the present city of Heath, Ohio, New York Governor De Witt Clinton turned the first shovel of dirt to start the construction of the Ohio Canal, a massive public works project that would forever change the shape of Ohio's lakes and rivers.

To get from the Muskingum River drainage system to that of the Scioto, it was necessary to bring the canal up the valley of the Licking River to the divide, where Governor Clinton had broken ground, so that it could then descend toward Portsmouth. Just beyond the glacial border and east of Newark, the Licking River passed between vertical cliffs of sandstone. On one cliff face, Native Americans had painted a large black hand. Since it was on a well-traveled canoe route to the nearby flint ridge area, where flint was quarried for arrow and spear tips, many people believe the hand signified that the land beyond this point was neutral ground for all tribes. At any rate, the name Blackhand Gorge was applied to the area, as well as Licking Narrows.

To get canal boats through the "narrows," a dam was built downstream to create slack water. The part of the cliff where the hand was painted was blasted away to allow construction of a towpath at its base. Though the black hand was gone, early geologists had already seen it and named the particular sandstone exposed there "black hand" sandstone.

A massive, coarse-grained, well-cemented sandstone with some iron impurities and often with embedded quartz pebbles, Blackhand sandstone is a prime player in the creation of some of Ohio's most scenic areas. Laid down perhaps 325 million years ago as a delta of outwash from eroding mountains to the southeast, Blackhand sandstone is present in a band 20 to 30 miles wide

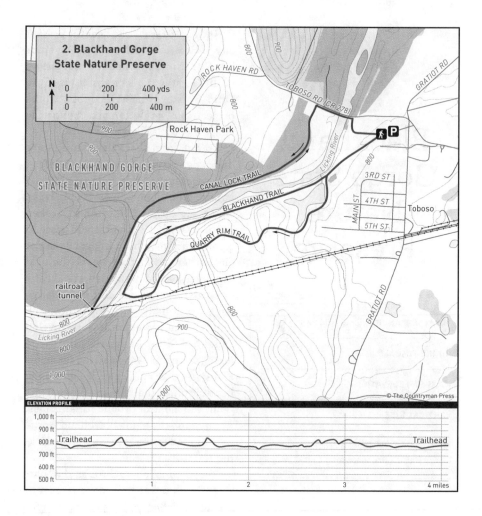

2. Blackhand Gorge State Nature Preserve

ELEVATION PROFILE

from the Ohio River to Wayne County. The rock shelters of the Hocking Hills region are all eroded from Blackhand sandstone, and Lancaster's Rising Park is of the same rock.

For nearly a century, Blackhand Gorge echoed to the "gees" and "haws" of the muleskinner as he towed canal packets north and south on the Ohio Canal. The 1913 flood brought that era to an end, but a new form of transportation had already entered the gorge. The Cen-

tral Ohio Railroad had acquired a right-of-way through the Licking Narrows and was operating a steam-powered railroad.

In the early part of the twentieth century, yet another form of transportation came to the narrows: the interurban railway. Instead of using the narrow ledge of the towpath, this electric railroad system chose to blast a tunnel through the Blackhand sandstone bedrock on the north side of the river. For nearly two decades, traction cars carried passengers from Newark to Zanesville through the Blackhand Gorge. The place was of such natural beauty that a recreation area known as Rock Haven Park was developed there, attracting revelers from far and wide. The interurban made a regular stop at Rock Haven Park and ran specials to the area on weekends and holidays.

By 1929, traction cars had given way to buses and, more important, to Henry Ford's mass-produced, inexpensive motor cars. The interurban right-of-way became a roadway, and Rock Haven Park continued as an attraction for many years. The old narrow road was finally closed to traffic when modern highways were built.

In 1975, recognizing the natural beauty of Blackhand Gorge, the state of Ohio set it aside as a state nature preserve. The boats, interurban cars, steam locomotives, and automobiles are all gone; only remnants of the artifacts remain. Nature is being allowed to take its course as the area returns to its original natural vegetation.

GETTING THERE

This 957-acre nature preserve is easily reached from the Columbus area by traveling approximately 10 miles east of Newark on OH 16, then turning right on OH 146 and, very shortly, turning right again on County Road 273. The preserve is located about 1.5 miles south on County Road 273 on the right. The driving time from downtown Columbus is about one hour. The hike at Blackhand Gorge is a good one to combine with the walk at Flint Ridge State Memorial, which is located only a few miles to the south.

THE TRAIL

A walk through Blackhand Gorge is a walk through history. The trail starts at the parking area along County Road 273 just outside the village of Toboso. This small community was moved from the low land along the Licking River to its present site when Dillon Reservoir was built downstream. Begin by looking over the pioneer log house that has been moved to the entrance for use in interpretive programs. Then walk out the driveway to the north and cross the Licking River on the left berm of County Road 273.

Since I first explored Blackhand Gorge, many changes have been made to the hiking route. I still recommend beginning by exploring the old traction line right-of-way on the north side of the Licking River. Between the trail and the river, the remains of a guard lock on the long-gone Ohio and Erie Canal can be seen. Farther down the trail you will reach the entrance to a tunnel through the hard Blackhand sandstone. Because the land above the tunnel is privately owned, this is as far as you should go. Retrace your steps, cross the bridge and start hiking west on the Blackhand bike path. Yield to the bikers but enjoy the spectacular streamside scenery. Use caution: Following a washout, the trail is undergoing repairs. The sandstone cliff face is where, before blasting for the canal towpath in the nineteenth century, there is said to have been an image of a black hand. Some have conjectured that it was a sign calling for truce between Indian tribes as they approached the sacred source of flint for tool and weapon making at Flint Ridge. We will never know.

"BLACK HAND" CLIFF IN BLACKHAND NATURE PRESERVE

When you come to a sign on the left marking the entrance to Quarry Rim Trail, begin your return trip to the parking lot and picnic area. This trail winds its way along the edge of the quarry that for many years supplied sand to the glass industry in Newark. The trail eventually skirts a buttonbush swamp to the south and east, an environment created a century ago by the construction of the old railroad grade. Returning to the bikeway, turn right and walk the few hundred yards to the trailhead.

LOG CABIN VISITOR CENTER AT BLACKHAND NATURE PRESERVE

3

Clear Creek Metro Park

TOTAL DISTANCE: 4.5 miles (7.24 km)	
HIKING TIME: 3 hours	
MAXIMUM ELEVATION: 1,100 feet	
VERTICAL RISE: 300 feet	
MAPS: USGS 7.5' Rockbridge; MPDCFC Clear Creek Metro Park brochure	

The narrow, forested valley of the small Hocking River tributary called Clear Creek has been a magnet for central Ohio naturalists for more than a century. I was first introduced to it in 1948 when I was invited to attend the annual weekend "hegira" of the Wheaton Club, a Columbus-based men's naturalist group. They gathered each year on the first weekend in June at a place called Neotoma (for the Eastern wood rat that once inhabited the rock ledges of the area), then owned by the late Edward S. Thomas, at the time curator of natural history at the museum of the Ohio Archaeological and Historical Society. The late-spring flora was at its peak and the trees were full of migrating warblers, vireos, thrushes, and the like. My eyes were opened to orchids and trilliums; lizards, salamanders, and snakes; toads and frogs; and much, much more—all new to a kid who grew up with the paved streets, storm sewers, and vacant lots of the city.

In the 65 years since, I have explored much of the Clear Creek valley in search of things that creep, crawl, sing, fly, and bloom. It is a place of splendid natural beauty where there is always a sight, sound, or smell to delight the senses and boggle the mind. In the early 1970s, I played a small part in helping fend off the threat of a Corps of Engineers dam in the valley; later, I urged public officials and private landowners to preserve as much of the valley as possible in a natural state in some sort of public or quasi-public ownership.

Scientists of many disciplines have explored the Clear Creek valley over the years. Many theses have been written and papers delivered about the natural history of the valley at conferences and meetings. The two best-known studies, published 35 years apart by the Ohio

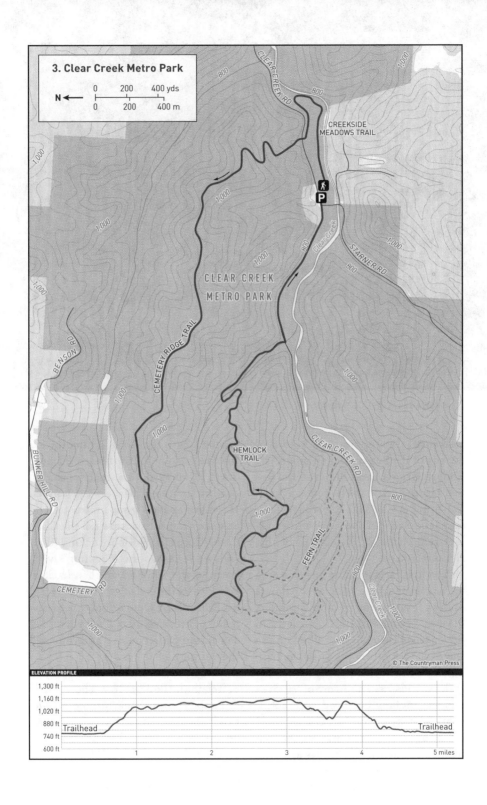

3. Clear Creek Metro Park

N ←
0   200   400 yds
0   200   400 m

CLEAR CREEK RD

CREEKSIDE
MEADOWS TRAIL

CLEAR CREEK
METRO PARK

CEMETERY RIDGE TRAIL

BENSON RD

BUNKER HILL RD

CEMETERY RD

HEMLOCK
TRAIL

FERN TRAIL

CLEAR CREEK RD

STARNER RD

Clear Creek

Clear Creek

© The Countryman Press

ELEVATION PROFILE

1,300 ft
1,160 ft
1,020 ft
880 ft — Trailhead   Trailhead
740 ft
600 ft
          1   2   3   4   5 miles

CLEAR CREEK RUNS ALONGSIDE THIS ROAD

Biological Survey, are "A Botanical Survey of the Sugar Grove Region," by Robert Griggs, and "Micro-climates and Macroclimate of Neotoma, a Small Valley in Central Ohio," by Wolfe, Wareham, and Scofield. Both are still excellent references on the nature of this treasured place.

The first Europeans to see this area were most likely the 1,900 or so soldiers under the command of Lord Dunmore, governor of the Virginia Colony, who in 1774 passed through the valley on the way west to confront the Shawnee Indians living along Scippo Creek, in the Pickaway Plains. The Army of Virginia and the Indians postured and met in council but never did battle. The Mingo chief Logan delivered his eloquent but poignant speech about his life and family under what came to be known as the "Logan Elm." An agreement was

reached between Lord Dunmore and the Shawnee chief Cornstalk. Though never formalized, this treaty is said to have brought some peace to the frontier. Dunmore and his troops retreated the way they came, back through the Clear Creek Gorge to the Hockhocking River (known today as the Hocking River), down to the Ohio River, then back to Fort Pitt. By the end of 1774 the army had been dismissed. One can only guess how many of those soldiers liked what they saw in the Ohio country and returned there to settle.

Probably no one knew the valley better than the late Tom Thomson of Columbus, whose book, *Birding in Ohio*, extols the diversity of bird life that can be seen there. What the book does not reveal is the hundreds and hundreds of birding trips Thomson made to the valley over the course of several decades to compile what must be one of the most complete records of breeding birds made for any such area anywhere. We can all hope that Thomson publishes his observations and data someday. Attesting to the special nature of this place is the fact that most central Ohio birders, when setting out to take a "big day" bird count, jump-start their list by birding the Clear Creek Road at the crack of dawn on a May morning.

Today most of the 7-mile Clear Creek valley is in public ownership, thanks to the foresight of the late Edward F. Hutchins, former board member and then-director of the Columbus Metro Parks. This large metro park now also includes within its borders the 4,769-acre Allen F. Beck State Nature Preserve. More than 800 species of vascular plants have been recorded from this preserve along with many species of animals. It is the largest preserve in the State Nature Preserve system.

Allen Beck was a Columbus industrialist who, in the early twentieth century, recognized the area's intrinsic value and began protecting it from exploitation by acquiring and nurturing it. Later, the lands he acquired were donated to the park district to become the nucleus of the preserve.

Since then, many improvements have been made to the park and the trails. What has not changed is the beauty of fern-covered sandstone, the towering hemlocks, or the call of the wood thrush, ovenbird, or pileated woodpecker. Considered by many to be the beginning of the western edge of the Appalachian foothills, the park is known to harbor more than 800 plant species and 150 species of birds, many of which are quite rare. Walk on a weekday and you may be the only person on the trail. Even on the weekend, few people visit the metro park, two counties away from the core of Columbus.

DWARF CRESTED IRIS

GETTING THERE

From I-270 on the south side of Columbus take US 33 southeast, going around Lancaster on the recently constructed bypass. About 12 miles beyond Lancaster a sign will alert you to the park, which you reach by turning west (right) onto Clear Creek Road. There is a gasoline station/convenience store there. The trailhead for the park is located at the Creekside Meadows parking lot along Clear Creek Road, about 2 miles from US 33.

THE TRAIL

Begin walking downstream on the east spur of Creekside Meadows Trail. After leaving the mowed grass area and entering an old field that glows with goldenrod in the fall, turn left at your first opportunity, heading toward the road. Across the tarmac, a sign introduces the 2.5-mile Cemetery Ridge Trail. Climbing an old driveway below a grove of spruce, the trail soon ascends the ridge and heads west on what looks like old township and gas-line service roads. The south-facing slope holds a good mixture of hardwoods, including several species of oak. An occasional non-native white pine appears along the trail, the results of human effort to reclaim abandoned hilltop farm fields of yore. Native hemlock and Virginia pine also show up among the dominant hardwoods of the ridge.

After traveling a little more than a mile, look for an old cattle barn on the left. It is quite obvious when the leaves are down, but may be well hidden during the summer. There likely was once a farmhouse nearby, but its setting is not clearly evident.

The barn sits at an elevation of 1,100 feet, about 325 feet above the elevation of the Ohio State House lawn in downtown Columbus. You still have another 20 feet or so of rise to the top of the trail. After swinging north, the trail heads west, again following the gas-line road on the side of the hill. The deeply cut route of the old rural road is quite evident uphill and to the right. To this naturalist, the crushed limestone the gas company uses to fill soft spots in the trail looks out of place in sandstone country. Incidentally, most of the gas wells in this area aren't in production, but are being used for underground storage of gas piped in from outside Ohio.

As the trail returns to the ridge, the trees are especially grand. In the head of the valley to the right is a nice stand of mountain laurel. And as I walked the trail among the large white oak and tulip poplars on an early November day, a monarch butterfly flew up from the leaves. What do you suppose its chances were of staying ahead of winter's arrival long enough to make it to the overwintering roosts of central Mexico?

After crossing a narrow saddle while still in the woods, the trail soon emerges at a meadow where it heads south and the gravel gas-well service road heads north; the juncture is marked by an arrow on a 6-by-8 post. Following alongside the thicket of abandoned pasture, the trail next crosses a nice high meadow, complete with bluebird boxes, before reaching its end. With Cemetery Ridge Trail behind, you now are traveling on the Fern Loop. A short distance farther, the trail splits. Going right will carry you around the hillside in a gentle descent toward the creek. Before reaching the road, you will have the option to turn left and ascend a valley and rejoin Hemlock Trail or to continue to the west spur of Creekside Meadows Trail.

If you turn left here, as I did, you will travel through young hardwoods and soon reach another juncture, where there is a sign introducing you to the 1.5-mile Hemlock Trail heading off to the left. This unimproved trail may leave you hanging onto the side of the hill, and at times walking it requires scrambling over blocks of sandstone. Suddenly the forest changes, and you are in the soft shade of a hundred hemlocks with the rustle of deciduous trees left behind. The trail drops off the nose of a point of land and switches back to cross the creek on a bridge that was under construction the day I walked it. With a ravine to the right, the trail

ROADSIDE VEGETATION AT CLEAR CREEK METRO PARK

follows the contour of the land, winding in and out before climbing steeply over a ridge. Quartz pebbles in the trail are evidence of a Blackhand sandstone outcropping above, and large oblong holes chiseled near the bases of less-than-healthy trees give away the presence of pileated woodpeckers, the "cocks-of-the-woods." The stump of a long-gone chestnut remains visible alongside the trail, and mountain laurel can be seen in this cool, moist environment. Passing large sandstone slump blocks and great patches of Christmas fern, the trail makes its slow descent through the hemlock forest toward the valley floor. As I reached what looked like an old logging skid or road, I stood quietly as two yearling does moved through the forest close by—one of the rewards of walking alone.

The trail crosses and re-crosses a small stream as it passes through the white oak, beech, and hemlock woods, and soon reaches a trailhead sign at Clear Creek Road. From there, it is a half mile of hoofing to the east on the west spur of Creekside Meadows Trail before you cross Starner Road and arrive at the parking lot. Among the many wonders of Clear Creek valley is Leaning Lena, the huge, leaning sandstone block that you must pass under on your way back to US 33. Because neither county in which the park lies spray the roadsides, this is an especially good place to enjoy the beauty of wildflowers as you leave the park, whether you go east toward US 33 or west toward Amanda.

PECULIAR POLLINATION

The mountain laurel (*Kalmia latifolia*) is one of America's most beautiful shrubs. (In the southern Appalachian Mountains, where rainfall may reach 200 inches annually, it can appear somewhat treelike, reaching heights of 30 to 35 feet. Natives there refer to it as ivy.) Growing native in 25 or so counties in un-glaciated southeastern Ohio, it is usually found on moist slopes, often near exposed sandstone outcrops. One look at its beautiful flower will tell you why mountain laurel is sometimes called calico bush.

According to the pioneering plant ecologist and botanist E. Lucy Braun, the pollination mechanism of the mountain laurel is particularly interesting. In fresh flowers, the anthers (the pollen-sac-bearing structures at the end of the stamen—the male organ) lie in the concavities of the corolla (the flower petals). In this position, the filaments (the slender structures of the stamen that terminate in the anthers) are under tension. When the tongue of a bee is inserted in the crevice between ovary and stamens, the tension is suddenly released, changing the position of the stamens and causing pollen to be thrown onto the head of the bee. The bee then moves on, carrying the pollen to the stigma (the female organ) of the next mountain laurel flower visited, thus effecting pollination—an out-crossing rather than a self-pollination. Braun says this trigger-release can be affected by a pin.

Conkle's Hollow State Nature Preserve

TOTAL DISTANCE: 3.5 miles (5.6 km)

HIKING TIME: 3 hours

MAXIMUM ELEVATION: 970 feet

VERTICAL RISE: 230 feet

MAPS: USGS 7.5' South Bloomingville; ODNR/DNAP Conkle's Hollow State Nature Preserve brochure

When W. J. Conkle carved his name on the face of the sandstone cliff of the hollow that now bears his name, he must have been struck by the beauty of the place. The year was 1797. The young German immigrant must have been one of the first white men to see the area, and he must have liked what he saw, for he settled there. Conkles of many generations are buried nearby, and many of his descendants still live in the region.

Conkle's Hollow truly is one of Ohio's most spectacular natural areas. A north-south oriented box canyon about 1 mile in length, it was carved into the bedrock by a small tributary of Big Pine Creek. The light gray and buff Blackhand sandstone and conglomerate bedrock were deposited in the region as a delta from mountains (no longer extant) to the south about 345 million years ago. Ranging from 80 to 250 feet thick, the rock layer is about 200 feet thick in Conkle's Hollow. Because the upper portion is structureless and well cemented, while the lower portions are cross-bedded and more easily eroded, cliffs with one or more levels of recesses or rock shelters have formed. These features dominate the scenic gorges of the Hocking Hills region and are found to a lesser extent in Licking and Fairfield Counties.

No visit to central Ohio would be complete without a walk along the trails of this very special place. To get a real feel for its grandeur and beauty, you should walk both the rim trail and the gorge trail, a hike of about 3.5 miles. Except for the 200-foot climb and descent to and from the rim trail, the hike is nearly all on flat, well-defined woodland trail. Even with stops for picture taking, the trip should not take more than 3 hours.

Though short, the Conkle's Hollow hike is very special. It is one that should be taken several times during the year

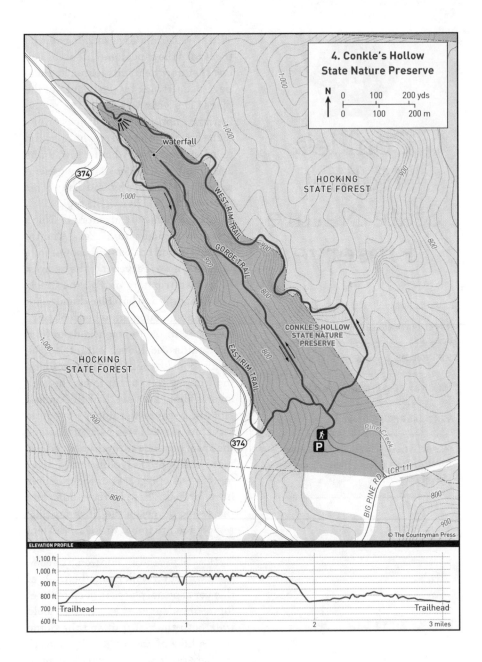

4. Conkle's Hollow
State Nature Preserve

waterfall

HOCKING
STATE FOREST

WEST RIM TRAIL

GORGE TRAIL

EAST RIM TRAIL

CONKLE'S HOLLOW
STATE NATURE
PRESERVE

HOCKING
STATE FOREST

Pine Creek

BIG PINE RD (CR 11)

© The Countryman Press

ELEVATION PROFILE

1,100 ft
1,000 ft
900 ft
800 ft
700 ft — Trailhead
600 ft

Trailhead

1   2   3 miles

to appreciate the ever-changing beauty of the area. Combined with the nearby Grandma Gatewood Trail (Hike 7), it provides a full day of hiking; by itself, it is a good walk for the end of a busy day in the city. The reward of an early-morning springtime walk might be the sound of a drumming ruffed grouse. An early-evening walk on a long summer day may serve up the haunting, flutelike call of the wood thrush or hermit thrush. Not even Michelangelo could match the

BLACKHAND SANDSTONE STANDS TALL AT CONKLE'S HOLLOW

colors of autumn, and the breathtaking beauty of a new-fallen snow is beyond description.

A number of improvements have been made to the trail system at Conkle's Hollow since I first described it in 1989 for the first edition of this book. The latest, completed in the fall of 2004, is the paving of about 2,600 feet of the gorge trail, to within 500 feet of the end of the hollow and the addition of some boardwalk and new bridges. With the earlier upgrading of the bridges near the entrance to the hollow, this allows visitors in wheelchairs to enjoy the grandeur of this special place.

GETTING THERE

Conkle's Hollow is easily reached from the Columbus area by two routes. From the east side of the city, travel US 33 southeast 10 miles past Lancaster, to where OH 374 originates as a right turn from the major highway. This scenic route takes the visitor to Hocking County, past all six of the Hocking Hills Park and Preserve sites. Follow the signs closely, as this is a twisty road in some places. Drive 13 miles on OH 374 and turn left on Big Pine Road (after passing Cantwell Cliffs and Rock House). A church adjoins a graveyard on the corner. For an interesting insight into the lives of the early residents of this area, spend a few moments reading the old headstones. The preserve entrance will appear 0.2 mile down Big Pine Road on the left. Unlike most state nature preserves, there is a restroom and some picnic tables near the entrance.

The other route from Columbus is US 23 south to Circleville, then east to South Bloomingville on OH 56. There, turn northeast on OH 664 and continue until it intersects with OH 374. Turn left and follow OH 374 about 1 mile downhill to where it intersects with Big Pine Road, then turn right to the preserve. Either way, the drive takes about an hour from the I-270 outer belt.

THE TRAIL

Upon entering the preserve, you are greeted by an uninspiring treeless area where there are picnic tables, latrines, and a pump. Unless you need those amenities, park at the next lot. There is only one way in and out of the preserve—over a footbridge across Big Pine Creek. Beyond the bridge, the trail takes a sharp turn to the left. A gathering place off the right side of the trail, about 50 feet beyond the bridge, has interpretive signs, including a large map of the area and a dispenser with brochures. Shortly after the assembly area, the trail reaches a set of wooden steps to the right. If you opt to walk the rim trail first, turn and climb these stairs. The paved main trail straight ahead will take you up the valley. Regrettably, an old arched stone bridge that once stood just up the trail from here did not survive the trail-paving project. It was built by the CCC in the 1930s. After 52 steps toward the east rim, you reach a wide landing where the first of many interpretive signs tells

about the rim trail and hillside ecology. In another 37 steps, you come to about 100 yards of steep, log-lined path through an insect- and wind-damaged pine grove. The trail then curves left as it climbs about the same distance through young hemlock and hardwood. A short scramble to the left up a clearly defined trail over bare rock brings you to the rim.

Almost immediately, the trail provides picture-postcard views of the valley, many nicely framed with scraggly pines. Upslope are more Virginia pines, oaks, mountain laurels, greenbriers, huckleberries, and reindeer lichen. Below are the tops of tuliptrees, yellow birches, hemlocks, and maples. At times the trail is on bare bedrock, and often it is near the cliff edge. Children should be kept close at hand since there are no railings. "Lucky stones"—quartz pebbles that weather their way out of the conglomerate rock—line the low spots on the trail, at some places making footing precarious. Two small footbridges span intermittent side streams set back from the gorge. In all but the driest of summers, the sound of cascading water gives away the end of the canyon. As you approach the 95-foot falls, you will see a large wooden deck at the cliff edge that affords a magnificent view. Seventy-five yards beyond, safely upstream from the edge, the stream that creates the fall is spanned by a footbridge, and signs direct you to the west rim return trail and a side trail to a nearby forest service road.

The path on the west rim lies only a short distance from the road and the forest headquarters, but it does not lose its feeling of wildness. Under towering white pines planted in 1931—legacies of the CCC and the Division of Forestry—you will likely focus on the cliffs across

AUTUMN EMERGES AT CONKLE'S HOLLOW

the valley. Canada yew grows above the edge of the cliff in this area. Wind blowing through the pines can magically obscure any intruding man-made noises. The trail takes two sweeping arcs above the rock shelters in the gorge wall. The woods above are dominated by oaks—white, red, chestnut, and scarlet—while below the forest is a blend of hemlock and hardwoods. When it's time to descend, steps in the bedrock, three steeply sloped switchbacks, and a 265-foot wooden staircase bring you to the valley floor only a few yards upstream from where you left the main trail. You have come 2.5 miles.

A left turn onto the main trail introduces a totally new environment: a deeply shaded, relict boreal forest dominated by hemlock. Although the glacial ice sheets of the Pleistocene period never reached this far (the last one stopped near Haynes, about 6 miles to the west), the colder climate of the times brought boreal forests to the gorges of the area. After the glaciers melted from Ohio, many of these plants continued to grow in the ravines and gorges because of the colder microclimates. Many songbirds breed here, and it is home to a variety of reptiles and amphibians. The northern copperhead is indigenous, but the likelihood of encountering one is very slim. The fern- and moss-covered slump blocks (chunks of bedrock that broke away from a stratum above, rolled down the slope, and eventually came to rest), the patches of Canada yew, the honeycomb-weathered sandstone, the picturesque waterfalls, and the clear-running stream all add to the ambience of the hollow. The .5 mile, 5- to 6-foot-wide paved trail crosses several small footbridges and some boardwalk before reverting to natural trail about 500 feet short of the .5-mile-long valley. Most of the year, water from the stream above slides over the rock and falls about 50 feet into a plunge pool. After drinking in the beauty of this verdant spot, head back to the parking area via the same valley trail. Note that there are different views to be had on the return trip. And, of course, remember that all things natural at Conkle's Hollow are protected as a preserve, including the critters that creep and crawl and the flowers that bloom—to be admired and enjoyed and perhaps photographed, but to be left for others to enjoy.

In the last couple of decades, a number of notable storms have left their mark on Conkle's Hollow, a reminder of nature's occasional wrath. On July 4, 1982, a small funnel cloud destroyed many of the hemlock in the front part of the valley. That area is now nicely recovered, the young growth providing good bird nesting habitat. In February 1986, a warm period followed by a heavy, wet snow wreaked havoc on the trees in the middle section of the canyon. A 20-inch snowfall on April 4, 1987, left its mark on the entire preserve, and a storm on March 4, 1988, that left the trees ice-glazed for nearly four days, took down more than 100 trees on the rim trail. Since the area is a nature preserve, none of these trees were salvaged for timber. Only trees that blocked trails were removed; the rest were left to rot slowly to provide homes for creatures large and small, their nutrients eventually returning to the soil.

Green Lawn Cemetery and Arboretum

TOTAL DISTANCE: 3.75 miles (6 km)

HIKING TIME: 2.5 hours

MAXIMUM ELEVATION: 735 feet

VERTICAL RISE: 25 feet

MAPS: USGS 7.5' Series Southwest Columbus; Green Lawn Cemetery & Arboretum map

The National Geographic Society lists Green Lawn Cemetery in its Guide to Bird Watching Sites, and birders have identified somewhere around 200 different species there. It's the location of seven state champion trees and many more outstanding specimens of native and exotic trees and shrubs. Founded in 1848, it is the final resting place for more than 145,000 of central Ohio's captains of industry and captains of war, poets and peasants, entertainers and entrepreneurs, founders and philanthropists, scientists and sorcerers—people rich and poor from all walks of life. Originally 83 acres in size, it now covers more than 360 acres. It is the state's second largest cemetery.

Located in the Columbus Lowland region of Ohio's till plain, the cemetery lies along the western margin of a Wisconsinan-age valley outwash, deposited in the southern part of what is now Columbus between 15,000 and 14,000 years ago when the last ice sheet was melting. For more than a century sand and gravel have been commercially removed from land close by, and similar material likely lies close to the surface in the nearly level eastern part of the cemetery. The base of the hill and the higher ground in the cemetery appear to contain larger-size glacial gravel—baseball- to softball-size well-rounded pieces of limestone and granitic material—along with the usual larger glacial erratics.

My introduction to the natural qualities of Green Lawn came in the spring of 1947, with the late Donald Borror's ornithology class field trips. As April turned into May, birds from warblers to warbling vireos, orioles to owls, appeared as if by magic each Saturday morning in the trees and shrubs of the cemetery. It has continued to be an oasis

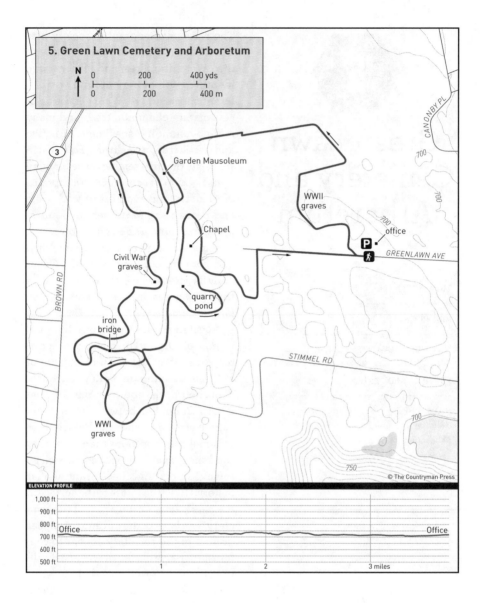

5. Green Lawn Cemetery and Arboretum

N

| 0 | 200 | 400 yds |
| 0 | 200 | 400 m |

Garden Mausoleum

WWII
graves

Chapel

office

Civil War
graves

GREENLAWN AVE

quarry
pond

iron
bridge

STIMMEL RD

WWI
graves

700

750

© The Countryman Press

BROWN RD

CANONBY PL

700

ELEVATION PROFILE

| 1,000 ft |
| 900 ft |
| 800 ft |
| 700 ft |
| 600 ft |
| 500 ft |

Office

Office

1   2   3 miles

for weary-winged travelers of the Scioto River corridor as they make their way north toward the wilderness nesting areas of Canada and beyond.

As for the trees and shrubs, I spent nearly a week roaming what is now called Green Lawn Cemetery and Arboretum in preparation for writing this chapter, and I was continually bedazzled by the size and beauty of what I saw. Early records suggest that this area was on the border between beech and maple forests and, on the higher sites, mixed-oak forest. Even with the many ornamental trees from around the world that have been planted at Green Lawn, you can still feel the presence of those early woodlands. Watch for 4-inch-by-

4-inch posts with slanted tops next to certain trees. Those with green plastic labels identify unusual specimens or unusually good specimens of usual trees. Gold labels identify state champion trees of a particular species, either native or non-native. There are too many to insert into this text or locate on the map, so keep your eye peeled for them as you explore.

Perhaps wandering through a graveyard isn't your idea of excitement, but I find it peaceful and educational. I learned a great deal about the history of Columbus and Ohio by reading the tombstones and monuments. And I would be remiss if I did not add that I was able to pay my personal, private respects to those I did not know but whom I know helped our great community grow and prosper, as well as to colleagues, mentors, acquaintances, relatives, ancestors, and many dear friends and family members who are among the 145,000 lying beneath the sod in this restful setting.

GETTING THERE

The entrance to Green Lawn is at the end of Green Lawn Avenue, 0.75 mile west of I-71. The Green Lawn Avenue exit from the interstate is the first one on I-71 south of its separation from I-70 on the west side of the Scioto River 70/71 bridge. It can also be reached by traveling south of SR 315 to where it joins I-71; again, take the first exit to the right past that point. The cemetery gates are open seven days a week, November through April 7 a.m. to 5 p.m.; May through October 7 a.m. to 7 p.m.. The management encourages passive recreation activities such as walking and birding in the cemetery. They do request that you show respect for the interred by not walking directly

on graves and, of course, by leaving no litter. If you park at places other than the lots, they ask that you keep all wheels of your vehicle on the pavement in order not to destroy the turf.

Park in the lot on the west side of the office, which is located on the right side of the road just inside the cemetery. Before you leave the lot, check the trees on each front corner of the building to get an idea of what the label posts look like. A large thornless honeylocust is on the west corner; a lovely, small, sweet bay magnolia was in full bloom on the east corner when I was there on D-Day (June 6), 2001.

There are approximately 25 miles of roads in Green Lawn Cemetery. The main thoroughfares are marked with centerlines of red, white, or yellow. The 3.75-mile walk suggested here avoids these roads as much as possible and, instead, uses the less-traveled tracks. It may, at times, seem circuitous, but it is designed to take you past special points of interest and through interesting habitat.

THE TRAIL

Walk west from the parking lot and turn right at the first opportunity. At the next corner, where the road swings west, to the left in the distance is a sign interpreting a butterfly and hummingbird garden established there by the Columbus Audubon Society in 1996. This area has been planted with native and exotic plants that are attractive to larval and adult butterflies, as well as to hummingbirds. You will recognize butterfly bushes (provided by Wild Birds Unlimited), purple coneflower, prairie gay-feather, and many other nectar-producing perennials. Notice, too, the beautiful specimen of shingle oak tree growing in an unmowed area just north and west of the garden.

West from this point you will see the mass of graves of those who fought and died in World War II. Pass the road to the right and walk to the Section 104 sign (it looks like a street sign). Turn right at that point and walk north past the anti-tank weapons and flagpole. From here you can see the skyline of downtown Columbus to the northeast. Walk clear to the road beyond the rows of government-issue grave markers, then turn right. Follow the road to the east as far as it goes. In Section 105, on the right side of the road, are the graves of veterans of more recent conflicts. Markers are of bronze and lie flush with the earth for easier maintenance. There are always more decorations on this section than on any other: the heroes leave behind widows and children. There were three freshly dug graves awaiting interments on my last visit. Yes, old men still send young men off to war.

A turn to the north affords a full view beyond the cemetery fence of Cooper Stadium, the home of the Columbus Clippers. Not many remember it as Jet Stadium when the local teams carried that name because of the city's pride in the air force jets that North American Aviation built on the eastern edge of the city. Fewer still remember it as Redbird Stadium, named for the St. Louis Cardinals triple-A farm club that played there when I was a lad. With 25 cents in my pocket, I could spend two nickels to ride the streetcar to and from the stadium. It took a dime to get in if I remembered to carry my "Knothole Gang" card. With

HUNTINGTON CHAPEL AT GREENLAWN CEMETERY

the other nickel, I could buy a Vernor's Ginger Ale or hot dog. That was 15 cents more than the Saturday matinee at the movie theater, but a whole lot more entertaining.

As you near the fence, make the sweeping turn to the left. To the right are single burial plots. Don't fret that there is little shade here. Soon you will be walking entirely beneath towering trees.

As you walk west in Section 106 on the left of the road, you will notice several tall ginkgo trees with distinctive fan-shape leaves. The species is an extant representative of the Ginkgoaceae family, which lived during the Mesozoic Area and is sometimes regarded as a living fossil. It represents an ancient line that is unlike any other living conifer. Though native to southeastern China, it has been widely planted as an ornamental in North America. It's a dioecious tree—there are both male and female plants. The females bear a yellow to orange fruit, circular or globular, with a thick fleshy layer surrounding the seed. When these fruits ripen in autumn, they fall and split, giving off a strong unpleasant odor that some call putrid, so few females are deliberately planted. In recent years ginkgo has gained notoriety as an herbal medicine. There is also an especially tall, straight sycamore to the right as you near the end of Section 106.

At the end of Section 107, beneath huge native hardwoods, stands a care-taker's building from earlier years. Jog slightly to the right here and continue walking west, against the one-way des-ignation. As you move uphill, you enter an older part of the cemetery. The road drops again and under tall maple trees continues west. After passing Sections S and Q, where the road once again begins to rise, turn left toward the Green Lawn

Garden Mausoleum. Just beyond this hillside structure is an Ohio historical marker discussing Civil War veteran Ovid Smith, who earned a Congressio-nal Medal of Honor by being with the Union outfit that captured "the Gen-eral," a Confederate locomotive. He had enlisted under an assumed name at the age of 16. He died of pneumonia at 22 and is buried here. Until 1985 he was the only one of the 24 raiders whose where-abouts were unknown by historians.

A few steps beyond this sign, if you look to the left and slightly to the rear, you can see in the distance what is considered one of the more distinctive monuments: a woman-and-child stone sculpture by the artist Rochman Reese. Now continue south with Section Q on the right. At the white-striped road, turn right, uphill, and cross the road to imme-diately turn left. On the left is a large monument honoring Lyne Starling, one of Columbus's pioneers, who with a gift of $35,000 founded the hospital that grew into The Ohio State University Medical Center.

Just beyond the Starling monument are those of the Sullivant family. Lucas Sullivant, a surveyor born in Mecklen-burg, Virginia, laid out the village of Franklinton (later incorporated into Columbus) on the west bank of the Sci-oto in 1797. It was the first settlement in the area. With statehood and the estab-lishment of Franklin County in 1803, it became the county seat and remained so until 1824, when it was moved to Colum-bus, on the opposite bank of the river. Lucas's son, William Starling Sullivant, whose monument lies to the south along with tombstones of members of his fam-ily, was a prominent Ohio botanist. The saxifrage-family plant sullivantia (*Sul-livantia sulivantii*) was named for him, by John Torrey and Asa Gray, from a specimen collected in Highland County around 1840. For interesting reading about the life and times of the younger Sullivant, see *Frontier Botany: William Starling Sullivant's Flowering-Plant Botany of Ohio (1830–1850)*, by Stuckey and Roberts. Many other members of the family were also involved in scientific pursuits.

On your hike, I suggest you now turn about and walk north, crossing the road with the white line where you will have Section C on the right. Almost immediately you will pass the dark stone monument to W. B. Hubbard and his family, all with matching headstones in rows facing one another. Hubbard was the founder and first president of the board of the nonprofit Green Lawn Cemetery Corporation. In the distance in this section is a monument with a sleeping child figure and the inscription "little Ida." Directly behind the Garden Mausoleum is a monument to Nathan Goodale, an officer in the Revolutionary War, that tells a story of migration to Ohio, then capture by Indians and death. Alongside is the monument to his brother, Dr. Lincoln Goodale, who at the time of his death was thought to be the oldest Ohioan. The Goodale name still lives in Columbus through the north-side park bearing the name.

Continuing north, you soon pass beneath the deep shade of a state champion native black maple tree. About 50 feet to the left stands the state champion Douglas fir tree, a native of the American West. At the end of Section C stands a large American beech tree and, behind it, a ginkgo with the Lazell family stones grouped around a sculpture of an open book.

As you turn west at the road, a large monument to the right commemorates prominent Worthington citizen Orange Johnson, whose home is now a museum. As you walk west, the original gate to the cemetery, off Brown Road, lies in the distance. The oldest graves in the cemetery are between here and the gate on the right side of the road. As I explored along here, I discovered gravestones with my family name that will prompt me to do more genealogy research.

In the middle of Section A, at the Deering family tombstones, turn left and head south, following the white-lined road for a short distance to where it turns left. Once there, go straight ahead on the old gravel road. At the base of the hillside to the left are several beautiful white oak trees. To the right in Section X, facing the next road to the right, is the well-known statue of five-year-old George Blount that is often adorned with a new cap and scarf during the winter months.

Walk past Sections F and H, then turn left with Section H still on your left and Section I on the right. There is striking specimen chinquapin oak on your left. Follow the curve to the right with Sections I and K on the right. As you do so you will pass the final resting place of P. W. Huntington, the founder of the bank that bears his name, and the Neil family monument. Turn right at the neoclassical statue to Gustavus Swan, with Section K on your right and N on your left. Follow the road alongside Section N, now heading south. In the woods to the left is an obelisk marking the grave of former governor Alfred Kelley, considered by many the Father of the Ohio Canal System.

Directly ahead is an unnumbered area of Civil War graves arranged in concentric circles. Walk clockwise around this section, noting that many markers on the far side are of unknown soldiers.

Many families from the border state of Kentucky pitted brothers against brothers in the tragic conflict. Behind the plot and mausoleum of the Lazarus family, the founders of the Lazarus Department Stores, stands the state champion Oriental spruce tree. This species has the shortest needles of all the spruces.

Leave the Civil War circle on the grass lane just east of the Lazarus mausoleum, heading due west. When you reach the yellow-lined road, turn left, then immediately turn right to pass between Sections 36 and 37. Walk straight on across the next intersection until Section 42 is on the right and 43 on the left. Walking with Section 43, you now approach another area flying the national emblem. Directly ahead are buried those who fought and died in the Spanish-American War. Though the 1898 conflict was short in duration, fathers, sons, and brothers from Ohio and the rest of the nation found themselves fighting on foreign soil in the heat of the tropical summer. Looking back more than 100 years later, it appears now to have been a case of rich old men sending poor young men off to war. Some paid the ultimate price for a victory that brought the country insular possessions, a newfound "world power" status, and a new hero, Rough Rider leader Teddy Roosevelt. A hundred years later we still soothe our children with stuffed toys in the shape of stylized bear cubs, named for the mustached soldier-politician who liked to hunt their real counterparts.

Turn right and march up the hill (seems appropriate) past the veterans. Look to the left to see an old iron bridge hidden in the woods. Stay to the right of the Hannah family monument and continue west, arcing to the south, with Section 58 on your left. At the first tri-angular intersection on the right there stands another state champion tree. It's easy to see how the cut-leaf European beech received its name. It turns golden-brown in autumn. Continuing on the curving road under the tall sugar maple trees alongside Section 68, you will soon be greeted by the smiling face of Captain Eddie Rickenbacker, a hometown hero, on his tombstone along the left side of the road. This World War I flying ace who grew up in Columbus went on to accomplish many things, including founding the now-defunct Eastern Airlines.

Continue walking with Section 58 on your left, turning onto the gravel road that goes to the left into a ravine between 58 and 54. Underfoot you can see the kind of large gravel that was quarried in the cemetery for use as a road base. These large pieces of round limestone and granite washed to the side of the Scioto outwash when glacial meltwater was carrying sand and gravel south from the edge of the melting Wisconsinan ice sheet. You will see the same kind of stone in the road base throughout the older part of the cemetery and even in the fill for new graves.

Pass the Smith family plot on the hillside before passing under the old bridge. Likely this ravine was made when gravel was removed for roads, at the same time creating a landscape feature. As you continue east beyond the bridge, stay right while noting the huge glacial erratics to the left. By now you have probably seen other small granite boulders throughout the cemetery, usually in the triangular intersections or on section corners.

Circle right and climb the hill headed west, keeping Section 55 on the right. A multi-trunk specimen of Scotch pine, with its orange upper branches, stands in the intersection ahead. Off to the right is the other end of the iron bridge, should you wish to explore it. Otherwise continue west to the next intersection, then make a hard left with Section 63 on your right and 64 on your left. Head toward a triangle where a group of spruce trees grow. Stay to the right of them and head due south past the old iron hand pump with Section 62 on your right and 69 on your left. Immediately ahead are the graves of those who died fighting in World War I, "the war to end all wars." Turn left past the row of birch trees guarding the final muster of our grandfathers and great-uncles, those who gave their all in the trenches of Europe. The grave markers pitch a bit, and fewer flowers adorn their resting places each Memorial and Veterans Day, as those who remember also answer the call.

Heading east now, keep Section 70 on your left while you turn to head north with Section 68 on the left. Continue north and then east alongside Section 68 until the road runs into Section 67. Henry Waldschmidt, one of the last blacksmiths in the German Village area of Columbus—and my wife's grandfather—lies buried not far from this point alongside his wife.

Turn left and head north with Section 57 on the right and Section 64 on the hillside to the left. Continue with 57 on the right, curving toward the east. Once again back at the yellow-striped road, cross it headed east so that Section 66 is on the right and M on the left. Turn left almost immediately, with Section 60 now on the right. On the left there is a stone bench carved to appear as if it was made from branches; the John Beales Brown mausoleum sits on the oppo-site corner. Here and elsewhere in the older part of the cemetery you may have noticed that some plots have curbstone steps to allow visitors to make a graceful step down from a carriage.

Near the end of Section 60, just beyond a tall stately tuliptree, you will pass the final resting place of the New Yorker writer, cartoonist, and best-selling author James Thurber, who died in 1961. It is marked with an unpretentious headstone matching those of others in his family.

The quarry or "pit"—short for gravel pit—lies ahead behind the trees and shrubbery. This has been a favorite haunt of birds and birders for as long as anyone alive today can remember. When the cemetery was established in 1848, it was the source of much of the gravel used to build the roads, but it has not been used for that purpose since the 1920s. The pond is kept filled naturally by the aquifer that exists in the outwash valley.

The "pit" is generally the first place birders go. In recent years the Columbus Audubon Society has worked with the cemetery to enhance the area as a special sanctuary for birds. There is a bulletin board there where bird sightings can be posted and several feeders that visitors frequently refill, especially during the winter months. Dr. Edward S. Thomas, the late curator of natural history for the Ohio Historical Society, often wrote of the birds he saw at Green Lawn in his weekly *Columbus Dispatch* nature columns. He and his wife are buried just north of the area.

Turn east to circle the quarry pond counterclockwise. Some of the most striking monuments, mausoleums, and tombstones are in this area. Immediately around the corner from the

CRYPTS COME IN ALL SHAPES AND SIZES

Thurber graves is the beloved statue of Emil Ambos, candy maker and amateur fisherman, sitting with pole in hand ready to make another cast. This bronze likeness is also at times enhanced with additions such as a fishing lure, scarf, sandwich, or cap.

Across the road is the Wolfe (publishing and banking) family grouping, including John W. Wolfe, with whom I played when I was young. Just east of that is the beautiful aboveground vault of Frederich Schumacher, a major contributor to Columbus Museum of Art. On the corner across the road stands yet another state champion tree—a Chinese catalpa, with fruits longer and narrower than those of our native species and leaves with "devil horns" toward their tips. When I was a youngster, I liked to pull off the corolla of the catalpa flowers from the tree alongside our home and suck sweet nectar from within. Around the pond are the plots of the Jeffrey family (mining equipment manufacturers), the Schoedinger family (funeral homes), the Vorys family (law firm and US congressman), and the Pace family, which includes a close personal friend.

Continue around the pond with Section 85 on your left, touching the red-lined road only momentarily as you do so. Amid the tall shade trees you will spot the neo-Egyptian mausoleum of well-known Columbus architect Frank Packard. Beyond that is the mausoleum of Gordon Battelle, a Columbus industrialist whose lasting legacy is the Battelle Memorial Institute, where, among other things, the "xerography" process was developed. Next is the Howald mausoleum. Like Schumacher, he was a major contributor to Columbus Art Museum. On the corner, facing the chapel, is the large C. H. Hayden mausoleum, the final place of peace for the son of financier Peter Hayden.

Moving to the right, clockwise on the road behind the chapel, you will pass the headstone of Samuel Bush, Columbus industrialist, president of Buckeye Steel Casting Company, and great-grandfather to President George Walker Bush. On the west side is a road of early-twentieth-century headstones of the Bancroft family with one military stone in the row, that of George Dallas Bancroft, Co. D, 16th Reg., Ohio Volunteer Infantry, July 9, 1869, aged 26 years, 1 month, and 27 days. The circumstances of his death remain to the imagination, but his next of kin obviously wanted him buried on their plot rather than in the military burial ground.

Back in Section 56, just before the chapel, there is group of three dawn redwood trees, the attractive deciduous conifer from China grown widely as an ornamental. As I passed behind the chapel, the carillon started to play as it does each hour during the day. Beethoven's "Ode to Joy" from his Ninth Symphony rang out, lifting my spirits as it never fails to do. As you pass behind the chapel, note the exquisite stained-glass windows. Across the road on the hillside are some very old headstones, and up the hillside near the end of Section O is the very unusual Tallmadge grotto—he was a stagecoach "king" in Lancaster, Ohio.

Follow around Section 34, momentarily along the right side of the busy white-striped road, to approach the front of the chapel. Across the road on the corner of Section 32 is the cottage-like Gay family mausoleum, with its beautiful stained-glass window visible as you approach it. Just before you reach the chapel, adjacent to a large specimen of the Ohio native cucumber tree stands the monument to Peter Sells, co-owner of Sells Brothers Circus that operated out of Columbus during my childhood.

When W. B. Hubbard addressed the cemetery board at its founding in 1848, he announced his intention "to erect a neat and permanent stone chapel" on the grounds. It was 54 years later, in 1902, when the Frank Packard–designed Roman-style marble structure was opened. Tiffany's of New York designed and installed two mosaic murals below the dome, representing "truth" and "wisdom." Peletiah Huntington gave two stained-glass windows, one picturing Peggy Thompson, first resident of Franklinton to die, and the other a representation of Isaac Dalton, who, too old to fight in the Civil War, cared for the sick and wounded of that conflict. When little use was made of it for services, it was remodeled to add burial crypts and a columbarium. Additional crypts were added later and the chapel was converted to a lounge, with chairs and sofas, and opened for meditation.

Still other improvements have been made through the years. It is open from 8:00 a.m. to 4:30 p.m. Monday through Friday and from 8:00 a.m. till noon on Saturday, but is closed Sunday and most holidays. As you exit the driveway to the south of the chapel, there is a European horse chestnut tree of about 30 inches in girth.

From the chapel driveway, cross the road, passing the Powell monument on the left, and head east between Sections

39 and 47. Beyond there, stay to the right of the spruce tree in a three-way intersection and cross the busy red-lined road to head southeast between Sections 77 on the right and 112 on the left. As you approach the Marks-Frank mausoleum you may see to the left the low pink marble Waldschmidt-Ramey monument, where Carolyn Ramey is interred and her mother and father will someday join her.

Continue counterclockwise with Section 122 on the left and you soon will be walking directly north, with recent burials on the right. At the stop sign, next to a native hackberry tree at the busy red-and-white-striped road, turn right onto the sidewalk. The hackberry is an important larval food species for a number of native butterfly species. Heading east now, notice the large round glacial stones in the base of the road. To the right in Section 120, about 60 feet from the road, stands a beautiful statue of a Native American with tomahawk in hand. The family name is Gabriel; I have no knowledge of the story behind the monument.

My wife's father was raised in a home adjacent to the present-day Schmidt's Sausage House in the German Village area. He lost his own father when he was seven. The family story is that his mother frequently walked to the cemetery via Greenlawn Avenue, two children in tow, to sit on an iron bench by their father's grave. The bench sits on our front porch, and instructions from my wife's father before he died were something along the lines of "don't spend time sitting at my grave site." Only time will tell whether the nearly 100-year-old bench will find its way back to Green Lawn Cemetery. I visited there often, mostly to walk and watch birds. I hope you will follow my footsteps.

6

Highbanks
Metro Park

TOTAL DISTANCE: 4.75 miles (7.6 km)

HIKING TIME: 2.5 hours

MAXIMUM ELEVATION: 910 feet

VERTICAL RISE: 110 feet

MAPS: USGS 7.5' Series Powell; CMPD Highbanks Metro Park brochure

The 100-foot-high shale bluffs that overlook the Olentangy River from the east in southern Delaware County have long been known as the Highbanks—hence the name of the 1,159-acre park that lies between US 23 and the river south of Powell Road. The bluffs are mostly composed of the massive formation called Ohio black shale that is also exposed at Alum Creek State Park, but the much-thinner Olentangy shale can be seen at the bottom near water level. Concretions—unique round rocks formed around an organic object in the shale—are found in the bluffs and in the rivers and streambeds below and downstream in the area. The Wisconsinan-age glacial till of the area is relatively thin, so the shale is also exposed in the deeply cut ravines that carry streams draining to the river from the east. Because central Ohio's bedrock dips to the east, not too far to the west of the Highbanks area the limestone rises closer to the surface, above the drainage system, giving rise to some solution caves.

Prehistoric Indians lived in this area, building mounds and earthworks. Later, with the arrival of settlers—many from Virginia, redeeming warrants issued in payment for service in the War of Independence—the beech forests of the uplands and much of the oak–sugar maple woodland of the ravines fell to the ax. Crop fields, pastures, meadows, and orchards took their place. Through the decades of change, many folks simply enjoyed the beauty of this part of the Olentangy River Valley, choosing to make their homes in the area.

The Columbus and Franklin County Park District acquired the land in the 1960s and opened Highbanks Park in the early 1970s. Play fields and picnic areas were laid out, shelters built, and

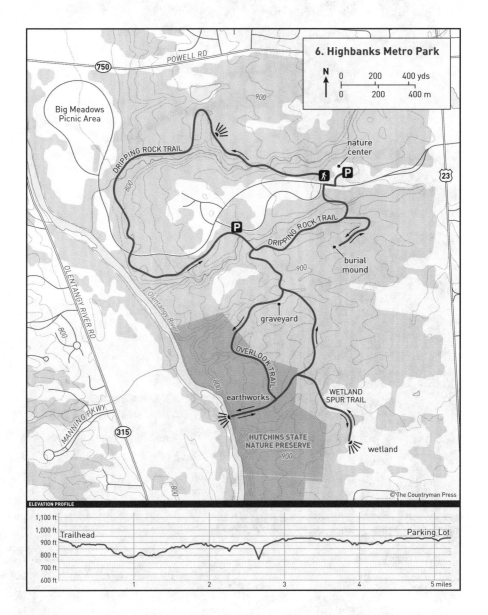

Big Meadows
Picnic Area

nature
center

DRIPPING ROCK TRAIL

DRIPPING ROCK TRAIL

burial
mound

OLENTANGY RIVER RD

Olentangy River

graveyard

OVERLOOK TRAIL

WETLAND
SPUR TRAIL

MANNING PKWY

earthworks

wetland

HUTCHINS STATE
NATURE PRESERVE
900

© The Countryman Press

ELEVATION PROFILE

1,100 ft
1,000 ft
900 ft
800 ft
700 ft
600 ft

Trailhead

Parking Lot

1   2   3   4   5 miles

an extensive trail system established, making the park a favorite of hikers. In the late 1990s, in pursuit of the park district's educational goals, a nature center was built. Programs for school groups and the general public are now offered throughout the year. A 206-acre plot within the park is registered as a national natural landmark and dedi-cated under Ohio law as the Edward F. Hutchins Nature Preserve.

GETTING THERE

To visit Highbanks Metro Park in the Columbus area, travel 2 miles north from I-270 on US 23. The park entrance is on the west side of the road.

THE OLENTANGY RIVER FLOWS BELOW THE OVERLOOK AT HIGHBANKS

THE TRAIL

The nature center is a good place to begin hiking at Highbanks. After viewing the exhibitions on the park's natural and cultural history, take Dripping Rock Trail just west of the building and turn right to head into the woods toward the river. Here the trail enters the largest and most heavily wooded ravine of the park. Notice the shale exposed in the ravine as the stream cuts its way downhill to the Olentangy. After crossing the stream, the trail climbs the north slope to eventually reach an observation deck designed for viewing wildlife such as white-tailed deer and red-tailed hawks.

From there, the trail continues a brief distance north to an educational study site, intersecting along the way with the pet/ski trail. To continue hiking, follow Dripping Rock Trail signs as the trail heads south and then west toward the Big Meadows play area. As it exits the woods, it intersects with an unpaved trail that goes to the right by the sledding area to join the paved Big Meadows Path at a parking lot to the north. Follow Dripping Rock Trail to the left along the edge of the woods; it soon meets a paved connector going right to the Big Meadows Path. Restrooms and drinking water are available at this area.

Dripping Rock Trail next reenters the woods and heads south to pass under the main park road. Then, following another ravine, the trail begins the slow 100-foot climb back to the upland area. Just after touching a parking lot and returning to the woods, Dripping Rock Trail meets Overlook Trail, off to the right. Follow this trail for a view of the shale bluffs of the Highbanks and a look at the earthworks.

Soon the trail passes through an area that is deliberately kept open as a habitat for non-woodland wildlife. Beyond, the trail forks to make a loop. Going to the right, you will soon see on your left a fenced area with tombstones within. During the development of the park, these tombstones were found together, having been moved many years earlier. Likely they were cleared from an old family graveyard to make way for agricultural activity after a farmstead had disappeared. The park district found it fitting to memorialize this pioneer family by re-erecting the stones at this new location.

Beyond this graveyard, the trail continues toward the overlook, soon entering the E. F. Hutchins Nature Preserve. Before long you will find yourself traveling alongside what looks like a ditch or trench, sometimes filled with water, on the right side of the trail. This semi-elliptical earthwork is considered to be a protective or defensive feature associated with the Late Woodland, or possibly Cole Indians. The bluff-top fortification has walls about 3 feet high; the depth of the ditch varies from 3 to 7 feet. There are three openings in the embankment. It is thought to have been built sometime between the years 800 and 1300 A.D. Overlook Trail is joined by an outgoing trail as it turns west to carry you to a wooden platform overlooking the banks of the Olentangy River.

On the return trip from the overlook, take the right fork in the trail to continue walking on the deep-woods trail. You will pass the 0.41-mile Wetland Spur Trail, leaving Overlook Trail to the right. A side trip will take you to a man-made wetland with a viewing shelter, another opportunity to see native wildlife close up.

RELOCATED HEADSTONES CELEBRATE A PIONEER CEMETERY ON PARK LAND

Back on Overlook Trail, continue through the woods to close the loop and return to the intersection with Dripping Rock Trail. After turning right onto that trail, you will find that it moves away from the congested picnic and playground area to continue into the woods. To the right, another side trail leads to Highbanks Park Mound II, also known as the Orchard Mound (there was an orchard there in the middle of the twentieth century) or the Selvey Mound (for the name of an earlier landowner). This semi-conical, 2.5-foot-high earthen burial mound is, because of its shape and upland location, presumed to be of the Adena culture.

Return to Dripping Rock Trail, turn right, and in a few moments the trail will take you to the main park road and a crosswalk to the nature center and your vehicle.

The other parks of the Columbus Metro Park System offer excellent hiking opportunities. Chestnut Ridge, Battelle Darby, and Clear Creek are described in detail in this book. Blendon Woods and Slate Run are also included elsewhere in this volume. Enjoy them all.

Hocking Hills State Park

TOTAL DISTANCE: 6 miles (9.6 km)

HIKING TIME: 5.5 hours

MAXIMUM ELEVATION: 930 feet

VERTICAL RISE: 183 feet

MAPS: USGS 7.5' South Bloomingville; ODNR Hocking Hills State Park map; BTA Old Man's Cave section map

Old Man's Cave, Cedar Falls, and Ash Cave are among the state's best-known natural features. The caves are not actually underground but are recess caves caused by differential weathering of the nearly 250-foot-thick Blackhand sandstone bedrock of Ohio's Hocking Hills region. All three of these features are spectacular and easy to reach on foot. This hike takes you past Old Man's Cave and Cedar Falls. Ash Cave is 2 miles beyond Cedar Falls, so the round trip would add 4 miles to your hike.

Many more trails crisscross the 12,311-acre Hocking State Park and forest complex. The state began purchasing land in this area in 1924 under an early state forest law. The scenic areas were transferred to the Division of Parks upon the creation of the Department of Natural Resources in 1949. Millions of Ohioans enjoy the area throughout the year.

In January 1998, a devastating flash flood through the Old Man's Cave gorge destroyed the original Civilian Conservation Corps (CCC) foot trail system, including all of the bridges. The trail was closed for more than two years, during which time the state spent more than 4 million dollars rebuilding bridges and upgrading and, in some places, rerouting the trail to make it safer and more enjoyable. The trails were reopened in May 2002. In 2003, a new park office, store, and camp office were opened at this popular park. There are Class A, primitive walk-in, and group camping facilities at the park.

I must confess to having a soft spot in my heart for the entire Hocking Hills region. I spent the better parts of the summers of 1946–48 as a counselor/naturalist at Big Brothers Camp (now Camp Oty'Akwa) a few miles up the road from

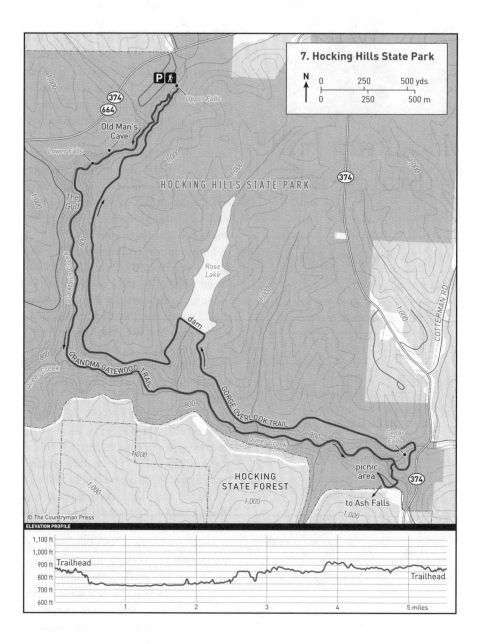

Old Man's Cave. Like a pied piper, I led walks through the forest along as many trails as I could on those hot summer afternoons and off-trail rambles and overnight campouts in places such as Saltpeter Cave, where I probably shouldn't have been. I will never forget standing on the sandbar below Cedar Falls watching my sweaty charges cooling off when the forest ranger walked up behind me, laid his hand on my shoulder and said, "Now Ralph, you know your kids are not allowed to be in there." Those naked boys were back in their

Levis in no time. After a friendly visit, we continued on our way.

Be warned, this trail traverses some quite rugged terrain, so should not be attempted by anyone less than able-bodied. On the other hand, Ash Cave, which is the turnaround point for this hike, can be reached easily on a short, level, paved walk from the Ash Cave parking lot just a few miles to the south. To reach that lot, take S.R. 374 east from OMC, following it as it turns south, passes the Cedar Falls entrance, and then tees with S.R. 56. Make a right turn there and after about a half mile, you will find the Ash Cave lot on the south (left) side of the road. The trail starts across the road from the parking area, so be cautious crossing this busy road. I will never forget a day in the spring of 1997 when I pushed my daughter, Carolyn, to Ash Cave along that trail to listen to a concert by the Lancaster Chorus. The ambience and the music were breath-taking. It was her last visit to Hocking Hills. (Note: The trail at nearby Conkle's Hollow is also handicapped accessible.)

GETTING THERE

From Columbus, the Old Man's Cave parking lot is reached by taking US 33 southeast to Logan and OH 664 south (right). Another option is to travel US 23 south to Circleville and then head east (left) on OH 56 to South Bloomingville, and from there, take OH 664 north (straight ahead where OH 56 turns right). Using either route, the trip takes about 1.5 hours.

Since the last edition of *50 Hikes in Ohio*, the Ohio Departments of Highways and Natural Resources have worked together to much improve the entryway and parking at the Old Man's Cave area of this park. The alignment of S.R. 374 has been changed by relocating it uphill from its old location. This much-needed change came about through the leadership of Mr. and Mrs. Clyde Gosnell and the Appalachian Alliance that they created to advance preservation in southern Ohio. From all of us who have many times dodged the traffic on that busy stretch of road: thanks.

THE TRAIL

Park at the east end of the Old Man's Cave lot, then take the wooden steps to OH 664 and carefully cross to the Grandma Gatewood Trail monument, where this hike begins. The plaque on the stone tells of Emma Gatewood, who was born in 1887, died in 1973, and began hiking after the age of 67. She walked the Oregon Trail once and the Appalachian Trail three times. This is a section of the Buckeye Trail and it was a favorite of hers. It was designated a National Recreation Trail and named in her honor in 1979. It was my privilege to have known her and to have walked this trail with her on several occasions.

Start hiking by crossing the stone arch bridge over Upper Falls. Turn downstream and take the steps to the valley floor. For the next mile the trail travels through what is known as "The Gulf." Through the Upper Gorge area, the trail goes beneath honeycombed cliffs. It crosses a bridge by the Devil's Bathtub before climbing stairs to the level where Old Man's Cave itself comes into view on the opposite wall. Like the floor of the Upper Gorge, this recess cave was formed when the weak middle zone of the sandstone was eroded by water and wind. The cave was named after a hermit by the name of Richard

CEDAR FALLS

Roe, a fugitive from West Virginia, who lived there after the Civil War. It measures 200 feet wide and 50 feet high and is 75 feet deep. Roe is said to be buried beneath rocks in the cave.

The trail begins by passing down a staircase inside a tunnel as it reaches the area above the Lower Falls. If you wish to explore the cave, cross the bridge and ascend a set of steps through another tunnel. Otherwise, look downstream toward the Sphinx Head profile, carved by natural forces, visible on the face of the cliff.

From there, the trail climbs to the base of the cliff before descending past the lip of the Lower Falls. It hugs the cliff before dropping down a set of steps to the valley floor below the falls. The Lower Falls is the only scenic feature in the Hocking Hills area that is located in the lower zone of the Blackhand sandstone. At the plunge pool level below the 60-foot waterfall, a deep recess cave has been carved in the underlying Cuyahoga shale, a soft stratum named for the spectacular exposures along the Cuyahoga River in the Cleveland area.

The trail now travels downstream on the left bank of Old Man's Creek. In many places it is unstable because of the seepage of water caused by the relatively impervious underlying shale, and there are places where you need to climb over rocks and roots. Large hemlock and yellow birch trees dominate the forest canopy, and Canada yew is seen in patches on the hillside, all relicts of an earlier, colder period. A 160-foot hemlock just across the small stone bridge near the Lower Falls holds a state record.

At the confluence of Old Man's

Creek and Queer Creek, the trail turns upstream toward Cedar Falls. The streams are not visible here but a sign points the way, and when the trail moves close to the creek you'll see that you are now going upstream. It follows the left bank, first traveling along the stream, then rising to the base of the sandstone cliffs and returning to the stream several times. In some places, the trail is difficult to navigate.

An old Native American trail that connected the Kanawha River region of West Virginia with Ohio's Chillicothe area is said to have run through here. Settlers knew it as the "Road to Hell" because prisoners were marched through during the frontier wars. Huge sycamores line the stream, and in some places the ever-present hemlock give a cathedral-like feeling to the woods. The trail crosses a 25-foot bridge as it approaches a beautiful waterfall, then moves through a football field-size grove of hemlocks before scrambling up and over lots of rock rubble. Next, it passes a lovely cave, then through another rocky area. For many years the trail continued ahead on the left bank, along a narrow ledge between the cliff base and the stream, as it approached Cedar Falls—it could be very dangerous in the winter when icicles sometimes broke loose from above and fell onto the trail, making the footing very slick. Now it crosses Queer Creek on a new steel bridge, at the other end of which there is a split in the trail. To go directly to the picnic area and parking lot, take the right fork. To visit the falls, follow the trail up the steps to the left. Another new bridge carries the trail back across the stream, bypassing the dangerous area. The sound of the falls can be heard from here, and there are several benches where you can rest and enjoy the beautiful scenery. Yet another bridge carries the trail to a sandbar area in front of the falls. It should be noted that there are no cedar trees at Cedar Falls. Early settlers didn't know their trees well, mistaking the hemlock trees for cedar.

After enjoying the view of the falls, take the stone steps that parallel a side stream and follow the narrow trail through the rocks to where it again branches. To go to the picnic area, restrooms, and parking lot, follow the trail straight ahead across the creek and up the ravine to the roadway, then turn right. There is a shelter house and drinking water there, so it is a good place for a lunch break. During the state's annual Hocking Hills Winter Hike, cornbread and bean soup are served here. If you want to hike on to Ash Cave and back, follow the blue blazes around the end of the loop road, then turn right up a forest service road. This will add about 4 miles, and probably 3.5 hours, to your hike, so before embarking on this additional leg of the trail make certain you have enough time to make it back to your vehicle before dark. The trail itself is well marked and easy to follow. It was first laid out and cleared in January 1967 by my colleague Norville Hall of the Division of Parks and Recreation and me, with the help of a group of Boy Scouts from Troop 417 of Upper Arlington.

To continue the loop hike back to Old Man's Cave, return to the split in the trail just above Cedar Falls, where a wooden staircase carries the trail above the falls. Just beyond the top of the steps the trail leaves the woods, crossing a grassy area above the falls. This is the beginning of Gorge Overlook Trail that will take you back to Upper Falls at Old Man's Cave,

UPPER FALLS AT THE OLD MAN'S CAVE AREA OF HOCKING HILLS

where you began walking. The trail is marked at frequent intervals by short 6-by-6 posts with red bands near the top.

Signs at the top of the falls warn of the danger of leaving the trail in this cliff-top area. A kiosk tells the story of the early years of Cedar Falls, when water from Queer Creek powered a mill there. Two old millstones lie nearby. An ornamental steel bridge carries the trail across the creek, to where steps carry it up to a seating area under a grove of pines. A sign indicates that Gorge Overlook Trail is 2.5 miles long.

Heading west from the seating area, the trail quickly returns to a hemlock environment. It rises and falls as it crosses streams that during part of the year provide water for the falls along the Queer Creek gorge to the right. Soon the trail begins a steeper climb and arcs to the right. In the distance a clearing can be seen, and in short order the trail arrives at the east end of the

dam that creates 17-acre Rose Lake, the main source of the park's drinking water. A purple bench beckons the hiker to rest at the dam. The red-banded posts indicate that the trail crosses the lake on its earthen dam and a short bridge over its spillway. At the north end of the lake, there is a wildlife observation blind built in 2006 by the Friends of Hocking Hills. Reach it via the fishermen's footpath along either lakeshore or a trail that runs from the main park campground.

At the west end of the dam there is another bench. Gorge Overlook Trail turns 90 degrees to the left, as indicated by red-banded posts seen down the trail. The trail quickly drops off to cross a ravine, and then begins rising to a ridge. Soon it makes a right turn to travel north along the rim of "The Gulf." An overlook offers a view of the forest below and a resting spot for the hiker. A sign indicates that it is 1.5 miles back to Cedar Falls and a mile to the visitor

ASH CAVE HAS UNUSUAL ACOUSTICAL PROPERTIES

center at Old Man's Cave. From here, the trail follows the gorge 20 or 30 feet back from the rim. It crosses a trail that leads left to Rose Lake before reaching the A-frame bridge that connects to the visitor center. A sign points straight ahead to Upper Falls, and it's not far before the trail passes the head of the steps that lead below the falls and the old CCC stone bridge comes into view. The hike ends as you pass the Grandma Gatewood monument and return to your vehicle at the parking lot across OH 664.

I began hiking this wondrous area in 1946, when I spent the first of three summers as a counselor/naturalist at a nearby youth camp. It has been my good fortune to be able to return to Hocking Hills many times in the intervening years. It was a special privilege to walk them again in 2006, as I prepared to update this book. There is no other place like it in the state of Ohio.

Ohio's State Trail

The Buckeye Trail is a long-distance hiking trail built and maintained by volunteers. The germ of the idea for the trail came from the late Merrill C. Gilfillan of Mount Gilead, who wrote an article for the magazine section of the *Columbus Dispatch*'s Sunday edition suggesting that Ohio ought to have a hiking trail like the Appalachian Trail, connecting Lake Erie and the Ohio River. Out of the article was born the Buckeye Trail Association, with the mission of providing such a trail—from Mentor Headlands, east of Cleveland, to Eden Park in Cincinnati. Now expanded to connect the four corners of the state in a continuous loop, the 1,200-plus-mile trail passes through 40 of Ohio's 88 counties; no population center is more than 75 miles from it.

The Buckeye Trail Association was incorporated in 1959 and began to develop the trail almost immediately. In 1967, the Ohio General Assembly designated the Buckeye Trail Ohio's official hiking trail. The famous septuagenarian and Appalachian Trail-hiker Emma "Grandma" Gatewood of Thurman, Ohio, was among the early volunteers who blazed out the Buckeye Trail in southeastern Ohio's hill country. Wherever possible, the trail keeps to public lands and is off-road. Where there is no other way to make connections, lightly traveled township roads are used, but the work to get the entire trail into the woods and fields or onto abandoned canal towpaths or railroad rights-of-way never ceases. Information about the trail, the trail-building organization, and available section maps and guides can be obtained by writing to the Buckeye Trail Association, P.O. Box 254, Worthington, OH 43085.

Malabar Farm State Park

TOTAL DISTANCE: 5 miles (8 km)

HIKING TIME: 4 hours

MAXIMUM ELEVATION: 1,320 feet

VERTICAL RISE: 260 feet

MAP: USGS 7.5' Lucas; ODNR Malabar Farm State Park map

Author and screenwriter Louis Bromfield, born in Mansfield, Ohio, established Malabar Farm in Richland County's Pleasant Valley in 1939. He built the country farmhouse mansion to be the Bromfield family homestead. Its design reflects the native Western Reserve architecture, even to the point that it was built to look as if it had been added to wing by wing over successive generations. He immediately began applying newly developed conservation farming practices to the worn-out land. During the following two decades, Malabar gained a worldwide reputation as a model farm, largely through the books Bromfield wrote about his experiences. In the 32-room "Big House" he built, he entertained his rich and famous Hollywood friends.

After Bromfield's death, in 1956, the farm was managed by an organization he helped form—Friends of the Land—and, after the organization folded, by the Malabar Farm Foundation. In 1972, the Foundation transferred ownership to the state of Ohio, to be operated jointly by the Departments of Agriculture and Natural Resources. In 1976, it became Malabar Farm State Park. Although the large amount of livestock from the Bromfield era is gone, the buildings and crop fields have been restored. Tours of the mansion, preserved much as Bromfield left it in 1956, have been an attraction throughout the years. The original dairy barn, which had been built in 1890 from the timbers of an old mill that dated back to 1830, burned to the ground in 1993. It was rebuilt with a barn-raising on Labor Day weekend in 1994, using mostly volunteers from the Timber Framers Guild of North America. People who have read Bromfield's books come to visit from around the world. Tours, special events, and interpretive programs help visitors

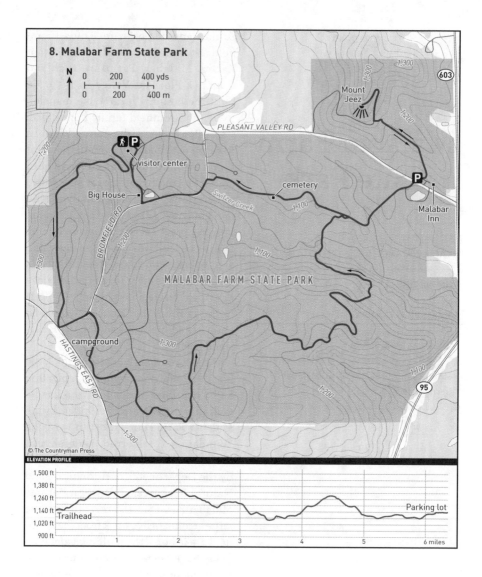

8. Malabar Farm State Park

N
0   200   400 yds
0   200   400 m

PLEASANT VALLEY RD

visitor center

Big House

BROMFIELD RD

Switzer Creek

cemetery

Mount Jeez

Malabar Inn

MALABAR FARM STATE PARK

campground

HASTINGS EAST RD

© The Countryman Press

ELEVATION PROFILE

1,500 ft
1,380 ft
1,260 ft
1,140 ft
1,020 ft
900 ft

Trailhead

Parking lot

1   2   3   4   5   6 miles

understand how much Bromfield cared for the land. A new visitor center opened in late summer 2006. The interior of the Big House has recently been restored to resemble as nearly as possible how it did when the Bromfields were in residence. It is once again open to visitors, but with shorter hours than in the past. Check in at the visitor center for further information.

GETTING THERE

To reach Malabar Farm from central or northeastern Ohio, travel I-71 to US 30, go east 3 miles to OH 603, and turn left (south). Travel 10.5 miles to Pleasant Valley Road on the right. Signs will direct the way west to Bromfield Road and the park entrance. Immediately after turning south into the park, make

THE VISITOR CENTER AT MALABAR FARM STATE PARK

a right turn into the driveway for the visitor center and walkways to the Big House and barns.

THE TRAIL

The trail entrance is uphill from the visitor center, across a hayfield. You will see a sign that reads "timber management trail." Usually there is a mowed path around the edge of the field, but be aware of the bees moving to and from their hives to the left at the edge of the woods. The alfalfa and red clover in the field are very attractive to butterflies in late summer, following the second hay harvest, when they rebloom.

Enter the woods on the interpretive trail. Take time to learn the basics of small woodlot management from the signs spaced along both sides of the trail in the maple/oak/walnut woods. Within 100 feet of entering the woods, the trail is joined by an old farm-lane-turned-

horse-trail coming in from the right. The path climbs the hill past sandstone outcrops on the left before opening onto another meadow. Remains of an early gas well can be seen on the left as you leave the woods. Turn right and follow the edge of the meadow, passing an old concrete stock tank, then make a sharp left turn onto a gas-line right-of-way. Sometimes deer can be seen grazing in the meadow downhill in the distance. Follow the right-of-way until it reaches the paved road. Pay no attention to the arrows on posts in this field.

This is another good area for summer butterfly watching, since they like to "hilltop" and the nectar on the alfalfa and clover. Just before reaching the end of the field, duck right and then left through the woods on the right side of the field. A sign there admonishes cross-country skiers to preserve their skis by removing them before going onto the road. Turn left (downhill) on the road, which at this point changes its name from East Hastings to Bromfield. About 150 yards downhill a driveway on the right leads you past an old barn, complete with a chewing tobacco ad, then uphill into the horsemen's campground. There are toilets located on the right, and drinking water is available from a Baker-type pump behind Campsite 5. The well is deep, so a strong arm is required to get it flowing.

To get off the pavement and back onto natural turf, continue up the road to the far end of the turnaround, where there is a sign reading PLEASANT VALLEY BRIDLE TRAIL—HORSE AND FOOTPATH ONLY. Avoid the poison ivy as you enter, then turn left. The trail gently rises to cross a gas-line right-of-way, then passes a neatly manicured picnic area. It soon swings right through another overgrown fencerow, then turns sharply left along the edge of an old field that is being invaded by trees and shrubs. After 200 yards, it emerges onto a gravel road that is still in use. Turn left. About 100 feet up the road on the right stands a double-trunk American chestnut tree that has somehow avoided the chestnut blight and actually reached nut-bearing age.

About 200 feet down the road another PLEASANT VALLEY BRIDLE TRAIL sign on the left indicates that it's time to reenter the woods. Here is a fine wood, with mature oaks and hickories dominating. After a short climb to the crest of the hill the trail descends the ridge to the right, and then crosses a bromegrass field and an old tree-lined lane before emerging into a field planted with hundreds of young sugar maples. To protect the trees from being browsed by deer, half of them have a short piece of snow fence wrapped around them, and the other half have been planted in pieces of plastic farm tile. The latter do not seem to be surviving well.

At the end of the maple planting, the trail turns left to enter the woods, then turns immediately right on an old lane. Still moving downhill, it eventually enters tall timber, then makes a sharp left turn down a talus slope below outcrops of sandstone. It then turns west along a bench, through rich mature woods with fern-covered slump blocks. At a 4-by-4 post, it makes a sharp right turn to drop to the stream valley below. An upstream/downstream glance will usually locate a reasonably dry crossing in all but the wettest of seasons. After the crossing you will hike 100 yards or so through riverine forest with aliens such as multiflora rose present. The trail then emerges onto the farm road alongside crop fields.

A turn to the right on the lane leads you to the famous Malabar Inn, which is still serving meals. The 165-year-old structure adjoins a vegetable stand that covers the equally well-known Niman Spring. Most of the water for the farm and garden operation comes from this spring. The barn across the road from the inn was chosen as the official Richland County Bicentennial Barn in 2003, and as such has the logo designed from the celebration painted on its east side. To the west of the inn parking lot a trail leads you up the hill that Bromfield dubbed Mt. Jeez, from the words he first uttered upon seeing the view. There is a great view of the entire spread from the overlook at the top of the meadow. Although the temptation is to descend the hill on the vehicle road and then head for the park entrance via Pleasant Valley Road, the better path is to follow the trail back past the inn to where it emerged from the woods. A quarter-mile beyond the trail entrance sign is the country cemetery where Bromfield, his wife, Mary Appleton, and other family members are buried. Pause and reflect on the words of William Cullen Bryant, a nineteenth-century poet, on Bromfield's gravestone: "to him who in love of nature holds communion with her visible forms, she speaks a various language."

Continue on the farm road, past the garden, to a barnyard area where there are restrooms and drinking water. Out the drive and across the road lies the farmstead where Bromfield lived while the Big House was being built. He didn't like the place, and referred to it as the "mail-order house." It is now a hostel operated by Hostelling International USA. Turn left and go downhill on the road, passing a pond and crossing the bridge. To your right is a good view of the main house and farmyard in the distance. Cows in the foreground complete the rural scene. On your left is the Doris Duke Woods, saved from logging after Bromfield's death by a contribution from the tobacco heiress, which was used to buy back timber rights Bromfield had sold during hard times. The park's sugar camp and buildings used for programs and meetings lie at the end of the road that enters the woods on the left, just beyond the bridge. The unsprayed roadside on the left between there and the Big House drive provides a show of native wildflowers in late summer.

Turn into the driveway on the right and walk by the Big House, then through the barnyard to return to the visitor center and parking lot. This 5-mile loop is a good hike to combine with the Mohican State Park hike. There is a 15-site primitive campground at Malabar, and more modern facilities are available at nearby Mohican State Park and Pleasant Mill Lake Park.

WRITER LOUIS BROMFIELD MADE HIS HOME HERE IN THE COUNTRYSIDE HE LOVED

Slate Run
Metro Park

TOTAL DISTANCE: 3.5 miles (5.6 km)

HIKING TIME: 2.5 hours

MAXIMUM ELEVATION: 910 feet

VERTICAL RISE: 110 feet

MAPS: USGS 7.5′ Series Canal Winchester;
CMPD Slate Run Metro Park brochure

From the northwestern edge of Slate Run Metro Park you can see the skyline of downtown Columbus, 16 miles away as the crow flies. Slate Run sits on the western slope of an end moraine that straddles the Pickaway-Fairfield County line, an area where elevations can reach more than 1,100 feet (for reference, the elevation at the corner of Broad and High Streets in the capital city is 768 feet). In between lies the Wisconsinan-age till plain called the Columbus Lowland, a relatively flat area with land that slopes and streams that drain toward the Scioto River basin.

The 1,708 acres of the Slate Run Metro Park mirror most of Ohio's variety of habitats, from wooded, rolling hills with deep ravines and steep ridges to former farm fields, and include a 14-acre lake and a 156-acre wetlands where sandhill cranes have been seen nesting. Northern bobwhite quail, once common in this area of Ohio, have recently been reintroduced to the park. The original oak–sugar maple forest was cleared in the 1880s, and much of the land has been farmed since. Lower Mississippian shale lies beneath the drift and is exposed in the deeply cut ravine, giving the name Slate Run to the creek.

The park district began acquiring the land for the metro park in the 1960s, planting trees and removing the land from agricultural use in preparation for a future park. A special feature is the Slate Run Living Historical Farm, located on the south edge of the park. For the hiker, there are more than 5 miles of trails, including some on which leashed pets are permitted.

The main park entrance to the park is on S.R. 674, 5 miles south of Canal Winchester. Once inside the park and past the ranger station, turn left where the

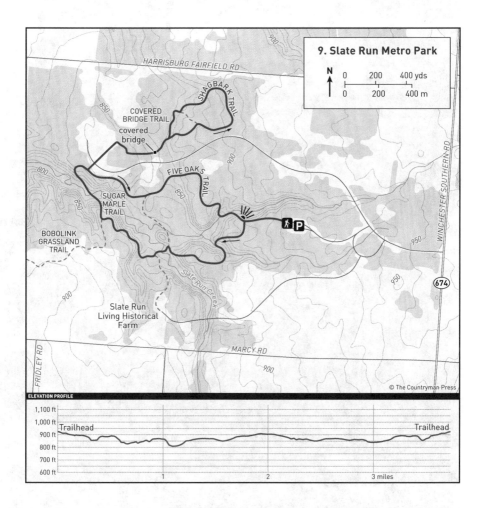

9. Slate Run Metro Park

sign points to a program area. Park at the far end of the lot to begin hiking on Five Oaks Trail. The trailhead is to the right, and the trail goes nearly due west from there. There are restrooms to the left of the trailhead.

GETTING THERE

To reach Slate Run from I-270, on the south side of Columbus, take US 3 east (toward Lancaster) to the Canal Winchester SR 674 exit. Turn right onto Gender Road/SR 674, and follow SR 674 south to the park entrance. From US 23, south of Columbus, travel east on Duvall Road to Winchester Road, south on Winchester Road to Marcy Road, east on Marcy Road to SR 674, then north on SR 674 to the park entrance.

THE TRAIL

The trail begins on tarmac that transitions to a fine gravel surface and is wide enough to hike side by side. A split-rail reminder fence soon runs out. There is a sign with a map and some reminders about trail behavior. The winding trail begins dropping gently downhill,

AUTUMN ON THE TRAIL IN SLATE RUN METRO PARK

paralleling a deep ravine to the right. Soon there is an overlook on the right where you can look through the tall trees toward the creek below. This is the junction where Five Oaks Trail splits to make a loop.

To continue hiking, turn left, heading downhill. Here there is a combination of pine plantings and native hardwoods. An occasional pileated woodpecker gives you the feeling that you are far away from urban environments. Follow the trail as it continues to drop into the narrow valley that the creek has cut through the deep glacial drift of this moraine country. The pieces of shale you will see in the creek bed are the best indicator that, not far to the east, the stream cut through the bedrock. Slate and shale are closely related and often confused—I suspect that the presence of the shale explains why the stream was named Slate Run.

A wood thrush was singing during my own visit, on the early-May morning when I crossed the bridge and began the steep climb beyond. There are some lovely large trees in the open woods along this section of the trail. Dropping once again, the trail reaches what is now called the family tree. This is a multi-trunk red oak, doubtless the result of sprouts growing from the stump of a tree that had been very much alive when cut. This particular specimen was formerly referred to as the Five-Oak Tree—hence the name of the trail. A nicely done interpretive sign tells of the interrelationship of this tree with other living things of the forest.

The trail next drops to the spot where a side trail branches off to the left and connects to Sugar Maple Trail. Five Oaks Trail, which you have been following, continues ahead and to the right

to return to the parking lot, making a 1.5-mile loop. For a longer hike, make the sharp left turn, travel downhill, and cross the main stem of Slate Run to meet Sugar Maple Trail, which runs from the Living Historical Farm parking lot to the Buzzard's Roost picnic area lot. Many of the violets that bloom beneath the sycamores in this stream bottom are white, not violet, but the wild blue phlox are blue and beautiful.

If you wish to explore the farm or use the restroom located there, turn left. Otherwise, turn right onto Sugar Maple Trail as it heads generally northwest, rising and falling among the many gullies leading to Slate Run. The patch of papaw trees in this area was absolutely loaded with deep mahogany-colored flowers when I passed by. Since I seldom see fruit in that kind of abundance, I wonder if pollination doesn't occur, and if not, why not; or perhaps lots of fruit does occur and I am too late to see it. There is also a grove of sassafras along the trail here. Since sassafras has been suggested as a possible cancer-causing substance, I no longer snag the young shoots and chew on the bark of their roots.

After traveling a considerable distance in the valley of Slate Run, Sugar Maple Trail climbs the left bank onto higher ground to move among young hardwoods. The creek valley is still visible downhill to the right. Just before the trail makes a sharp turn to the north, a new trail, Bobolink Grassland Trail, exits to the left. This is a 3-mile-long unimproved trail that leads through mostly old field habitat and connects with the 1.5-mile Kokomo Wetland Trail in its newly established wetland. The latter includes a sizable length of boardwalk. This trail can also be accessed from a parking lot near the northwestern corner of the park off Circleville-Winchester Road. Sections of this natural-surface trail can be a bit muddy during rainy periods.

After passing a bench and trash barrel at a wide spot, the trail descends to again cross Slate Run. My May morning walk turned up a box turtle using the same trail as me; several first-hatch zebra swallowtail butterflies also found it easier flying along the trail corridor. A gentle climb leads to the edge of the woods and a road crossing, then to the Buzzard's Roost picnic area parking lot. At the far end of the lot are restrooms, and drinking water is available nearby. There is a barnlike shelter and trails leading to Buzzard's Roost Lake.

In the metro parks, trails in mowed areas are generally paved, even though they are continuations of nature trails. South and east of the barn/shelter parking lot is a trail intersection where signs point two directions to nature trails. To begin a return trip to where you started, head south back across the road to reenter the woods. To add nearly a mile more to your hike, turn left onto Covered Bridge Trail. Be aware that hikers may have leashed pets on this trail, as well as on Shagbark Trail to which it connects. Canada geese also frequently use this trail. Need I say more?

The improved Covered Bridge Trail leads through old fields and thickets to a 56-foot-long covered bridge of multiple kingpost design that was relocated to the park in 1998. Originally known as Blackburn Covered Bridge, it was moved from Muskingum County by Arthur Wesner to a site on private property in Franklin County, where it was thereafter referred to as the Wesner Bridge. Though at least two Ohio counties have erected some new covered bridges in recent years, the bridges of the nineteenth century have continued to fall victim to age and road relocations, so the wooden structures are not frequently seen. A number of the old-timers have been preserved by groups of concerned citizens. I count myself among that group, and once moved a covered bridge 25 miles to a new, protected site in Glen Helen.

Beyond the bridge the trail climbs through young open woods, and soon comes to another junction. Here the unimproved Shagbark Trail exits right to travel in a counterclockwise fashion for 0.5 mile, rising and falling through young woods and thickets. For most of the trek, you may wonder why the trail is called Shagbark. Suddenly you will be in the midst of a nearly pure stand of this species, and you will understand. Shagbark Trail will shortly wind its way back to Covered Bridge Trail. There is a lot of multiflora rose in the understory of this trail.

Go straight ahead to follow Covered Bridge Trail in a counterclockwise manner as its return leg carries you back onto blacktop of the nature trail intersection you encountered earlier. On a bright day, this is a good area in which to observe many of the smaller species of butterflies in the open field. When you reach the trail intersection, turn left onto Sugar Maple Trail and head across the road to begin your inbound trek.

At a "T" in the trail just inside the woods, turn left (the opposite direction from which you earlier came) to follow a trail that will connect with the return leg of Five Oaks Trail. The trail runs 15 to 25 feet inside the woods as it heads in a generally eastern direction. There are many glacial erratics lying on the hillside just inside the woods, dragged from more level land more than a cen-

THE BLACKBURN BRIDGE AT SLATE RUN METRO PARK

tury ago to make room for crops. Buckeye trees grow along this trail, and the maroon-blossomed sessile trillium or toad trillium blooms on the forest floor.

When you reach the intersection with the Five Oaks Trail, turn left and continue on the high ground parallel to the park road. The trail emerges from the woods to a managed grassland area where, in the warm months, you will be entertained by butterflies and dragonflies. As I left this opening to reenter the woods, a flock of crows was making a terrible racket overhead. I suspect they were badgering an owl somewhere nearby, but I was not able to spot it.

A switchback carries the trail to the creek and a crossing. Turning upstream, the trail follows the stream for a short distance. For the first time on the trail, bedrock is visible in the creek bed. Look also for shale in the bottom of the streambed and blocks of sandstone on the hillside. From here the trail makes a long, steady climb through a beautiful forested ravine to close the loop at the overlook. It's but a short walk to the parking lot and the end of a good day's hike.

While you are in the area, take time to visit the Slate Run Living Historical Farm. A brochure giving information about the farm and its hours of operation can be picked up outside the ranger station.

Tar Hollow State Park and Forest

TOTAL DISTANCE: 12 miles (19.3 km)

HIKING TIME: 9 hours

MAXIMUM ELEVATION: 1,200 feet

VERTICAL RISE: 498 feet

MAPS: USGS 7.5' Hallsville; USGS 7.5' Laurelville; USGS 7.5' Londonderry; USGS 7.5' Ratcliffburg; BSA Troop 195, Columbus, Logan Trail map; ODNR Tar Hollow State Forest map

Tar Hollow State Park and Forest lies just east of where the glaciers ended, close to the intersection of Ross, Hocking, and Vinton Counties. When the area is approached from Circleville, the unglaciated hill country can be seen to the east from the high hills of the Marcy Moraine, located about 5 miles east of that city. The country is rugged, with little mineral wealth. Its major asset at the time of settlement was the trees that covered the steep hillsides and narrow ravines. Now dominated by several species of oak, the forest once included the American chestnut and, on some of the ridges, pitch pine. When cleared, the rocky hillsides of the area could barely grow enough crops for a family to eke out a living; so, in addition to cutting the virgin hardwood for lumber, the settlers distilled pine tar from the pitch pine. Pine tar was commonplace on the shelves of many nineteenth-century households. It was blended with grain alcohol and used as an expectorant or, in viscous form, as an antiseptic salve. It also served as a sticky lubricant for the wooden gears and axles of early implements. With the advent of petroleum distillates, pine tar fell into disuse. What probably was never a very lucrative enterprise died out, leaving only another place-name derived from a long-gone economic activity—in this case, Tar Hollow.

Tar Hollow is a special place for wildlife. Turkey, deer, squirrel, ruffed grouse, pileated woodpeckers, and many species of woodland songbirds abound. So do reptiles and amphibians like the northern copperhead and timber rattlesnake, though in far fewer numbers. The rattlesnake is listed as a threatened species in Ohio, and the capture of reptiles is tightly regulated.

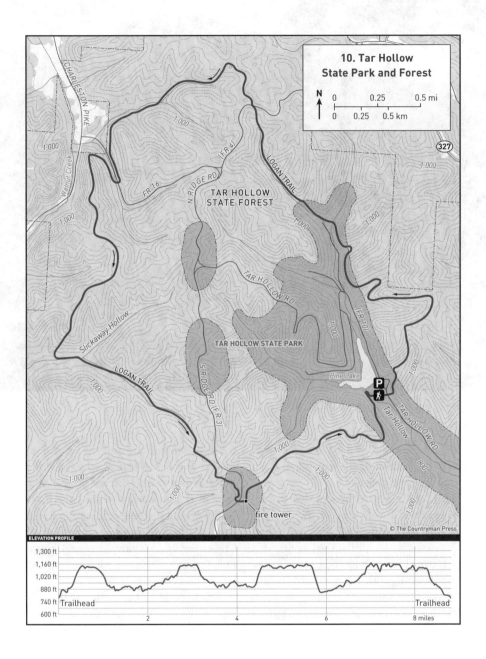

10. Tar Hollow State Park and Forest

N

| 0 | 0.25 | 0.5 mi |

| 0 | 0.25 | 0.5 km |

TAR HOLLOW STATE FOREST

TAR HOLLOW STATE PARK

Pine Lake

fire tower

© The Countryman Press

ELEVATION PROFILE

1,300 ft
1,160 ft
1,020 ft
880 ft
740 ft — Trailhead — Trailhead
600 ft

2   4   6   8 miles

Since all but the park area is open to public hunting, it is a good idea to avoid coming here during the week of deer gun season in the fall and turkey season in the spring. The wildflowers are beautiful during the last week of April and the first two weeks of May, and dozens of species of mushrooms can be seen after a rain during the warm months of the year. Tar Hollow should be visited often, for despite its size and nearness to the well-known Hocking Hills parks,

PINE LAKE IS LOCATED NEAR THE CENTER OF THE PARK

it is not very heavily used. It deserves to be better known, for its excellent Logan Trail if nothing else.

Unlike many other parks in the region, the hiking trail at Tar Hollow owes its existence to neither the Civilian Conservation Corps nor the Department of Natural Resources. The present-day Logan Trail, with its north and south loops originating out of the park area, was developed and is maintained by Boy Scout Troop 195 of Columbus. Named for the famous Mingo Indian chief, the trail was originally opened in 1958, using park and forest roads. It was not popular with Scout units, however, who felt that in a state forest hiking should be on woodland trails. Completely shut down and carefully rerouted off roads and into the woods, the trail was reopened

in 1965. I walked the trail with my Scout troop shortly after its reopening. Like most Scout trails, a badge is available to Scouts who complete the hike. Unit leaders can get more information about the trail from Roy Case, Logan Trail Treasurer, 643 Weyant Avenue, Columbus, OH 43213. He can also be reached by phone at 614-235-7026.

The hike described here utilizes only part of the 21-mile Logan Trail. Because of the rugged nature of the terrain, hiking the entire trail requires 15 or 16 hours of daylight. Logan Trail is well marked. There are directional and checkpoint number signs on 4-by-4 posts at road crossings and other appropriate points along the trail. In some places, red metal arrows are nailed to trees. The trail is blazed with red paint, but because it is designed to be walked in one direction only, it is blazed only in the direction of the numbered checkpoints. If you do not see a blaze after 100 feet or so, retrace your steps, as you probably missed a turn. Although road crossings are minimal on this neatly laid-out trail, the few that there are allow you to walk shorter loop hikes utilizing the forest roads. The trail is divided into named segments between numbered checkpoints. Most of the checkpoints are at road crossings.

There is no potable water along the route, so you must carry a supply for the full trip or cache some at one or more of the checkpoints. Camping is not allowed along the trail. A primitive, pack-in camping area known as Camp N. A. Dulen, located about a mile south off the south loop of the trail, is available for Scout units only. Troops or posts planning to camp there must inform the park ranger in advance. There is a drive-in campground in the park for family camping by the general public and there is an area designated for group camping that can be used by groups before or after hiking the trail. Backpackers are permitted to camp at the fire tower area, but they must self-register at a registration box on the porch of the general store, beyond the beach at the upper end of Pine Lake, before heading up the trail. This is a matter of safety, so rangers can locate you in the event of an emergency.

GETTING THERE

Tar Hollow is reached from the Columbus area by traveling south on US 23 to Circleville, then east 28 miles on OH 56 to OH 180. There, turn right (south) and travel 0.7 mile to Adelphi. Next turn left (south) onto OH 327 and travel 7.5 miles to the park entrance on the right side of the road. The trip takes about 1.5 hours. From Cincinnati, take either US 50 or I-71 and US 35 to Chillicothe, then continue on US 50 east for 12 miles to OH 327 at Londonderry. Take OH 327 left (north) 9 miles to the park entrance. From the Dayton area, use US 35 to reach Chillicothe and the route described for Cincinnati travelers. The parking lot for the trailhead is located about 1.2 miles inside the park, below the dam at Pine Lake. A sign at the entrance to the lot reads LOGAN TRAIL PARKING.

THE TRAIL

All the signs along this trail have been made and put in place by volunteer Boy Scouts and/or their adult supervisors. They are not uniform in design and, since they are almost always near park or forest roads, they are subject to frequent vandalism. Paint blazes on trees are the most dependable indications that you're on the correct path. Do not attempt to walk this trail in reverse, as the signs and blazes have been placed to be read in one direction only. When you reach a road crossing, the continuation of the trail is not always directly across. It may be a short way to the right or left and may not always be easily recognized. A sign may be missing. Be certain that you are on a red-blazed trail before proceeding.

The north loop trail begins on a hard-to-recognize gravel service road at the southeast corner of the parking lot, opposite the launching area near the dam. The trailhead sign is frequently missing, but the red blazes on the trees to the right of the trail indicate the correct route. Just before the trail reaches a small creek, there is supposed to be a "Checkpoint 1" sign pointing left to the beginning of the Hocking Segment of the trail. It too is sometimes missing. In any event, the trail goes to the left before the service road reaches the creek crossing. Follow the trail uphill along the stream bank to the park road. There is a large paint blaze on a tree here instead of a checkpoint sign, and perhaps a small sign across the road indicating the continuation of the trail. After crossing the road the trail climbs sharply, making a left turn through the pines. Beyond the pines, the trail enters deciduous forest as it drops to a creek crossing. It then turns right up a ravine, climbing smartly up the left slope. This difficult climb of more than 300 feet to the ridge is a little more than a half-mile long and is the only such climb on the north loop.

After following the ridge for a short distance, the trail turns left to descend on the spine of a side ridge. A red arrow points right as the trail drops off the ridge and into a hollow, where it makes a T with another trail. The red-blazed trail turns right, then left across a stream, and then left again as it begins climbing the hillside. Partway up the slope, it levels off to follow the hillside above the group camping area driveway. At a fork in the trail it goes right, through the woods above the campground. There are a number of "wild" trails in this area, so it is especially important to keep the red blazes in view. Turn right at another T, this one with a trail coming in from the campground. Eventually the trail drops to the valley to cross a small stream. The number on the tree here identifies Checkpoint 2, almost 2.5 miles from the start of the trail.

The 1.75-mile Ross Segment begins by climbing out of the streambed. The trail leads up the slope a short distance

before turning to the left to round the end of a ridge. There are more wild trails here, used by hikers starting from the campground. Shortly thereafter the trail drops to the bottomland, goes straight across the streambed, and then heads uphill. It eventually levels off, turns left, and curves to the right around the end of a ridge. Drop into a small ravine to cross a side stream and cross another stream after 125 feet. At yet another T, the trail turns right to start a moderate climb up the valley to a crossing with the blacktopped North Ridge Road. The trail reenters the woods across the road, slightly to the left. Look for a red arrow on a tree along the road. The post announcing Checkpoint 3, where the trail turns to the right, is about 30 feet off the road.

Going north, the trail occasionally uses an old wagon road as it passes through a brushy area and then to the right of a small pond. Reentering the oak/hickory woods, the trail leaves the old road and turns left to begin dropping into a hollow. Now headed in a westerly direction, it moves back and forth across the streambed and up and down the valley wall, then passes near an old dump and a rotting slab pile. Moving down the hollow, the trail hugs the left slope as it approaches Swamp Hill Road (Forest Road 16). Instead of dropping to the road as it draws near, the trail swings left around the hillside to parallel it for several hundred yards before turning toward it. This approach detours around a private inholding at the mouth of the valley and keeps the trail on state-owned land. Just across the road is Checkpoint 4, the end of the 2-mile Sawmill Segment.

After reentering the woods the trail crosses a stream, then turns right, angling up the slope on what may have once been a logging skid. At an easily missed left turn, the trail begins its steepest climb. Fortunately the climb is short, and at the top there is a nice grassy spot under oaks that begs to be used for a respite. For the next mile the trail follows the ridge in heavy forest. Turning left onto an old wagon road, it shortly reaches Checkpoint 5, where a sign on the right indicates a right turn off the old road. Here ends the appropriately named American Discovery Trail in Ohio.

If you are out and about on the trails of southern Ohio, sooner or later you will see a slightly bulging triangular sign that reads American Discovery Trail (ADT) on a tree or a post. From the beginning, the creation of the ADT was a grassroots volunteer venture. Like the Appalachian Trail, the Buckeye Trail, and the North Country Trail, the ADT is a work in progress. Its 6,300-mile route passes through 15 states. It leads to 14 national parks and 16 national forests and visits more than 10,000 sites of historic, cultural, and natural significance along the way. Tens of thousands of hours of volunteer effort have gone into its making and thousands of folks "under their own steam" have traveled sections of it in forest, field, mountain, and prairie across this great land. The 11 sections of the ADT in Ohio cover 511 miles, using public lands and private lands with landowner permission. It enters the state from the east at Belpre. Before leaving Ohio for good, a southern route crosses into Kentucky via the Roebling suspension bridge to allow exploration of sites in the Covington area. It returns to Ohio by way of historic Anderson Ferry then, after passing the tomb of President William Henry Harrison, enters Indiana on State Line Road near Elizabethtown. The Northern

THE TAR HOLLOW FIRE TOWER DATES BACK TO THE 1930S

Midwest Route of the ADT also enters Indiana on State Line Road, but east of Richmond. On its last gasps in the Buckeye State it passes Miami Whitewater Forest, through Governor Bebb Park, Hueston Woods Park and State Nature Preserve, and Indian Creek Preserve, and finally passes through Harshman Covered Bridge.

On the hikes detailed in this book, you will tread on the ADT on Archers Fork Trail in Wayne National Forest, on Gorge Trail at Fort Hill State Memorial, at Tar Hollow State Forest, at Hocking State Park, at Shawnee State Forest, at East Fork State Park, and at Hueston Woods State Nature Preserve, and you will come within a whisker of it at Wildcat Hollow in Wayne National Forest. When you see the red, white, and blue symbol on a post or tree, it's an invitation to explore beyond state boundaries on a trail like the one on which you're walking, built by hands like yours and mine for those of us who want to explore the world using what my mother used to call "shank's mares."

1.5-mile Lookout Segment. Next, the trail follows the ridge for another half mile, then begins a steep descent into Slickaway Hollow. There are no switchbacks, and the trail is badly eroded and quite rocky in places. Exercise due caution. At the bottom, the trail crosses the hollow and turns to the left to begin a mile-long climb back to the ridge. The trail crosses the stream several times and occasionally follows an old road that once came all the way up the valley. Toward the head of the ravine the trail follows a fork to the left, hugging the right slope as it makes a gentle climb. Just before reaching the ridgetop and the edge of the woods, the trail hits a T. A sign identifies Checkpoint 6, the junction with the south loop, which goes to

the left. The trail to the right goes to the fire tower area and the continuation of your north loop hike. A sign also points to the right to Camp Dulen for Scouts, who are now about 5 miles away from that overnight spot. The Slickaway Hollow Segment has covered 2.3 miles.

At this point you have traveled a total of 10 miles. Another 2 miles of easy hiking will complete the north loop. Proceed via a left turn at the T. The trail climbs a few feet and emerges from the woods onto a logging road, which takes you to the left. Shortly up the logging road, your red-blazed trail exits to the right. It goes down and around the head of a ravine, then up and over a knob. After you cross a stream, you climb steeply and then more gently to the Brush Ridge fire tower. The trail emerges onto Forest Road 3 (South Ridge Road) directly west of the tower. This is the end of the half-mile Fire Tower Segment. The "official" trail through the woods can be bypassed for a slightly longer but less rugged route by continuing on the logging road until you reach pavement, where you turn right to the fire tower.

Checkpoint 10, the beginning of the Pine Lake Segment, is identified by a red-topped 4-by-4 post, but this sign is also subject to frequent vandalism and is not always there. Normally it is to the left of the fire tower across the gravel loop driveway. There is also a forestry sign there identifying the trail as the 1.5-mile Brush Ridge Trail, which Logan Trail uses to complete the loop.

Here Logan Trail comes close to the Buckeye Trail (BT), which passes through the area both on and off the road. The entrance to a short, white-blazed connecting trail is marked by a round post near where the fire tower loop drive meets the paved road just south of the tower. About 100 feet beyond the post, there is a T where the blue-blazed BT leaves Logan Trail, going to the right. Brush Ridge Trail is easy and well defined. It is probably the most used trail in the park/forest, since many day-hikers travel it between Pine Lake and the fire tower.

After rounding the head of a ravine, the trail rises gently to go out to a ridge. After a quarter mile, there is a fork. The left branch goes to a resident camping facility in the valley below. Logan Trail continues on the right fork, where it rises gently to and over a 1,100-foot knob before starting its descent to the Pine Lake area. Near the bottom of the hill it crosses a power-line right-of-way. Beyond is the Brush Ridge Trail sign pointing back the way you came. The red-blazed Logan Trail continues along the hillside past another sign that announces the end of the trail and the location of the trailhead. Yet another sign points back up the trail to the BT, 1.5 miles away. The trail comes out at dam level and follows the spillway downhill, which it then crosses on a bridge. The trail ends on the mowed lawn of the earthen dam within sight of the Pine Lake parking lot, where there are restrooms and a shelter house. Having sampled the rugged terrain and the solitude of Tar Hollow State Park and Forest on the north loop of Logan Trail, you will want to plan for another day, perhaps in another season, in the area. Before you leave, pick up a state park and/or state forest brochure with information about other hiking and camping facilities in this 18,026-acre public area.

II.

NORTHWESTERN OHIO

Cedar Bog Nature Preserve

TOTAL DISTANCE: 1.5 miles (2.4 km)

HIKING TIME: 1 hour

MAXIMUM ELEVATION: 980 feet

VERTICAL RISE: 6 feet

MAPS: USGS 7.5' Urbana West; Cedar Bog Nature Preserve map

ACCESSIBILITY: Accessible elevated boardwalk with edge-boards.

FACILITIES: Education Center with accessible restrooms

Many people refer to Cedar Bog as Ohio's premier nature preserve. With its combination of fen and white cedar stand, it is, in the true sense of the word, unique. Simply in sheer numbers of state-listed plant and animal species that have been found there, with additional ones still being reported, it stands head and shoulders above other preserves. Published studies of the area date back to at least 1912, and it has been officially protected since 1942 when the state purchased 100 acres for management by the Ohio (Archaeological and) Historical Society.

Once accessed with great difficulty, the quicksand-like wetland of this preserve can now be easily viewed from a 1.25-mile-long boardwalk. Expanded from the original purchase to 1,450 acres with the help of The Nature Conservancy and the Division of Natural Areas and Preserves of the Ohio Department of Natural Resources, the preserve is now managed by the nonprofit Cedar Bog Association, which also operates the Cedar Bog Education Center that opened in spring 2009. The preserve includes swamp forest, marl meadow, sedge meadow, arborvitae forest, and original and reestablished prairie. Studies of the hydrogeology, microclimate, ecology, and flora and fauna of the preserve continue.

The wetlands in this preserve are all that remain of a wet prairie-fen complex that at one time covered at least 600 acres along Cedar Run in the broad valley of the Mad River north of Springfield. Early in the twentieth century, the Mad River was channelized for most of its length, with ditches dug and tiles installed, in an attempt to make the entire valley tillable. A major tributary of the Great Miami River, the

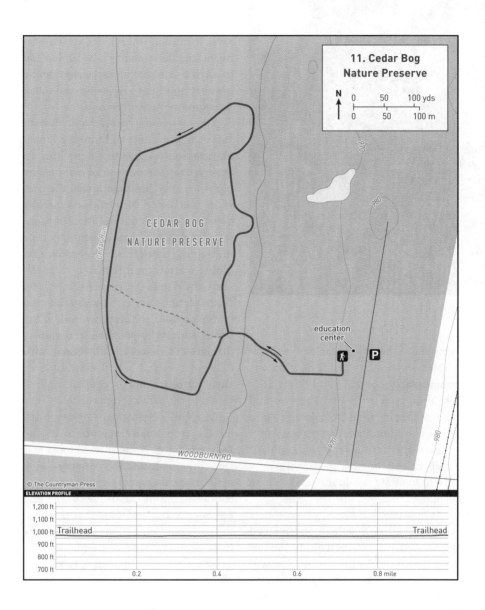

11. Cedar Bog Nature Preserve

N

0   50   100 yds

0   50   100 m

CEDAR BOG
NATURE PRESERVE

Cedar Run

education
center

P

WOODBURN RD

© The Countryman Press

ELEVATION PROFILE

1,200 ft
1,100 ft
1,000 ft Trailhead   Trailhead
900 ft
800 ft
700 ft

0.2   0.4   0.6   0.8 mile

Mad runs clear and cold because of the many springs that make up its source. Attempts to drain the headwaters of the spring-fed Cedar Run never met with success.

The field notes from my first visit to the area on October 16, 1948, refer to it as Dallas Arbor Vitae Swamp. When first acquired by the historical society, it was called Cedar Swamp. A decade or so later, the name was changed to Cedar Bog. Though retaining that name, the unforested part of the preserve that is wetland is now generally referred to as a fen because of the alkalinity of its water.

A walk through Cedar Bog with an interpretive naturalist is an exciting adventure into Ohio's past. It is a

SPIDER WEB IN THE BOG MEADOW

remnant of the vegetation of a postglacial time when the climate of Ohio was considerably cooler. In addition, it is a refugium for other plant and animal species that invaded Ohio during a dry, warm period that occurred as recently as three or four thousand years ago. All species blend together in a special mixture of habitats not found in the same combination anywhere else.

Your guide will explain to you how scientists believe that this area remained unchanged while eastern hardwood forest covered most of the state. You will learn about the source of the alkaline water upon which the fens "float" and perhaps have an opportunity to jump up and down on the social surface to see the ground shaking. The special relationships between plants and animals and the fen and forest environment will come alive when you observe them firsthand. Five of the six species of swallowtail butterfly found in Ohio frequently can be seen in the preserve, for the food plants of all five grow there. The spotted turtle with its yellow spotted back shell survives in the bog, where it can avoid freezing during the winter by hibernating and can avoid overheating in the summer by aestivating in the even-tempered muck under the surface of the bog.

Like so many preserves, threats from the pressures of human endeavors are no stranger to Cedar Bog. In the 1970s, construction of a four-lane highway to be built alongside the preserve was halted. Nevertheless, nearby development, reconsideration of highway construction, overutilization of the underlying aquifer, air pollution, and global warming all threaten to accelerate the demise of this special place. Alien plants such as honeysuckle and garlic mustard, which grow well on the fertile soil of the preserve, threaten to displace the native flora. Raccoons, with no predators and only disease to keep their numbers under control, pose a threat to the rare spotted turtles.

The Ohio Historical Society, with advice from many scientists in the Department of Natural Resources and from others around the country, apply modern management techniques to try to prevent the loss of special species and habitat. Cedar seedlings that threaten to shade out populations of rare plants have been removed by hand, and programs have been instituted to control plant and animal pests.

GETTING THERE

Located in Urbana Township, near the southern boundary of Champaign County, Cedar Bog Nature Preserve is easily reached by traveling 1 mile west on Woodburn Road from US 68, approximately 4.5 miles south of the center of Urbana.

Except for members of the Ohio Historical Society or the Cedar Bog Association, there is a small admission charge. The area is open to visitation only during public tours, which are conducted by a naturalist at 1:00 and 3:00 p.m. on Saturdays and Sundays, from April through September. Group tours between 9:00 a.m. and 5:00 p.m., Wednesdays through Sunday, from April through September can be arranged by calling 513-484-3744. For group tours during other months, call the same number or (in Ohio) 1-800-686-1541. Access to trails without a guide is prohibited.

The bog is a permanent wetland where mosquitos as well as deer flies are often present in large numbers during the warm months of the year. Do not enter the bog unprepared. The uncommon massasauga rattlesnake also makes its home in the preserve, but it is extremely unlikely that this small, non-aggressive snake will be encountered or even seen by a visitor.

THE TRAIL

The trail into Cedar Bog begins along the left (south) side of the Education Center. At the rear corner of the building it turns left, then shortly makes a right turn and drops onto a boardwalk heading toward the bog. At this second turn, there is a glacial erratic (a large granite boulder) with a plaque in memory of my late daughter, Carolyn Ramey. Confined to a wheelchair most of her short forty-two-year life, she loved joining her mother and I on trips into the bog. The field that the trail next passes through usually features many plant species attractive to small birds and butterflies during the warm months.

The trail into the bog is open at most times throughout the year, even when the Center is closed. It is however, occasionally closed for maintenance or special programing. For up-to-date

A SPOTTED TURTLE

BOARDWALK WITH SIDE RAILS

information on hours of operation for the Education Center and open hours for the trail, call the Cedar Bog Association toll-free number, 800-860-0147 or contact their website at cedarbognp.org.

There is a fee for visiting the Cedar Bog Education Center, but there is no charge for access to the trail.

Upon reaching the bog, the hiker will immediately be surrounded by the white cedar (arborvitae) for which the bog is named. From early spring to late summer there are dozens of species of wildflowers that line the trail. To try and list them all, let alone place them in the location and sequence in which they will be seen, would be quite an impossible task. Blooming skunk cabbage opens the show in late February before the last frost of spring and fringed gentian closes it in late September or October after the first frost of fall. In between come the beds of marsh marigolds and golden ragworts of April, the trilliums and jack-in-the-pulpits of May, the showy lady's-slipper of June, the marl

intersection where, beneath the limbs of a large, multi-trunk tuliptree, it turns right, left, and then continues straight ahead. Your guide will most likely lead you to the right to travel through the swamp forest. Once considered an elm-ash-map association, the elm is gone except for the occasional young tree that has yet to succumb to Dutch elm disease. Tuliptree is now a co-dominant species with ash and the soft maples in this environment.

The trail soon emerges through the forest to pass through arborvitae hummock, marl meadow, and sedge meadow. Wide platforms along the trail provide places to gather around your guide to learn more about the unique habitat. After winding north parallel to the East Branch of Cedar Run, the boardwalk turns west and then heads south along the West Branch. There it runs atop a spoil bank where earth was dumped when the creek was dredged, the result of an unsuccessful attempt to drain the bog for "muck farming" in the early part of the twentieth century. It is along this reach that, in the spring, I have occasionally seen a spotted turtle basking on a log.

Shortly before reaching the chain-link fence along Woodburn Road, the trail turns east, then north through the swamp forest to return to the main intersection. There is a shorter cut-off trail that runs from east to west across the middle of the preserve, but most visitors cover the entire loop with their guide.

A walk through Cedar Bog is an experience you will not soon forget. Since first visiting the area in 1948, I have returned to explore the bog hundreds of times, and find some small reward during each visit. This is a treasure that everyone interested in the natural world should get to know.

meadow plants of July and the prairie plants of August. At no time between the last frost of spring and the first frost of autumn will there not be a flower in bloom. Note that, because of the cooler microclimate of the bog, the "growing season" is considerably shorter than that recorded at the local weather station and frost has been recorded in nearly every month.

Several hundred feet into the bog and after crossing the East Branch of Cedar Run, the boardwalk reaches an

Charleston Falls Preserve

TOTAL DISTANCE: 2 miles (3.2 km)	

HIKING TIME: 1.5 hours

MAXIMUM ELEVATION: 900 feet

VERTICAL RISE: 65 feet

MAPS: USGS 7.5' Tipp City; MCPD Charleston Falls Preserve map

Charleston Falls Preserve is a 216-acre sanctuary located north of Dayton, 3 miles south of Tipp City. It is a facility of the Miami County Park District. Charleston Creek and its falls get their names from the small community of West Charleston, which lies less than a mile to the east. The creek arises from a spring just east of the park. The central feature of this petite preserve is the beautiful waterfall where Charleston Creek tumbles over a 37-foot limestone escarpment into a cool shaded ravine. Here, rocks of lower Silurian age, formed from material deposited in the bottom of warm, shallow seas perhaps 400 to 440 million years ago, lie at the surface. The small stream is making its way downhill to the Great Miami River, less than a mile to the west.

The rock exposed at Charleston Falls is essentially the same age as that exposed at the escarpment at the eastern end of Lake Erie. The formation near the surface at the top of the falls is Brassfield limestone. It is especially blocky and tough here, referred to as Bioclastic Brassfield, because it is rich in fossils. Below it are limestones of the Belfast Beds, which are layered and cross-bedded, allowing water to penetrate easily. Freezing and thawing action breaks this rock apart, leaving the layer above it. The next stratum down in this valley head is Elkhorn shale, an Ordovician-age (440 to 500 million years since deposition) member of the Cincinnatian shale. Loose, crumbly, and relatively impenetrable to water, the shale forms a slope away from the base of the rocks above. This remarkable little gorge was cut by the massive amounts of glacial meltwater that flowed along this drainage route as the last glacier melted, until it was gone from the divide 33 miles to the north.

Managed not as a park for active rec-

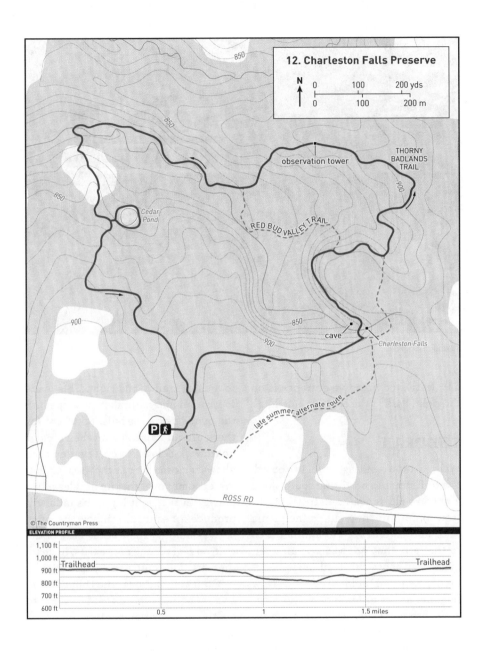

12. Charleston Falls Preserve

observation tower

THORNY
BADLANDS
TRAIL

RED BUD VALLEY TRAIL

Cedar
Pond

cave

Charleston Falls

late summer alternate route

ROSS RD

© The Countryman Press

ELEVATION PROFILE

Trailhead	Trailhead

1,100 ft
1,000 ft
900 ft
800 ft
700 ft
600 ft

0.5   1   1.5 miles

reation but as a natural area, Charleston Falls has a trail system that allows visitors to observe its special natural features without damaging them. The only picnic area is close to the road, away from the falls and stream. Restrooms are located at the rear of the parking lot. Maps at intervals throughout the preserve show where you are.

GETTING THERE

Take OH 202 north off I-70 (Exit 36). Travel 3 miles to Ross Road and turn

SIGN IN CEDAR POND

left (west); the preserve entrance is on the right. Park at the only parking lot.

THE TRAIL

Walk east 100 feet, past a bulletin board, to a trail running north and south along a shaded old fence-line. To the right (south), toward the road, is the picnic area, and an entrance to another trail to the falls that goes across an open meadow. Choose this trail in late summer, when the goldenrod and New England asters are in bloom and monarchs are nectaring in preparation for their flight toward Mexico. There is an observation deck where you can look out over the top of the vegetation. At other times of the year, turn left and follow the .3-mile trail north and then east through the forest to the falls.

In all but the driest of seasons, the falls will be heard before it is seen. Walk to the top of the falls for a careful look from above, then backtrack 50 feet to a short trail to the right. This leads to wooden and natural stone steps into the ravine below the falls. Take care, for there are no handrails on the steps or boardwalk below. An observation area allows a closer look at the escarpment. Water comes over the rim in at least two places. In the right light, the falls will produce a beautiful rainbow. Because of the slumping shale at the base of the cliff, no real plunge pool exists. Instead, the water falls onto a rocky talus slope.

Continue across the boardwalk, and then climb more wooden steps to another observation platform for a look at the falls from the left side. From there, scramble up the natural rock "steps" to the base of the dolomite cliff. Follow the trail for about 700 feet below the cliff face, passing a small limestone cave, until it climbs on a few wooden steps to double back on itself. The calcareous soils derived from the limestones of this gorge are especially conducive to the growth of such plants as Virginia bluebell, purple cliffbrake, walking fern, and columbine; look for them along the way. Turn left at a sign that reads RETURN LOOP. Take this trail about 200 feet to where it intersects with another trail. Turn left on the trail to the Thorny Badlands.

There is a less rigorous alternative route to continue hiking the Charleston Falls Trail. Instead of taking the steps to the observation area beneath the falls, follow the trail to the east from the overlook area above the falls. Very soon, it curves toward the north and then reaches Charleston Creek, where you have the option of crossing on a bridge, fording the creek, or carefully crossing on artificial stepping-stones.

Continue directly ahead on the wide path and soon you will be on the trail to the Thorny Badlands. At the top of the first rise, there is a split in the trail. The left fork is the Redbud Valley Trail, which follows a low route downstream. I suggest opting for the Thorny Badlands Trail, which sticks to the high ground. Here and there to the side of the trail you will see glacial erratics, reminding you of the glacial past of this part of Ohio. At another intersection the Thorny Badlands Trail is joined by the trail connecting to the falls and rim trails. There is a nice bench at this juncture, one of many you will find along the trail.

After the bench area, the trail dips

CHARLESTON FALLS

THE FALLS AT CHARLESTON FALLS STATE PARK FLOW YEAR-ROUND

to cross a bridge, then rises to an area where white pines were once planted to halt an erosion problem on the abused slope to the left. Here you can see many special year-round residents, like barred owls and chickadees, and transients like purple finches and pine warblers. You can easily discern when the pines were planted because each whorl of branches represents one year's growth. These trees are lovely now and have served their purpose in controlling erosion. In due time, they will die out as they become overtopped by invading deciduous trees. This is hardwood country.

At the high point on the trail stands a wooden observation tower where you can look over the treetops on the hillside below. When the trail system was designed, this hillside was covered with hawthorn trees. In this part of Ohio, when land is taken out of pasturage, invasion by hawthorns often follows invasion by old field grasses and forbs, and leads eventually to invasion by forest hardwoods; as such, these hawthorns are now being overtopped by tuliptrees, maples, and oaks. Beyond the tower, the land is still recovering from its agricultural past, with sumac trees and old field species along the trail.

Soon there will be a marked change in environment, as the trail enters a forest tunnel. Too dark for many plants, this place is ideal for fungi, the decomposers of the natural world.

At the trail juncture with the Redbud Valley Trail, continue straight ahead. After a short distance, a spur trail to the left leads to a bench overlooking the stream. This is a good place to rest body and soul and to contemplate the words of others, such as Henry David Thoreau, who wrote, "I went to the woods because I wished to live deliberately, to front only the essential facts of life, and see if I could not learn what it had to teach, and not, when I came to die, discover that I had not lived."

Once you're back on the main trail, continue downstream. You will soon cross Charleston Creek on man-made stepping stones. The path climbs uphill from the stream, and in about 100 feet comes out into the open at the edge of a small planted prairie. Using seeds gathered from remnant prairies within 50 miles of here, the park staff—under the leadership of the former Miami County Park District director, the late Scott L. Huston—created a prairie where one never before existed. Given its thin soil over limestone, the eroded slope was a good place to plant native prairie grasses and forbs. Small patches of original prairie occur along the Stillwater River not far from here in Miami County, on a variety of mesic and xeric sites. (A good example of these prairies can be seen in the Miami Park District's Stillwater Prairie Reserve off OH 185, 9 miles west of Piqua). Leave the main trail and walk the narrow path uphill through the prairie, noting how it looks in this season. Be certain to return to this site during the last week of July or the first week of August for a spectacular show of native prairie flora. For a better understanding of what the pioneers faced when they encountered the prairies of west-central Ohio, turn left and walk through this hilltop prairie.

Returning to the main trail, turn left and walk uphill. Look left at the serene setting of small, man-made Cedar Pond. There is a sign in the pond that reads correctly only in its reflection. Stay long enough to let the green frogs or cricket frogs return to their calling and take time to contemplate how the dragonflies, damselflies, red-winged blackbirds, and swallows fit into the natural world.

Heading due south, follow the main trail to where it turns left (east) along an old fencerow. Ignore the side trail to Locust Grove that leaves the main trail to the right at this corner. After traveling about 600 feet, take the trail to the right as it swings southeast past a small meadow, then heads to the shaded trail leading to the parking lot. Take home some good pictures and lots of good memories; leave only footprints, and return often to walk the trails here at all seasons of the year.

Goll Woods State Nature Preserve

TOTAL DISTANCE: 3 miles (4.8 km)

HIKING TIME: 2 hours

MAXIMUM ELEVATION: 715 feet

VERTICAL RISE: 10 feet

MAPS: USGS 7.5' Archbold; ODNR Goll Woods State Nature Preserve booklet

The first European to explore the northwest corner of Ohio was, in all probability, the French fur trader Robert Cavelier La Salle. He visited the valley of the Maumee River in 1679, finding it inhabited by Chippewa, Ottawa, Wyandotte, Delaware, and Pottawatomie Indians. More than 150 years later, German pioneer families became the first whites to settle in what is now German Township, in Fulton County. By 1834, the Native American tribes that La Salle encountered had been pushed out of Ohio, the Shawnee who replaced them had long since been defeated, and only a handful of Wyandotte Indians remained on a reservation near Upper Sandusky.

In June 1836, Peter F. Goll, his wife, Catherine, and their young son, Peter Jr., immigrated to America from Dobs, France. The next summer, Goll made his way to the federal land office in Lima, where he purchased 80 acres of what we now know as Goll Woods for $1.25 an acre. Goll's farm prospered, and he continued to buy land, eventually owning 600 acres.

The timber at that time was described as "dense throughout the whole area: it was tall and the whole of an extremely vigorous growth. The varieties included elm in abundance, basswood, oak of several varieties, hickory, black walnut, whitewood (tuliptree), butternut, sugar maple, and a sprinkling of beech in some parts, and in the lowest lands black ash, and white ash prevails throughout the township." Timber wolves howled in the forest close to settlements and cougars roamed at will, as did bison, elk, black bear, Canada lynx, and many other mammals that have long since vanished.

The area was the wet forest of Ohio's

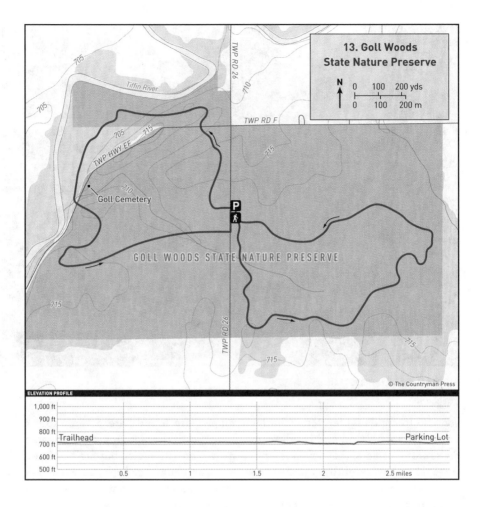

ELEVATION PROFILE

1,000 ft					
900 ft					
800 ft					
700 ft	Trailhead				Parking Lot
600 ft					
500 ft					
	0.5	1	1.5	2	2.5 miles

Great Black Swamp, land that was under the western extension of Lake Erie after the exodus of the Wisconsinan ice sheet from what is now northwestern Ohio. The land was flat, with soils that did not drain well. They were black from the decay of vegetation that flourished in the shallow postglacial lake basin and rich enough to grow big timber.

Settlers needed that timber when they first arrived—to build houses, barns, and wagons. But they needed more than trees to survive and raise families: They needed tillable land, and every farmer knew that any land that could raise such trees as these of the Black Swamp could surely raise great corn and wheat. In 1859, therefore, the county commissioners passed a law providing for extensive ditching, and in a few decades the swamp that once covered two-thirds of the county was almost gone.

Almost gone, that is, except for this 80-acre tract we call Goll Woods. The Goll family stayed on the land for four generations. The land was passed on from Peter F. Goll Sr., to Peter Goll Jr., to George F. Goll, and then to his

TALL OAK ALONG GOLL WOODS TRAIL

son and to his daughter, Mrs. Charles Louys. Although Goll and his descendants were farmers, they loved the big trees, and they carefully guarded the Big Woods from the timber operators. At the urging of citizens and conservation groups from northwestern Ohio, the Ohio Department of Natural Resources (ODNR) purchased 321 acres of land, including Goll's 80-acre Big Woods, from Mrs. Louys in 1966. It was dedicated as Goll Woods to the people of Ohio in 1969 and in 1975 became Goll Woods State Nature Preserve.

The closest thing to a stand of old-growth woods in northwestern Ohio, Goll Woods holds visitors in awe. Many of its magnificent trees were large when the Pilgrims landed at Plymouth Rock. Trees commonly found in three different types of forest—elm/ash/maple swamp forest, mixed mesophytic, and beech/maple—are found here. Swamp forest is found in the wet area, beech/maple grows on the moist but well-drained sites, and mixed mesophytic, a blend of many species, frequents the transition areas between.

Goll Woods is a place of beauty during all seasons. Many special creatures, such as tree frogs, barred owls, redheaded woodpeckers, red foxes, and several species of salamanders, make their homes here. So, too, do many kinds of ferns and wildflowers, including the delicate purple, white, and yellow Canada violet and the three-bird orchid. Unfortunately, it is but a small remnant of the once vast forest of this part of Ohio.

We can only hope that some of the countries of the world just now undergoing "development" will do better than we did protecting larger tracts of these original forests.

GETTING THERE

Travel I-80/I-90 (the Ohio Turnpike) west from Toledo to Exit 3. Turn left (south) on OH 108 and go 1.5 miles to Alternate US 20. Turn right (west) and travel 8.3 miles to OH 66 in Burlington. Here, turn left (south) and go 1 mile to Township Road F. Turn right (west) and travel 3 miles to Township Road 26, where you turn left (south) to the preserve entrance.

THE TRAIL

A walk through Goll Woods is a walk through a precious remnant of the primeval forest characteristic of northwestern Ohio's Great Black Swamp. Start exploring by heading into the eastern 160-acre tract. Take the right fork at Post 1 on the Goll Woods self-guided nature trail. A guidebook is available at the kiosk at the parking lot or by mail from the ODNR's Division of Natural Areas and Preserves office in Columbus.

The area near Post 2 was probably swamp forest at one time, but with the water table dropping in recent years it is undergoing a transition. The red maple and ash are still there, but so too are trees that don't tolerate being in standing water all year, such as tuliptree, basswood, bur oak, chinquapin oak, sugar maple, and shagbark hickory. This is the transitional mixed mesophytic area.

Goll Woods' vernal flora is special. On a May trip, I was struck by the light color of the wild blue phlox compared to what I've seen in central Ohio, where I grew up. The trail guidebook provides a checklist of the more common flowers of the preserve. Remember: "Let them live in your eye ... not die in your hand." Between Post 3 and the next stop on the

trail, a side trail enters from the right. This will be your inbound trail at the end of our hike.

At Post 4, let the statistics speak for themselves. Bur oak (*Quercus macrocarpa*) diameter at breast height (DBH): 56"; height: 112'; estimated board feet: 4,270. Here, a bur oak that stood at Post 5 was struck by lightning in 1970 and has now fallen. The lightning scar is still visible along the full length of the trunk. After Post 4, the trail turns east to explore more of the Big Woods. Every Ohioan should know the tree at Post 6. This is the buckeye from the Native American word *hetuck*—"the eye of a buck deer"—and it is the official state tree.

Perhaps by this point you will have discovered one of the nuisances that plagued early settlers in the Black Swamp region—mosquitoes. A good warm-weather walker is always prepared with a head net or repellent close at hand. In early Ohio, mosquitoes were more than a nuisance—they were a hazard, because they carried malaria. The papaws at Post 7 are Temperate Zone members of the largely tropical custard-apple family. Dark maroon flowers in May change to yellowish-green, banana-like fruits in the fall—food for opossums and raccoons. Before reaching the next stop, you'll pass a trail to the left that takes a short route back to the trailhead. Continuing on this hike, however, you will come to Post 8, where the "Elder of the Woods," a 122-foot-tall bur oak, has occupied the site for close to 500 years. It died in 1984, but when I last visited the woods it was still standing. What stories it could tell! No hiker needs to be told about the poison ivy pointed out by Post 9: "Leaves of three, let it be."

Nature is the grand recycler. Post 10 reminds the visitor that letting dead trees rot and return to the soil allows their nutrients to be used again. That philosophy is central to the management of nature preserves. White ash like the one at Post 11 provide the wood for products such as baseball bats, tool handles, and furniture. The giant specimen shown there is 104 feet tall with a 32-inch DBH. Four of North America's 18 species of ash grow in Goll Woods.

The cross-section of the bur oak that fell during the winter of 1968 at Post 12 is nature's time capsule. From the growth rings, you can read of dry years and wet ones, lightning strikes, fires, and the disease and death of the old oak.

All along, the elevation of the trail has been changing subtly. At Post 13 the forest has become true swamp forest, with black ash, red maples, and silver maples dominating. Swamp white oak also occurs, but the American elm has been gone for nearly 40 years. The trail rises now, only a few feet, to a well-drained sandy knoll, and once again the composition of the forest changes. At Post 14 American beech and sugar maple dominate. In time, as the area becomes better drained, this combination will probably dominate all of Goll Woods.

People who live downwind from a cottonwood like the one at Post 15 have probably wondered aloud about the value of these trees. The "cotton" can be a real nuisance! The red squirrels that live in this one, however, could easily sing the cottonwood's praises, as could the other mammals and many birds that are cavity dwellers. The much larger fox squirrel also abounds in these woods. By examining the tooth marks on the opened acorns, you should be able to distinguish which of the two squirrel species found in Goll Woods made them: the smaller or the larger species?

Now heading west, the trail reaches Post 16. This is the location of a tall tuliptree, a living fossil. Geologists have found evidence that this genus has existed for as long as 100 million years. Because it grows tall and self-prunes its lower branches, it was often used by pioneers for log structures in this part of Ohio. A relative of the magnolia, its green and orange tulip-like blossoms grow on the top of the tree, usually out of sight. Small ponds such as the one at Post 17 support life of all sorts, including frogs, salamanders, dragonflies, and mosquitoes, which only spend one phase of their life there. Others, like fairy shrimp, are tied to the pond throughout their lives. Bigger creatures like raccoons and skunks feed off the turtles and frogs in ponds.

Ferns similar to those at Post 18 have been around for 400 million years. They need moist environments like this one to survive. Lichens, such as the greenish white Parmelia lichen on the trunk of the tree at Post 19, are examples of two different life-forms that coexist to their mutual benefit. The plant is composed of both a fungus and green alga cells, living harmoniously as one structure. Hummingbirds and eastern woodpewees use bits of this species of lichen for lining the insides and outsides of their nests.

The shortcut side trail enters from the left as you approach Post 20. The giant white oak at this stop would provide enough wood to construct half of a small frame house. This tree is 44" in DBH. At the time of settlement, thousands of trees like this one were felled and burned in huge piles to clear the land for agriculture. Forests like that at Post 21 were often burned by Native Americans to keep the brush from growing up and hindering hunting. When

WINTER IN THE BLACK SWAMP

pioneers found these burned areas, they called them oak openings.

As this interpretive trail ends, continue exploring the other environments of Goll Woods by taking the trail across the road from the other end of the parking lot. While passing through the pine planting east of the manager's residence, try to figure out what year it was planted. The planting will probably be crowded out by hardwoods eventually. Here the trail crosses the road toward the Tiffin River. Here there is an especially large patch of toadshade, the maroon sessile trillium, in April and May. The trail goes through a stand of beech/maple and tuliptree between the river and the Goll Cemetery. Take the time to read the tombstones in the graveyard and to reconstruct the lives of those buried here from the facts gleaned from the stones.

The trail reenters the woods on the east side of the road 200 feet to the right (south) of where it emerged. From there it swings south through more pines and secondary-succession scrubland. It passes a parking lot before turning left (east) past more large trees. After a half mile, the trail reaches the road that bisects the preserve. Angle across the road to the right to enter the trail and connect with the east woods loop. Upon reaching the T intersection with the nature trail, turn left to return to the parking lot.

Lichens: Complex Organisms

Lichens are the pioneers of the plant world. They grow on rocks, soil, and wood in the harshest weather conditions and are found in forests, fields, backyards, and urban parks. They are sensitive to acid rain and air pollution, a characteristic that allows them to be used as monitors of air quality.

Found in unique shapes and colors, lichens are not really a single organism but two different organisms, comprising a photosynthetic organism and a fungus that have formed a symbiotic mutualism. Each organism gains some advantage from this cooperative living arrangement. In most lichens, the photosynthetic partner (or photobiont) is a green alga and/or a cyanobacterium (what we used to call blue-green algae). The other partner is a fungus and is referred to as the mycobiont.

There are estimated to be 13,500 species of lichens. They grow in four general forms: crustose, growing closely attached to the substrate; squamulose, which are scale-shaped with a free edge; foliose, which are flattened from top to bottom or leaf-like; and fruticose, which are bushy and most often attached at the base. The familiar reindeer moss is an example of the last.

To photograph lichens, you need a good macro lens. I prefer to use a 90 to 105 mm focal length, so as not to make a shadow with my camera. Their study requires a hand lens and a reference book or two. *How to Know the Lichens*, by Mason E. Hale (Wm. C. Brown Co.), has good keys, and *Michigan Lichens*, by Julie Jones Medlin (Cranbrook Institute of Science), has topnotch color illustrations. How many different lichens can you find on your next wilderness walk?

14

Kelleys Island State Park

TOTAL DISTANCE: 7.5 miles (12 km)

HIKING TIME: 6 hours

MAXIMUM ELEVATION: 615 feet

VERTICAL RISE: 40 feet

MAPS: USGS 7.5' Kelleys Island; ODNR Lake Erie Islands State Parks map; KICC Kelleys Island map

Early maps call it Cunningham Island, but for more than a century the 2,800-acre solid limestone island that lies in Lake Erie, 11 miles north of the mainland city of Sandusky, has been known as Kelleys Island. Between 1833 and 1841 the Kelley brothers of Cleveland, Datus and Irad, purchased the entire island for $1.50 per acre. The name Cunningham—that of a squatter who had built a house on the island in 1808—was lost to geographers forever. With the establishment of the Kelleys Island Stone Company, quarrying—the industry that was to bring people and fame to the island—was under way in earnest.

By 1842, grape cuttings had been set out on the island, marking the beginning of the second industry that was to carry the name far and wide. Fermented from grapes grown on the sweet soils of the island, the products of the Kelleys Island Wine Company were known for their quality. The 1990 census listed 200 residents on Kelleys Island, where there were once several thousand people working in jobs related to the fishing, quarrying, and winemaking industries. Though now supplemented by air service, the principal way to reach Kelleys Island remains, as it was in the 1830s, by boat. The ferries do haul cars and trucks to and from the island year-round (weather permitting), but the number of vehicles on the island remains small. It is thus a wonderful place to explore on foot.

In addition to the artifacts from the early industries, the island has other points of interest. Inscription Rock, on the south shore, is covered with Native American drawings. The glacial grooves scratched into the limestone bedrock that are visible at Glacial Grooves State Memorial are world famous. There are also homes and churches left from the

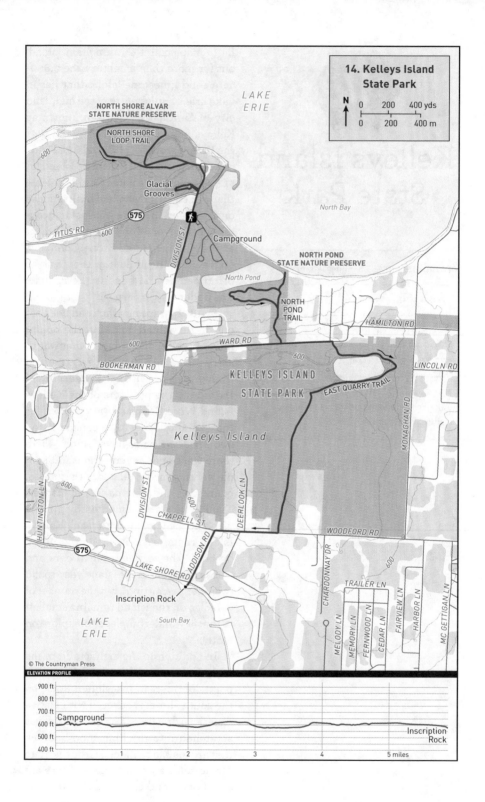

island's heyday to be admired. The Ohio Department of Natural Resources (ODNR) operates a 661-acre state park with a beach, boat-launching ramp, and campground on the island. Local merchants and restaurateurs ply their goods to tourists during the vacation season. The Kelleys Island Chamber of Commerce will gladly send you a packet of material with a map and information about local businesses, including accommodations. Its phone number is 419-746-2360, its website is kelleys islandchamber.com, and its e-mail address is kelleyschamber@aol.com.

GETTING THERE

At least two ferry operators serve Kelleys Island. The Kelleys Island Ferry Boat Line (419-798-9763) runs from a dock at Marblehead year-round, with an expanded schedule from early May until late September. It will transport vehicles and their passengers as well as pedestrians. Between Memorial Day weekend and mid-September, Jet Express operates catamaran passenger ferries out of downtown Sandusky (1-800-245-1538).

Sandusky is 54 miles east of Toledo via I-80/I-90 and US 6; 105 miles north of Columbus via US 23 and OH 4; and 64 miles west of Cleveland via I-80/I-90 and US 250. To get to Marblehead, which is only 3.5 miles from the island, take OH 2 west from Sandusky across the Sandusky Bay Bridge. Turn right (north) on OH 269, then right (east) on OH 163. Free parking is available at both terminals. Each of the ferries will bring you to the south shore of Kelleys Island and Water Street. When you get off the ferry, be sure to note the time of the last returning boat. If you plan to take the last one, get to the dock early, as it is often crowded.

If you are carrying camping gear, you should proceed to Kelleys Island State Park at the north end of Division Street to obtain a campsite and to stow gear. The Kelleys Island Ferry comes into the Seaway Marina, less than a half mile east of Division Street, the center of town. The park campground entrance is not quite 1.5 miles north on Division Street, on the right side. Use the sidewalk and take time to study the homes and other structures along the route. You may want to stop at the Kelleys Island Historical Society's stone church museum on the right side of the road, just north of the business district. Be sure to walk through the cemetery, studying the names and inscriptions, and don't miss the Butterfly Box, where you can walk amid live butterflies in a plastic hoop house and shop for butterfly- and beetle-related gifts. Islanders have had a long love affair with butterflies, especially the monarch, as the island is an overnight resting place for that long-distance flier in the fall. The chamber of commerce can provide details about the butterfly festival held each September.

THE TRAIL

After setting up camp (or leaving your luggage at some other accommodation), I suggest that you walk north from the campground entrance to the Glacial Grooves. There is excellent interpretive signage along the grooves, or you can stop at the park office and purchase an inexpensive booklet, entitled "A Glacial Grooves Fossil Walk on Kelleys Island." The grooves are nothing short of awesome—400 feet long, 30 feet wide, and 15 feet deep. They are scars that were scratched along the surface of the limestone bedrock by the mile-deep glacial ice as it advanced to the south many

GIANT SWALLOWTAIL NECTARING

millennia ago. The glacial groove site is a state memorial owned by the Ohio Historical Society but operated by the Division of Parks and Recreation.

The 1-mile North Shore Loop nature trail originates just north of the grooves. It enters the quarry only briefly, and then swings to the right to travel through woods to the rocky shoreline. As you would expect on an island that is solid limestone, the woods are composed of trees that do well on sweet soils: hackberry, redbud, blue ash, water ash, basswood, chinquapin oak, and, early in succession, red cedar. Where the trail continues west, paralleling the shoreline, the sparse vegetation on the rock surfaces between the trail and the lake is an unusual natural community known as a stone alvar. At a point just after the trail turns west, back from the shoreline, a path leads over to the shore and a low-to-the-ground display case with interpretive material about the alvar plant community. This is a dedicated state nature preserve. I recommend that you not try to descend to the bare rock for a better look. I did, and I tripped and fell against the rocks and into the poison ivy, bloodying myself badly. (One of the best examples of this kind of habitat is found at Lakeside Daisy State Nature Preserve, just south of the mainland village of Marblehead. It is open to the public during May, when its namesake plant is in full bloom.) Back on the North Shore Loop Trail, turn right and continue going west. The trail eventually swings south and east to return to the parking lot. One summer I walked it in the evening and saw many deer in the scrubby area along the way.

Return to Division Street via the driveway and walk south on the sidewalk on the east side of the road. The next area to explore is North Pond Trail. To reach this, continue walking south along Division Street to Ward Road. Turn left (east) and follow the sidewalk 0.4 mile until you reach the entrance to the 20-acre North Pond State Nature Preserve, managed jointly by the Division of Natural Areas and Preserves and the Division of Parks and Recreation. Turn left to enter the trail system. A sign along the trail speaks of the designation of the site as an important birding area by Ohio Audubon. The trail leads north down a considerable slope toward the lake. A pile of granite boulders (glacial erratics) to the right indicates that at one time the area was cleared for agricultural use. Soon it reaches a fork where a sign describes the mission of DNAP. Continue north toward the lake. After 150 feet the trail changes to boardwalk, where signs provide information about the trail's construction and the plastic lumber used. Just beyond is a five-paneled kiosk where the natural history of the area is illustrated with pictures and text.

From there one trail goes north to the beach. There are interpretive signs and a bench along the way. After looking at the beach community, return to the kiosk and take the other trail. At another fork in the trail there is a raised observation area, allowing a view of North Pond from overhead. The winding trail continues through the heavily vegetated sand-dune community. The pond does not always contain water; it's dependent upon rainfall and the very fickle nature of the level of Lake Erie. When I visited, in July 2006, it was essentially dry and completely overgrown with emergent vegetation. From the tower I could see neither waterfowl nor wading birds. The trail circles the pond counterclockwise, the boardwalk ends, and the environment becomes more "old field" in nature. When the loop trail meets the access trail, turn right (south) to exit the preserve where you entered.

Now, back at Ward Road, turn left (east), walk on the sidewalk, and look for the entrance to the East Quarry Trail area of the state park on the right (south) side of the road. It's a distance of about a quarter mile. Stop and look at the map of the area on the trailhead sign to fix the lay of the land firmly in your mind. There are so many exits that it's unlikely you'll get lost. On the other hand, it is easy to end up somewhere other than where you intended. If it's a sunny day, it's a good idea to check the position of the sun before you enter the area. That should enable you to reorient yourself any time you wonder what direction you are moving. The object is to go in from Ward Road on the north, circle around the east end of Horseshoe Lake, and then exit to the south onto Woodford Road. Go around whatever is blocking the road and walk toward the lake. If you can find them, follow the green blazes around the east end of the lake between red cedars, planted pines, and brush.

After you have rounded the lake and are more or less heading west, turn left at the second exit headed south. If you take the first, or the third or the fourth, you will still get there. And if you choose to go straight west you will eventually come out on Division Street Road, knowing exactly where you are. A self-guided trail brochure with a map of East Quarry Trail is available free at the park office. The trail is about a mile from north to south, and it shouldn't take more than 40 minutes unless you loiter too long while basking on the rocks overlooking the lake. Be careful with your scrambling if you decide to explore the lakeshore.

Once on Woodford Road, continue your Kelleys Island hike by turning right (west). If you need nourishment, the new Kelleys Island Wine Company is on the left. At Addison Road, St. Michael's Church stands on the right. Turn left on

Addison Road toward the lake. The Kelley Mansion, built in 1863, sits on the left corner of Addison and Water Streets. About a dozen years ago, 78 archaeological sites and 316 buildings—including this mansion—that are associated with the settlement and history of the largest American island in Lake Erie, were added to the National Register of Historic Places as the Kelleys Island Historic District. And the work of sorting out the interesting history of the island goes on, carried out in no small part by the active Kelleys Island Historical Association. (If you have time, visit their museum on Division Street about a third of the way up the road to the state park.) Prehistoric sites on the island show evidence of human occupation from Paleo-Indian times through the Late Woodland period, or from 12,000 B.C. to A.D. 1,300. Among those sites is Inscription Rock, which sits under a protective shelter to the right across Water Street from the mansion.

Many more places to explore and things to see await you on Kelleys Island. There are excellent eating establishments on the island, and fishing trips can be arranged on the waters of Lake Erie. The route that I have suggested is about 7.5 miles long, but you can easily pick a route to suit your interests. Bicycles and electric golf carts can be rented on the island. For a day, a weekend, or a week of walking, leave your automobile on the mainland and visit this enchanting island.

GRANITE BOULDERS BESIDE THE TRAIL ARE EVIDENCE OF ANCIENT HISTORY

Kendrick Woods State Nature Preserve

TOTAL DISTANCE: 3 miles (4.6 km)	

HIKING TIME: 2 hours

MAXIMUM ELEVATION: 810 feet

VERTICAL RISE: 20 feet

MAPS: USGS 7.5' Series Spencerville; JAMPD Kendrick Woods South Trail Guide

When, in the spring of 1794, the army commanded by "Mad" Anthony Wayne moved down the valley of the Auglaize River to its confluence with the Maumee River, they were moving through virgin forest. Where they passed the mouth of Six-Mile Creek, where Kendrick Woods State Nature Preserve is located in what is now western Allen County, they were traveling through spectacular beech–maple forest on rich glacial till.

By the time they reached what was later to be called Six-Mile Creek, the small stream that empties into the "Glaize" at Kendrick Woods, the army was already north of the major recessional moraines left 10,000 years earlier by the receding Wisconsinan Glacier. Only a few miles farther north the going would get more difficult as they encountered the mire of the Great Black Swamp. Occupying the old bed of one of a series of lakes that developed in front of the glacier as it melted from the Ohio countryside, the swamp forest consisted of elm, ash, and soft maples, along with bur, pin and swamp white oak—all trees that grow well with their roots close to the water table. When the troops reached the Maumee River—the main stem of the river system that drained the Black Swamp—they built Fort Defiance. Then they moved downriver to do battle with the Indians. The rest, as they say, is history.

The Greeneville Treaty that resulted as a result of Wayne's victory at Fallen Timbers did not immediately open this part of Ohio to settlement. But Ohio became a state less than 10 years later, and settlement began to occur in waves all across its territory. Lima was surveyed in 1831, and from 1835 to 1843 the federal government had a land office there, right in the heart of the congressional lands of this part of Ohio, making

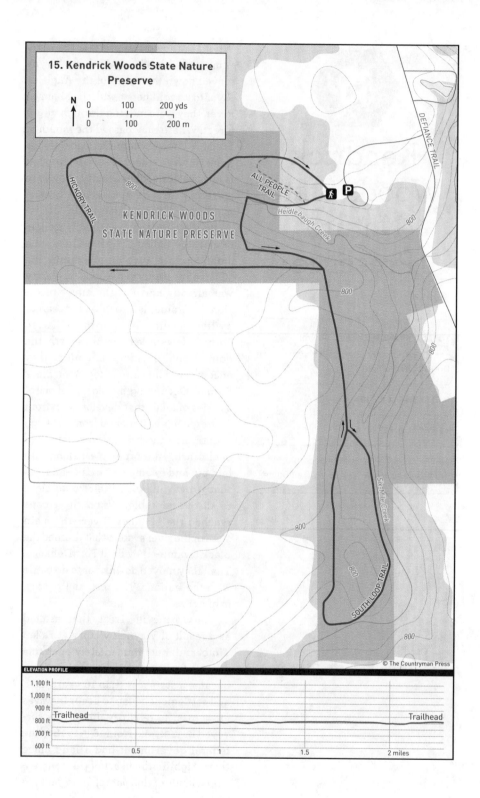

15. Kendrick Woods State Nature Preserve

KENDRICK WOODS
STATE NATURE PRESERVE

HICKORY TRAIL

ALL PEOPLE TRAIL

DEFIANCE TRAIL

Heidlebaugh Creek

SOUTH LOOP TRAIL

Six-Mile Creek

800

© The Countryman Press

ELEVATION PROFILE

1,100 ft
1,000 ft
900 ft
800 ft
700 ft
600 ft

Trailhead

Trailhead

0.5   1   1.5   2 miles

it easy for settlers to file land patents. Allen County was created in 1846. Timber was an impediment to progress, and logs went to sawmills by the wagonload. In 1884, a man drilling for gas discovered oil. A year later Lima found itself at the heart of the largest oil field on the globe. Thousands of oil wells were drilled, and the Standard Oil Company built the earth's largest oil refinery in Lima.

As the twenty-first century gets under way, the largest contiguous tract of woods extant in Allen County is the one preserved as Kendrick Woods. Though the USGS Kendrick Woods topographic map still carries the label "oil field," the oil is depleted and the wells are capped. The beech and maple trees that Wayne and his men passed beneath were felled for firewood and construction timber centuries ago. With tile fields and ditches drying out the land, young oaks and hickories now dominate the upland forest. Fortunately, more than a dozen huge white oak trees, estimated to be near 300 years old—trees that were likely saplings when General Wayne and his men passed nearby—still grow in Kendrick Woods. Yet throughout all the clearing and row-cropping, drilling and pumping, successive generations of landowners did not clear-cut these woods. Strayer's Woods, as it was called locally, stood when the local park district was born.

In 1976, the district received money from the estate of Florence Kendrick to be used to buy land to serve as a memorial to her late husband, Raymond W. Kendrick. An avid outdoorsman who loved the woods and wildlife, Kendrick felt a personal closeness with the out-of-doors, and Mrs. Kendrick wanted the gift to be used to share this feeling with others.

It took 10 years to acquire the needed titles and easements to protect this 218-acre tract, but in 1987 it was opened to the public as Kendrick Woods. In May 1992, when I was serving as chief of the Division of Natural Areas and Preserves, Kendrick Woods was dedicated as a state nature preserve. Interestingly, the purchase of the original 182 acres in 1976 specified no development or disturbance of the woods. The people who owned the land at the time it was bought were planning to develop a mobile home park there and had to be persuaded by local conservationists to sell the woods to the park district.

GETTING THERE

The entrance to Kendrick Woods is on the west side of the Defiance Trail, less than 1 mile north of SR 81 and approximately 12 miles west of Lima. The open area in front of the woods includes restrooms and picnic and play facilities. There are said to be a total of 5 miles of trails within the park. The best access is just beyond the bulletin board, which is located at the far corner of the first parking lot. Note: From mid-May until mid-September, the woods are generally full of mosquitoes. The park district does not run programs during that period of the year. If you plan hiking then, be very well prepared.

THE TRAIL

Begin walking on the All People Trail, a boardwalk of less than a quarter mile that is accessible to those with wheelchairs and walkers. My late daughter, Carolyn, lived most of her 42 years in a wheelchair, so I am particularly pleased to find more of these sorts of facilities in Ohio's outdoor recreation areas. Just

SOME AREAS OF KENDRICK WOODS TRAIL REQUIRE A BOARDWALK

inside the woods, a monument notes that this trail is the gift of the Lima Rotary Club. There is also a plaque alongside the trail illustrating the layout of the trail system. I suggest that you begin walking by turning left to travel the boardwalk in a clockwise direction. Pick up a trail guide from a dispenser at the first left-hand trail exit, then take the exit and follow the earthen trail, reading the interpretive material in the guide in the proper sequence. Posts numbered from 1 to 10 along this trail are keyed to the trail guide; you will find the first one alongside the trail shortly after you leave the boardwalk.

White, red, and occasional bur oak and shagbark hickory stand close to the wide winding boardwalk. Almost immediately into the woods I encountered a fat fox squirrel, as might well be expected given the abundance of what is called mast—acorns and hickory nuts. In some parts of the woods there are large trees; in other areas they look to be 50

to 100 years old. There is a good understory and, in some spots, a good layer of spicebush and other native shrubs. The spring wildflowers of these woods are spectacular. I do not remember seeing large-flowered trillium blossoms this big anywhere else, and the abundance of wild blue phlox reminded me of that which grew in the wet beech forests of eastern Franklin County during my youth. How well I remember the day when workers began digging a hole for the basement of a home in the exact location of my favorite patch of "sweet williams." Unfortunately, the invasive alien garlic mustard is present in a growing number of places along the trail, probably brought in on the soles of hikers.

Upon leaving the boardwalk, the trail tread is unimproved forest floor. Watch out for the occasional protruding root. It drops into the valley of Heidlebaugh Creek, the small stream that drains the northern part of the park, then climbs the hillside gently before dropping to a trail intersection. The park people have made navigation in Kendrick Woods easy, by placing at strategic points small plaques with a map that indicates your location with a red dot. You have already passed one numbered post; to continue past them in succession, turn left. A humpback bridge carries the trail across the major channel, and a smaller plant bridge across a lesser channel. Then the trail climbs and winds its way to the east on high ground.

At the next intersection, go straight ahead. The trail to the right is the Hickory Trail, which circles the west end of the park and returns to the All People Trail. If you were to take that, you would miss the interesting South Loop Trail. Continuing ahead, you soon come to a trail exiting to the left. It goes back to the parking lot (in case you need to abort your hike). The trail continues east and then swings south to join with a trail coming in from the right. On a single trail, continue south, traveling downhill to cross a small bridge and travel upstream on the floodplain of Six-Mile Creek. (Incidentally, the name of this creek probably dates from after 1812. In that year Colonel Poague of General Harrison's army built a fort that he named Fort Amanda in honor of his wife, along the Defiance Trail 6 miles upstream from here. Travelers coming north likely put the six-mile name on the stream because of its location 6 miles up the trail from Fort Amanda.) Note the absence of glacial gravel and boulders in this stream. At one spot, the trail goes very close to the stream edge. Channel posts have been installed with brush tucked in behind in an attempt to halt erosion with natural material. By now, the trail has passed five of the numbered posts.

Your nose probably tells you that post 6 is not far ahead. You will pick up the smell of the sulfur-bearing artesian spring before it comes into sight, off to the right of the trail. Like the water, the origin of the spring is not very clear. Either it was formed when an aquifer was drilled as the area was being explored for oil, or the aquifer naturally meets the surface here. In either case, there is a spring flowing from the broken upturned end of what looks like a buried concrete tile. It is surrounded by an area of wetland that is fed by natural seeps rising year-round out of the ground. The spring flowed at a considerably faster rate before the city of Delphos developed a well field directly west of the northern part of the woods. At one time the spring was used to water cattle that grazed nearby. A similar spring close by along the Auglaize River was formerly called the "Fountain of Youth"—visitors filled bottles with the sulfur water thinking that it possessed medicinal qualities. At the outflow for the spring there is a sluice and some instruments, which of course should not be disturbed.

Beyond the spring the trail crosses another small side stream on a bridge that looks as if it has a bite out of its right side. It is, of course, a circle cut out of the deck to accommodate a tree that's no longer there. The trail next moves closer to Six-Mile Creek on what looks like dredge fill from a channelization project. Off to the right is what appears to be the natural channel.

As the trail rises from the flood, a large stump to the right gives you some indication as to the size of trees that stood in this part of Allen County at the time of settlement. Beyond, on the higher ground, the trail passes the large white oaks mentioned earlier. These scattered forest-grown trees must be close to 300

EVEN SMALL CREEKS AT KENDRICK WOODS NEED TO BE BRIDGED

years old. Imagine what this area must have looked like when trees like these were widespread across the landscape. One early Ohio settler, writing in 1817, reported that "The white oak is the glory of the upland forest. I measured a white oak by the roadside, which at four feet from the ground was six feet in diameter and at seventy-five feet is measured nine feet around." If you look closely at some of these trees, you can see a faint blue color. Sometime in the not-too-distant past, a timber buyer probably marked these trees to be cut. How fortunate we

are that someone felt these woodland monarchs were worth saving for future generations to see and admire.

The trail remains now on the high land. Groundhog burrows give evidence to the ease with which a critter can dig into this deep glacial till. Traveling parallel to the edge of the woods, the trail now begins its return to the northern part of the park, crossing several small bridges across streams that drain the farm fields to the left. More oaks and hickories dominate the woods, with sugar maples in the understory. As

the parking lot. Otherwise, turn left and head due west on a wide trail that looks like a former farm lane. Kendrick Woods is like most parks and natural areas: tucked into a corner is the spot where former occupants of the land disposed of unwanted appliances and equipment. Nature hides it during the green time of the year, but not so in winter.

After a good distance, the South Loop Trail meets the Hickory Trail coming in from the right. Continue west on the Hickory Trail to where, at a park bench, the trail turns right. This section is one of the best places to photograph spring wildflowers without leaving the trail.

At the bench, look due south across the fence. There lies the only glacial erratic that I found in the area. What a contrast with the "boulder belt" areas of the moraines of west-central Ohio, where granite boulders are everywhere. From here the trail travels to the north on flat ground, then turns east and drops to broad floodplain—Heidlebaugh Creek (named for the owners of the land to the west) in the deep woods. After crossing another bridge, the Hickory Trail reaches a T. Turn left amid tall oaks and hickories and follow the trail as it arcs right to meet the All People boardwalk. A left turn and a short walk soon bring you back to the bench and monument area near the trailhead and parking lot.

It was fall the first time I walked this trail, but I was so impressed by the quality of the forest that I returned at the end of the following April. I was rewarded with a beautiful display of spring wildflowers in a woods very different from those I more frequently walk in central Ohio. I believe that you will share my enthusiasm for Kendrick Woods and the 150-acre, state-designated Kendrick Woods State Nature Preserve that it includes.

the trail drops to the valley of Six-Mile Creek, it passes a big honey locust, one you would not try to climb. Here there is a side trail to the right that leads to an area where skunk cabbage and marsh marigolds grow. I suspect a small hillside spring provides water year-round.

When you reach the trail you came in on, continue north, then turn west to climb and descend before crossing a bridge. After turning toward the west, the trail arrives at a split. If you want to cut your hike short here, go right, then take the next right across a bridge to

16

Kiser Lake State Park and Kiser Lake Wetlands State Nature Preserve

TOTAL DISTANCE: 2.5 miles (4 km)

HIKING TIME: 2 hours

MAXIMUM ELEVATION: 1,150 feet

VERTICAL RISE: 80 feet

MAPS: USGS 7.5' Series St. Paris; ODNR Kiser Lake State Park brochure

I knew I was in for a special treat the moment I set foot on the Kiser Lake Wetlands trail. It was a warm cloudy-bright early-April morning, and 20 feet down the trail I was greeted by the sunny face of a marsh marigold in full bloom. As I hit the boardwalk, I thought I heard the call of a single western chorus frog, so I began a slow, stealthy walk along the edge of the wetland. At the end of the short section of boardwalk, just inside the preserve, the trail returns to a dirt track and follows the east bank of Mosquito Creek upstream. I could see a huge bed of marsh marigolds (really a species of buttercup) across the creek where I could only enjoy them from a distance. And then it happened: the lone frog I had heard earlier turned into a full chorus. I froze, for the slightest movement will often return them to silence. As their confidence grew, their numbers did too. Soon they were joined by the chirping of male spring peepers also advertising their presence to would-be suitors. As if that weren't enough, from deeper in the wetland came the trilling voices of male eastern American toads singing of their readiness to mate. The final member of this anuran symphony, a single northern leopard frog, began its snore-like calls from across the waters, hoping that some lady-in-waiting leopard frog would choose him. It was almost too much: four of the nine species of frogs and toads known from Champaign County present and singing in one place. Anything that was to follow would be anticlimactic.

The wetland that I was exploring may well have resulted from the work of humans—flowage from springs being blocked by road fill or stream-dredging spoil. But this wetland has been here in one shape or another since soon after

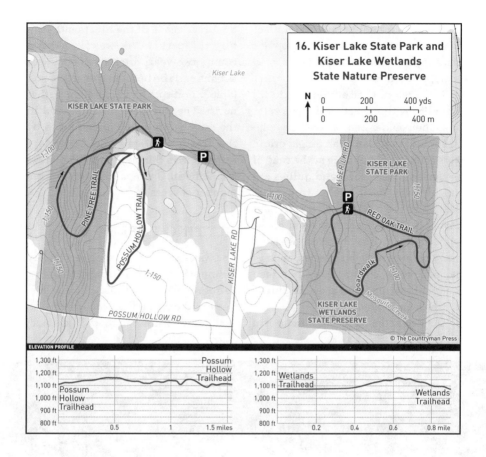

16. Kiser Lake State Park and
Kiser Lake Wetlands
State Nature Preserve

Kiser Lake

KISER LAKE STATE PARK

KISER LAKE
STATE PARK

PINE TREE TRAIL

POSSUM HOLLOW TRAIL

KISER LAKE RD

KISER LK RD

RED OAK TRAIL

boardwalk

Mosquito Creek

POSSUM HOLLOW RD

KISER LAKE
WETLANDS
STATE PRESERVE

© The Countryman Press

ELEVATION PROFILE

the melting of the last ice sheet. Mosquito Creek drains the runoff and seepage from springs on the western side of a large area of hilly Wisconsinan-age moraine, along the western edge of Champaign County, carrying it northwest to eventually empty into the south-flowing Great Miami River near Sidney. The moraine east of Kiser Lake is the divide between the Mad River drainage to the east and the Great Miami. Mosquito Creek, nestled in a valley between the moraines, was a slow-flowing stream fed by numerous hillside springs as well as runoff. It created a wetland known as the Mosquito Creek Swamp in the valley now occupied by the lake. It was the dream of local resident John W. Kiser and other members of his family that the area be dammed and made into a lake.

In 1932, the Kiser family offered several hundred acres in the Mosquito Creek Valley to the state. In 1939, a dam was constructed at that time, creating the 396-acre Kiser Lake, which became part of the state park system operated by the former Division of Conservation and Natural Resources. A bronze plaque commemorating the gift of the lake site by John W. Kiser and his mother, Thyrza Kiser, is attached to a large glacial boulder in the picnic area on the south side of the lake. As a part of the terms of the gift, motors are not permitted on Kiser Lake, so it has always been a popular place for enjoying small sailboats, rowboats, and canoes.

This area of the southern Ohio till plain lies within what geologists refer to as the boulder belt, where large glacial boulders of Canadian Shield origin were found in abundance at the time of settlement. Fencerows and gullies are full of them, most hauled from farm fields, and great piles can be seen near barns. No creek bed or stream cut is without them. Beech forest, with its many other associated species, such as oak and maple, covers the well-drained land, with swamp forest occurring in the poorly drained areas.

Opened to the public for purchase in the first decade of the nineteenth century, this part of Ohio was formed as a county two years after statehood, with Urbana early on becoming an important jumping-off spot for exploration farther north. The Shawnee Indians lived in the area before being forced north by the Treaty of Greeneville. Legendary frontiersman Simon Kenton also made his home in Champaign County for a number of years.

GETTING THERE

The Kiser Lake area can be reached by taking SR 235 north from I-70 above Fairborn to Possum Hollow Road, a distance of about 24 miles. Once there, turn east, drive 1.5 miles to Kiser Lake Road,

KISER LAKE SUNSET

and then turn north to the park and preserve. An alternate approach is to take Kiser Lake Road from the center of St. Paris, which is located on US 36 about halfway between Urbana and Piqua.

THE TRAILS

Begin hiking, as I did, by parking on the grass next to the bulletin board and trailhead—just east of the sign identifying the Kiser Lake Wetlands State Nature Preserve—on Kiser Lake Road, at the southeast corner of the lake. The best way to reach this point is by driving east from SR 235 on Possum Hollow Road (located a little more than a mile south of the lake dam). SR 235 dead-ends onto Kiser Lake Road. Turn left and follow the road as it heads north toward the lake, then turns right (east). At the bottom of the hill you'll find a short side road, along with the entrances to the wetlands trail and the state park's Red Oak Trail.

Enter the wetlands trails on the right side of the bulletin board. A boardwalk carries you across the seepage area and outlet to the marsh; then the trail uses a dredge spoil on the left bank of Mosquito Creek to head south, adjacent to the wetland. Another section of boardwalk, this time plastic, bridges a seepage as the trail works its way upstream. Other bridges span small outlets from the marsh to the stream. After a turn to the east along the meandering stream, the trail makes a sharp left turn to travel a long, winding boardwalk northeast across the wetland to the base of the moraine.

At the end of the boardwalk it looks like the trail goes both left and right, but it really doesn't: go left as the arrow on the Carsonite post indicates. Follow the trail as it climbs over and winds its way between the loam-covered piles of

gravel that constitute the moraine. As you approach the end of the trail, it dead-ends with the Red Oak Trail. If you have time, turn right and follow this 0.7-mile-long trail as it climbs the moraine to the right and loops south along the park boundary before returning to this intersection. As you go to your parking area, there is an old cellar hole uphill and to the right among a large patch of daylilies. Scramble up there, taking a moment to examine the stone foundation and, perhaps, to contemplate what living in a small house on this site might have been like 100 or more years ago, looking out not onto a beautiful lake but toward the well-known Mosquito Creek Swamp. I suspect that making a living and raising a family was tough.

To continue exploring the Kiser Lake area on foot, drive due west on Kiser Lake Road to the spot where it makes a right turn up the hill toward St. Paris. Instead of turning, take Park Road 7 straight ahead for about a half mile to signs on the left introducing the 0.7-mile Possum Hollow Trail and the half-mile Pine Tree Trail, in the state park. Have fun exploring this habitat, which is very different from the wetland. The trail follows the high bluff to the east of Possum Hollow, then returns via the valley floor. Huge patches of blue cohosh, skunk cabbage, and many other woodland wildflowers, including the uncommon twinleaf, grow near the trail. When I walked it, on Earth Day in 2001, the shrill voices of tree frogs echoed throughout the valley at high noon.

Kiser Lake has a pleasant campground with about 100 campsites where you may want to overnight. Boats are available for rent at two locations, and there is a swimming beach on the north side of the lake. During the warmer part of the year, interpretive programs

KISER LAKE WETLANDS REQUIRE A BOARDWALK

and exhibitions are offered at a small nature center and amphitheater near the campground.

While you are in Champaign County, you might enjoy hiking at other state nature preserves. Siegenthaler-Kastner Esker is located on Couchman Road between Calland and Church Roads in Harrison Township. Davey Woods is located off Lonesome, Smith, and Neal Roads north of US 36 in Concord and Mad River townships. Cedar Bog State Memorial, with its mile-long boardwalk, is reached by traveling west on Woodburn Road from US 68 south of Urbana. Walks in all three are described in *Walks and Rambles in Southwestern Ohio.*

Lake La Su An Wildlife Area

TOTAL DISTANCE: 5 miles (8 km)

HIKING TIME: 4 hours

MAXIMUM ELEVATION: 990 feet

VERTICAL RISE: 60 feet

MAPS: USGS 7.5' Series Nettle Lake; ODNR Lake La Su An Wildlife Area map

Lake La Su An sits high on the edge of the Wabash End Moraine in the northwest corner of the state, only a stone's throw from Michigan. The Wisconsinan-age loamy till soil of the hummocky terrain lies atop Mississippian-age Coldwater shale. It features rolling hills, closed depressions, wetlands, few streams, deranged drainage, and interspersed flats. Beech forests dominate the uplands, with swamp forests present in the poorly drained areas. It is land like none other I have seen in Ohio.

Most of this Steuben till plain, as the geologists call it, is located outside Ohio in Indiana and Michigan. In fact, the area where Lake La Su An Wildlife Area is today was claimed at one time by both the state of Ohio and the territory of Michigan. It lay between what was known as the Fulton Line—the line Michigan claimed as its southern boundary— and the Harris Line, which Ohio was certain was its northern border. War almost broke out over the conflicting claim in 1835. The dispute over the 8-mile strip was settled when the Upper Peninsula was added to Michigan in return for it giving up its claim on the disputed turf.

Hardly anyone lived in this far corner of the state until the 1830s, when people from the Middle Atlantic area began to settle the western end of the Michigan survey lands. Timber was cleared, and subsistence farming began. I suspect that the rolling land was used for grazing livestock.

Much of the land along the West Branch of the St. Joseph River that is now the 2,430-acre Lake La Su An Wildlife Area was purchased beginning in the 1950s by the late Edward Brodbeck. Largely working alone, he cleared brush, removed deadfalls, built dikes and

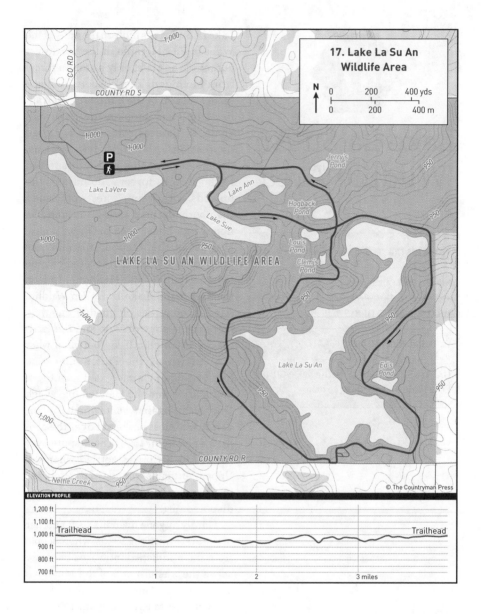

17. Lake La Su An Wildlife Area

N

| 0 | 200 | 400 yds |
| 0 | 200 | 400 m |

CO RD 6

COUNTY RD S

Lake LaVere

LAKE LA SU AN WILDLIFE AREA

Lake Ann

Lake Sue

Jerry's Pond

Hogback Pond

Louis Pond

Clem's Pond

Lake La Su An

Ed's Pond

COUNTY RD R

Nettle Creek

© The Countryman Press

ELEVATION PROFILE

| 1,200 ft |
| 1,100 ft |
| 1,000 ft | Trailhead | | Trailhead |
| 900 ft |
| 800 ft |
| 700 ft |

1　　2　　3 miles

dams, and expanded the original 6-acre pond known as Hays Lake to about 82 acres, naming it La Su An after the middle names of his daughters. After years of hard work, Brodbeck intended to open the lake to the public as a paid attraction called Dreamland Acres. However, his health failed before this dream could be recognized, and he died in 1986.

Those who had fished La Su An knew it as a source of premier bass and bluegills. The state began purchasing the area in 1981 and opened it to the public in 1983. Originally, fishing required an advance permit, but that is no longer the case. The area is now opened to licensed anglers on a restricted schedule available on the Lake La Su An

Wildlife Area website. Lack of available parking presents some limitation. Hikers and wildflower- and bird-watchers are welcomed on days that the area is open. I was especially pleased to see American columbo among the wildflowers. Redheaded woodpeckers, prothonotary warblers, and black-crowned night herons are but a few of the species of birds that reside or pass through La Su An. There are at least a dozen named bodies of water to find, all with interesting names.

Public hunting and trapping are also allowed on some parts of the area. Information can be obtained from the area office or from the Division of Wildlife in Columbus. Hikers must, of course, be aware that hunters may be present during open season, though I have hiked the area in fall and found no one around but me.

GETTING THERE

This unusual wildlife area is located approximately 60 miles west from Toledo, 41 miles north of Defiance, 1 mile south of the Ohio-Michigan state line, and 5 miles from the Ohio-Indiana state line. To reach it, take US 20 west from Toledo to SR 15 in Williams County. Turn north and go 1 mile to the center of Pioneer. To reach the headquarters of the area, turn west on County Road R and travel 7.5 miles. To reach the parking lot suggested above, drive 1 mile farther north on SR 15, then turn west onto County Road S and travel 8 miles. The entrance to the Area A parking lot is on the south side of the road.

Plan to spend a day hiking and a day fishing and/or canoeing (you must bring your own canoe).

THE TRAIL

I suggest that you begin your hiking at the Area A parking lot outside the gate on Williams County Road S. That is the northwest corner of the property. As I assembled my kit to begin walking on a beautiful May morning, a male eastern bluebird flew to the top of a post close to my car. Eastern towhees were singing their drink-your-tea song from nearby established territories. And a chorus of frog calls was coming from the closest lake.

Head into the area on the entry road and turn to the left, uphill, to continue on the gravel road overlooking Lake Lavere off to the right. There are 14 lakes in the area, many of which you will pass on your hike. The clockwise direction of travel is my choice to give me some backlit scenes of the lakes and possibly some pictures of wildlife with the sun behind me. The shagbark-hickory-dominated woods between the road and the lake along this first part of the walk are full of yellow trout lilies in spring. A first-hatch tiger swallowtail butterfly flew alongside me here on a May day, nectaring on dandelions beside the road.

At the east end of Lake Lavere, continue walking east on the service road with fields to the left and woods to the right. The road rises, then turns right and drops to a parking lot sitting between Lake Sue on the right and her smaller sister, Lake Ann, on the left. There are wood duck nesting boxes on nearly all of these lakes, so keep your eyes open for these spectacular woodland waterfowl.

Beyond the parking lot, follow the deteriorating old road as it makes a long climb through the woods, past an old field at the summit, and descends

WOODLAND TRAIL AT LAKE LA SU AN

to another pair of ponds. These are the much-smaller Hogback Pond on the left and Lou's Pond to the right. There are several clumps of white bark birch growing in this area. Not native, they may be either the European white birch or the paper birch found farther north on this continent. Some old apple trees alongside the trail must surely be enjoyed by the white-tailed deer of the area.

With Lake La Su An directly ahead through the woods, the service road turns left. A side road goes left toward the Hogback Pond dam, and another heads to the right around the west edge of Lake La Su An. Don't take either, but continue straight ahead, traveling east, parallel to the north shore of the lake, which is about 20 feet below the trail to the right. This is a nice wooded trail with a good show of spring wildflowers. Off to the left is buttonbush swamp. The endangered copperbelly water snake is a known resident of this part of Williams

the gentian family has not been reported in the literature as occurring in this part of the state. When seen in spring, before it sends up its flowering stalk, it has a resemblance to a cultivated tobacco plant. When it blooms in late spring, it has large paniculate clusters of four-lobed, purple-spotted, greenish yellow flowers on stalks about 6 feet tall.

Soon the trail makes a right turn to cross the dam and, heading south now, begins its ascent to the high open land east of Lake La Su An. As I traveled this area, I was not alone. Several unnamed dragonflies and a six-spotted (green forest) tiger beetle moved along the trail at about my pace. Both are predators, carnivores if you will; they were looking for other flying insects upon which to feed.

It is about a 75-foot rise from the dam to where the gravel service road turns 45 degrees to the right to travel a ridge through open grassland above the lake. There is a mowed trail parallel to the fence if you prefer, but I chose the route closer to the lake. There was a male prairie warbler singing his up-the-scale song as I passed through. From here you get the best view of Lake La Su An. The track you are following begins dropping as it swings to the left to cross the dike to Ed's Pond. A single redbud tree was in full bloom down the hill toward the lake during my hike.

A sign indicates that this is the nesting area of an endangered species. Upon inquiry, I learned that the Henslow's sparrow nests here. To the right of the trail is a planting of several acres of big bluestem grass, a native of Ohio's tallgrass prairies. Short-eared owls are seen in this wildlife area during the winter months. This crepuscular species occasionally nests in Ohio, but most of those seen are winter migrants from farther north. They fly low to the ground in the

County. This is the kind of habitat it prefers. It is, of course, illegal to collect or harm these creatures. Like their cousins the common water snakes, they are aggressive when encountered, but not poisonous.

Trees that were obviously felled by beavers give away the presence of a bank den along the lakeshore, downhill from the trail. It was also here that I found American columbo growing. This rosette-producing perennial member of early morning and late afternoon hours, hunting meadow voles.

Another bird that is considered uncommon in Ohio but is occasionally seen here during migration is the sandhill crane. They breed not far to the north, in Michigan, then fly south to spend the cold months in Florida and other Gulf states. Their breeding range seems to be expanding, so it is not unlikely that they may be seen nesting here in the not-too-distant future.

As the trail makes its way around the upper end of the lake, you are about as far from where you started as you will get. After passing a pump, the old road you have been following goes by a dock, then heads to the local checking station,

where fishing permits are issued and catches checked.

After a short rest, it's time to begin the return leg of the hike by heading west along the road, then turning back into the wildlife area to follow a mowed path uphill among pines and open meadow. As I crossed the area, a tree swallow emerged from a bluebird box, a brown thrasher entertained with its mocking song, and a towhee sang from a branch close by.

At the end of the pines, the trail passes a large sycamore that seems out of place so far from the water's edge; then, after a short stretch of more old field, it enters the woods. As the trail drops rapidly toward the lake level, it

LAKES, PONDS, AND TRAILS ARE ALL SIGNED AT LAKE LA SU AN

passes another small pond, this one through the woods to the left. The trail is surfaced with crushed gravel in this area. When I walked the trail through these more mesic woods there were some large patches of wild blue phlox in bloom. Among the oaks, hickories, and maples, the wide trail heads east on the level. To the left and right you can see where the road was located in an earlier time. Spring beauties and large-flowered trilliums, Ohio's official state wildflower, were in full flower in mid-May. A little-used track heads off to the right toward Lake La Su An, but do not follow it. Though this is not one of Ohio's boulder belts, an occasional glacial erratic sticks up through the surface of the ground.

After crossing another ravine, the trail returns to high ground and heads east once more. You can see Lake La Su An through the trees to the right and another small impoundment, Clem's Pond, to the left. The trail makes a hard left turn to cross in front of Clem's Pond. This is a picturesque spot where I could not keep the camera in my pack. The first green frog I had heard that spring gave its banjo-like call from the water's edge, and male toads were trying hard to seduce the opposite sex. Set a good many feet higher than La Su An, Clem's Pond is several acres in size. A blue jay scolded as I moved on down the trail; the shadow of a turkey vulture passed over the trail, as it had many times that day.

As the trail nears the top of yet another rise, the presence of old-fashioned garden iris in the young woods seems to indicate the earlier existence of a homestead in years past. A sign on the right identifies Lake La Su An, and the trail has returned to a familiar intersection. The outbound trail route has passed from left to right. Turn left, if you wish, to return to your vehicle by the route you entered, or continue straight across the intersection and cross the dike of Hogback Pond, which lies to the left. I interrupted a common water snake's sunbath on the dike, but enjoyed watching it navigate through the water. This pond has been stocked with amur carp to try to control aquatic vegetation. At the far end of the pond, a pair of Canada geese took to the water from their nest.

Next, follow the road uphill to where you can see Jerry's Pond on the right. There is a tower here that looks like a nesting tower for ospreys; these towers have been successful in many places around the country and should work here as well. There are a couple of other small ponds beyond this point, but they are neither accessible nor visible from the trail. Take the grass trail to the west to head through the woods, past the construction disposal area, and reconnect with the service road to the parking lot. Lake Lavere is visible to the south.

When you reach the mowed path to the Lake Lavere dam, turn left and walk to the dam. In spring you will likely be greeted by Canada geese using the earthen dike for nesting. Follow the trail beyond the dam and into the woods. American columbo also grows among the oaks and hickories on the slope. Eventually the trail comes out into a grassy field where there are more towers. Walk past them, heading northwest, to reach a service road that will lead you to the parking lot.

Camping is not permitted at Lake La Su Ann, but Harrison Lake State Park, which has a fine campground, is located about 20 miles to the east, just inside Fulton County.

Lockington Reserve

TOTAL DISTANCE: 3.5 to 6.5 miles (5.7 to 10.7 km)

HIKING TIME: 2 to 3.5 hours

MAXIMUM ELEVATION: 960 feet

VERTICAL RISE: 70 feet

MAPS: USGS 7.5' Piqua East and Piqua West; SCPD Lockington Reserve map; BTA Buckeye Trail map; St. Marys section map

The 1913 flood devastated the Great Miami River valley. Nothing on the floodplain was spared, and farmers and city folk alike suffered. Downtown Dayton was awash with water like no one had ever seen. City fathers decided that such a flood should never recur. The Miami Conservancy District was thus created, and five flood-control dams were built on the great Miami and four of its principal tributaries. These dams are unique because they impound no permanent pools and have no gates to close, even in times of flood. Only when the rainfall upstream exceeds the amount of water that can pass through the dam does water pool behind it. As the rain lets up and the water drains out, the water level drops. When no floodwater is being retained, which is most of the time, the hundreds of acres behind the dams are available for recreation. The genius behind this design was Arthur Morgan, later to become the president of Antioch College at Yellow Springs.

In Montgomery County, those lands form the heart of four park district reserves. Lockington Dam on Loramie Creek, in southern Shelby County, is the fifth of the conservancy's flood-control reservoirs. The Shelby County Park District now manages 200 acres around the reservoir as Lockington Reserve. Because it is a flood-control area, at times of heavy rainfall the trails may be inundated. If in doubt, call the park district office at 937-773-4818.

Loramie Creek, the West Branch of the Great Miami, originates on the flatland of Shelby County between the Lake Erie and Ohio River watersheds. It gets its name from Pierre Loramie, a Frenchman who operated an Indian trading post, Loramie's Station, at the present site of Fort Loramie from 1769 until 1782. In the early 1840s, the headwaters

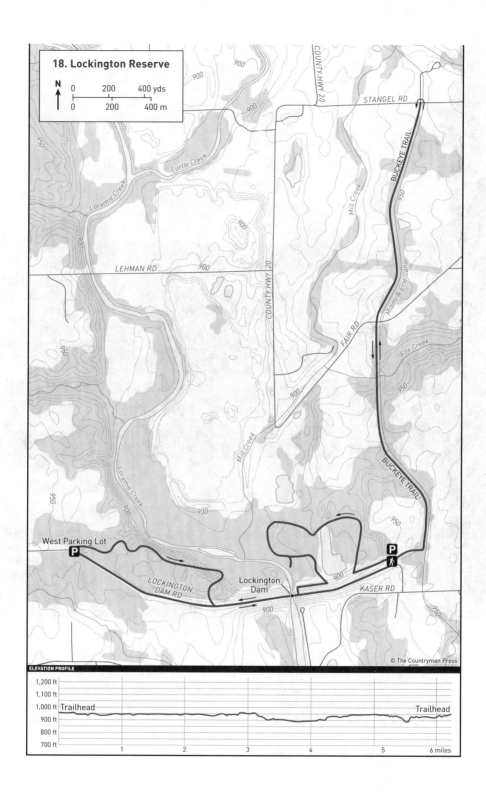

18. Lockington Reserve

N

| 0 | 200 | 400 yds |
| 0 | 200 | 400 m |

COUNTY HWY 20

STANGEL RD

Turtle Creek

Loramie Creek

900

950

Mill Creek

BUCKEYE TRAIL

950

Miami & Erie Canal

LEHMAN RD

900

COUNTY HWY 20

FAIR RD

900

Fox Creek

950

950

Loramie Creek

900

Mill Creek

900

BUCKEYE TRAIL

950

West Parking Lot

P

950

LOCKINGTON DAM RD

Lockington Dam

900

KASER RD

P

900

950

© The Countryman Press

ELEVATION PROFILE

1,200 ft						
1,100 ft						
1,000 ft	Trailhead				Trailhead	
900 ft						
800 ft						
700 ft						
	1	2	3	4	5	6 miles

LOCKINGTON RESERVOIR

of Loramie Creek were dammed to make Loramie Reservoir, which fed the Miami & Erie Canal. The summit at Loramie was 512 feet above the level of the Ohio River at Cincinnati, so a series of locks was needed to allow boats to make the 99-mile trip. The first of these, Locks 1-5, were at the village of Lockington, 18 miles from the feeder that brought water from Loramie Reservoir to the canal. During the late 1800s, Lockington thrived, and in its heyday it boasted 19 industries. The 1880 census reported a population of 219, and those are only the ones who were counted. But by 1913, when floods sounded the death knell for

When the flood-control reservoir was built on Loramie Creek it was named for the closest town on the 15' USGS quadrangle, Lockington (those were the days before every reservoir was named for a politician). The area includes trails for hiking and cross-country skiing, several bird blinds, a camping area available for a fee by reservation, and two picnic shelters. The park district offers an already assembled "Rent-a-camp" if you do not have, or do not want to bring, your own gear. The Buckeye Trail passes along the eastern edge of the preserve, and there is a connecting trail to the BT from the shelter and restroom area. Due to the vagaries of public wells, carrying water from home is advisable.

GETTING THERE

Lockington Reserve is reached by taking US 36 west from I-75 into Piqua. Turn right (north) on OH 66 and follow it 4 miles to Hardin Road, where you turn right. At a T with Fessler-Buxton Road, turn right. After crossing Loramie Creek, turn left onto Kaser Road, which leads to the park entrance at Lockington Dam Road.

THE TRAIL

The Buckeye Trail and the trails of the reserve start at the parking lot at the east end of the dam. To walk the section of the BT north of here, along the Miami & Erie Canal towpath, go east from the parking lot 200 yards, following the blue blazes. Turn left at the towpath. For the next 1.5 miles, the BT follows the path once trod by horses and mules as they towed canal boats between Cincinnati and Toledo. At Stangel Road, the BT leaves the towpath for pavement. Turn around there and return to the picnic area at the reserve.

the canal system statewide, water traffic had already ceased in Lockington. The locks, located in the middle of the village, are preserved by the Ohio Historical Society in cooperation with the Shelby County Park District. The canal towpath, north of the town, is the route of the Buckeye Trail (BT).

A relatively new trail leaves the picnic area going north along the edge of the old field, hugging the forest on the left. It is headed for high ground where there is an observation deck from which you can see the pond in the valley below. It's a dead-ender. Return to the parking lot to begin your exploration of the main area of the preserve.

To continue the hike for another 3 miles, head downhill on the service road at the base of the dam. Turn right and go down a set of steps. After crossing a bridge that spans a stream between a small pond on the right and a large borrow pit pond on the left, the trail crosses a smaller bridge. As it reaches a pine growth, it splits. Follow the right fork as it goes uphill and curves left through the pines. It soon reaches a point where a trail to the right leads to the group camping area. Make a partial right turn. There will be an area of successional forest (an old farm field now reverting to forest by the process of natural succession) to the left and woodland on the right. Watch for a wildlife-viewing area; you may want to spend some time there.

Soon, a quarry pond becomes visible on private property to the right. After 100 feet, the trail reaches a spot where you can see another meadow being overgrown with shrubs and young trees a short distance ahead through the woods. Follow its left edge. Shortly, the trail splits. The right fork is a spur that leads through the woods to Loramie Creek for a good view of the dam. After studying the unusual open dam, return on the same spur trail and turn right to continue on the main trail.

After 100 feet, the trail turns into the woods and approaches two bird blinds, where you can view birds at feeders.

Departing the bird blinds, continue toward the dam on the paved trail. Where the trail reaches an old road, turn right. The borrow pit pond will be on the left. When this trail reaches the base of the dam, turn left (east). There you have a choice. To bring your hike to an end, continue east up the old road to the parking lot where you began. If you want some more hiking, travel up the road to where you can climb to the abandoned road on top of the dam. Travel this path west for 1 mile, across the dam and over the spillway to the west parking lot. There, turn right where you see the trail entering the brush and forest to the north. A colored marker there indicates the trail, but sometimes it's difficult to see. The trail crosses a boardwalk between two ponds, then passes another pine planting as it heads to the 90-foot-high bluff overlooking the creek. Upon reaching the edge of the bluff, the trail turns right to loop back to the trail along the foot of the dam. This west loop trail is not heavily used and may be a little difficult to follow; however, the dam is always in view, so there is no chance of becoming lost, even if you end up bushwhacking around a deadfall or a place where the trail has grown over. Return to the trailhead parking lot via the old road atop the dam.

A visit to the Lockington Reserve area would not be complete without spending some time in the village viewing the locks and the 150-year-old homes that remain from the canal days.

Maumee Bay State Park

TOTAL DISTANCE: 2.25 miles (3.6 km)	

HIKING TIME: 2 hours, at a scenic pace

MAXIMUM ELEVATION: 575 feet

VERTICAL RISE: 5 feet

MAPS: USGS 7.5' Reno Beach and Oregon; ODNR Maumee State Park brochure; Maumee Bay Boardwalk map

ACCESSIBILITY: This trail and its ancillary facilities meet the standards of the federal Americans with Disabilities Act (ADA).

Ohio is said to be second only to California in its loss of natural wetland habitat. Since settlement, millions of acres of fens, bogs, swamps, wet prairies, and marshlands have been drained for agriculture or to make managed "duck marshes." At Maumee Bay State Park, a small expanse of Lake Erie marsh has been preserved and a boardwalk constructed to allow visitors to have a closer look at this rare habitat. The Milton B. Trautman Nature Center, with exhibitions that interpret the natural and cultural history of the Lake Erie marshes, is located at the entrance to the boardwalk. No matter how many times you walk this trail, you will always have a unique experience. Visit it in different seasons, when different land birds and waterbirds are using the area. Experience the various weather moods Mother Nature throws at the boardwalk. See how many different species of dragonflies, damselflies, and butterflies you can see on a summer walk. Come when the male frogs are singing their "aren't I pretty, come mate with me" call over the months of spring. Learn the blossoms of the plants of the wetlands by visiting often during the growing season, with short-focusing binoculars, a 100 mm macro lens on your camera, and a wildflower book in your pack. And remember, it's a wetland, so be prepared for the six-legged hummers. These female mosquitoes need a blood meal to ensure that there will be a next generation to help feed the birds and other insects.

GETTING THERE

To reach Maumee Bay State Park, with its lodge, cabins, campground, Milton B. Trautman Nature Center, and Maumee Bay Boardwalk, take OH 2 east from

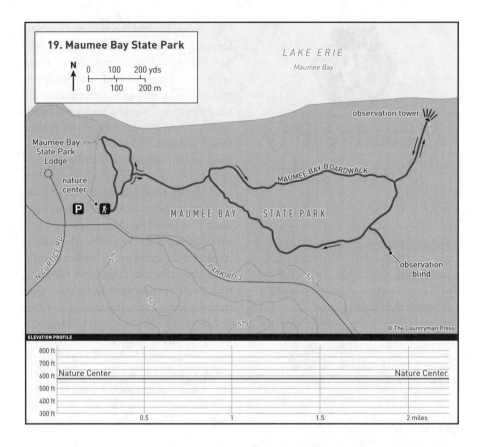

19. Maumee Bay State Park

N

| 0 | 100 | 200 yds |
| 0 | 100 | 200 m |

LAKE ERIE
Maumee Bay

observation tower

Maumee Bay
State Park
Lodge

nature
center

MAUMEE BAY BOARDWALK

MAUMEE BAY   STATE PARK

N CURTICE RD

575

PARK RD 3

575

575

575

observation
blind

© The Countryman Press

ELEVATION PROFILE

| 800 ft |
| 700 ft |
| 600 ft | Nature Center | | | | | | Nature Center |
| 500 ft |
| 400 ft |
| 300 ft |
| | 0.5 | 1 | 1.5 | 2 miles |

I-280 on the east side of Toledo. At North Curtice Road turn left (north) toward Lake Erie. This road will lead you into the park, where signs will direct you to the nature center.

THE TRAIL

This hike begins with a visit to the Milton B. Trautman Nature Center, reached by sidewalk and a bridge over a small pond. Note the cutout steel artwork in the pond to the right. The center is dedicated to the memory of Drs. Milton B. and Mary A. Trautman. Milton was author of the monumental treatise *Fishes of Ohio*, and Mary was his steadfast helpmate during the writing of this book and the completion of many other projects. They were dear friends of mine and of the community of naturalists in Ohio and beyond. How fortunate we are that they passed our way. There is an exhibition related to their lives in the nature center. During the spring and summer, the nature center's hours are 10:00 a.m. to 5:00 p.m. Monday through Friday, and 1:00 p.m. to 6:00 p.m. Saturday and Sunday. In the off season, the hours are 1:00 p.m. to 5:00 p.m. Wednesday through Friday, and 10:00 a.m. to 5:00 p.m. on Saturday. The nature center's dedication ceremony was May 21, 1993.

The 2-mile boardwalk system that reaches out into the coastal marsh from the nature center was built in 1992 by the proud young people of the Ohio Civilian Conservation Corps, a division of the Ohio Department of Natural Resources. In addition to serving park visitors, the center offers special programs for visiting school groups and people of all ages from the surrounding communities. To the left of the center is a wooden screen house, named the Doris N. Stifel Monarch Gazebo in honor of The Monarch Lady of Toledo, who ran monarch rearing and tagging programs here each summer. Beyond the gazebo is a handicapped-accessible butterfly garden maintained by staff and volunteers. It is an official Monarch Way Station in the program run by Monarch Watch, based at the University of Kansas.

On the opposite side of the nature center there is a small pond and a bird-feeding area that can be viewed from a window in the center. Restrooms available from the outside are open even when the center is closed. The elevated trail through the marsh begins from the right rear corner of the center and is accessible by stairs or ramp. The 5-foot-wide trail was built of treated wood to the standards of the Americans with Disabilities Act. There is a quarter-mile loop close to the center that can be reached from the center and the park lodge, a 1-mile loop available via a single connecting trail from the smaller loop, a connecting trail to the cabin area, a spur trail to a two-level observation deck, and a spur trail to an observation blind. There are large interpretive signs with color photos and text at nine places along the trail. Most, but not all, are at trail entrances or intersections. At the bottom of each you'll find a map routed in wood with a red dot showing the location and station number, not necessarily in sequence.

The numbers are useful in giving hikers the approximate location of plants or animals that have been spotted by others. I have not provided the information on the signs here, as they are better understood when you read them onsite. In addition, at least eight smaller interpretive signs on tall posts scattered along the trail provide information about such topics as reptiles, poison ivy, dead trees, bat boxes, wood ducks, swamp forest, and decaying logs. On the short loop, small red signs with white letters (also in Braille) are located on the top of a handrail and are keyed to an interpretive guide for the disabled, including those with a visual handicap. Ask for the accompanying material at the nature center. There are places to sit and rest at each of the nine stations, plus at a few other good places for wildlife watching along the way.

A lake and shoreline marsh represent a dynamic environment, changing over time spans both short and long. I have walked this trail perhaps a dozen times since its construction and it has never been the same. In the 1990s, the lake level was high and there was standing water along much of the trail. As I write this, Lake Erie is near a historic low level, thus the marsh and adjoining swamp forest have been devoid of water. Most woody plants, such as the swamp forest trees and the stands of buttonbush, survive those changes, but some do not, and you will see standing dead trees. These become feeding and nesting sites for many creatures. Herbaceous plant populations tend to respond more quickly to changing water levels; needless to say, so too do the populations of reptiles and amphibians.

On the left side of the boardwalk,

BOARDWALK AT MAUMEE BAY STATE PARK

just beyond Station 1, there is a concrete slab on the forest floor that identifies the imprint of eight mammals that might be seen along the trail. This is one of several Scout projects along the trail. Study it closely so you can recognize any tracks you come across. Rabbits have sometimes been fairly abundant along the trail, but the presence of the canine carnivores such as red fox and coyote make that a balancing act that tilts back and forth between predator and prey. White-tailed deer are nearly always seen in the swamp forest. I counted nine on a recent early November day. Some folks I talked with on one autumn walk reported seeing 28.

The boardwalk starts out through swamp forest with only an occasional open area. At Station 2, turn right and continue through the woods along the outer part of the handrailed short loop. Soon you will reach Station 3. The short loop continues straight ahead toward the lake. Take the trail to the right to access the long loop, the observation tower, and the blinds. This is a good area in which

to spot deer. Soon you will emerge from the woods and experience the first large stand of Phragmites along the trail. This very tall grass with its plume-like inflorescence is often called reed grass. It competes with cattails for dominance in the marsh. In the early spring, red-winged blackbirds can be seen swaying back and forth near the tops of last year's reed grass, advertising their availability with a squeaky kiong-ka-ree song.

At the next station, No. 6, turn left toward the lake. From here on the swamp forest will give way to stands of herbaceous reed grass, cattails, or the woody buttonbush. On one June walk I saw several viceroy butterflies along here, and photographed one that was basking. This is typical habitat for that monarch-look-alike species. There are cottonwoods and willows here too, both species that are known to be host plants for viceroy larvae. After nearly a half mile of walking, you will really feel that you are out of the woods and wholly into a Lake Erie marsh. Notice that both the common cattail and narrow-leaved cattail are present here—and probably the hybrid between the two.

At Station 7, take the spur to the right to a two-level observation tower. On the upper level there is a map that will help you identify the man-made objects you can see across this broad sweep of Lake Erie's western basin. Note the Little Cedar Point National Wildlife Refuge jutting into the water along the shore to the right. As a naturalist, it grieves me to see that the shore-vine visible from here is armored with rip-rap, but this is probably necessary to protect the area against further shoreline erosion. A great egret was fishing in the marsh beyond the tower on one early summer day when I walked this way. The nearest egret rookery is on West Sister Island, more than 16 miles northeast from Maumee Bay in Lake Erie, so these wading birds make a long flight back and forth daily to feed in these shallow protected waters.

Backtrack on the spur to the main trail. Note that enough people get confused about where they are that directions have been painted on the decking at most intersections. A hard left turn will carry you past more marsh, but soon you will reenter the swamp forest. If the alien emerald ash borer that is spreading across Ohio reaches this area, as it is quite likely to do, another important element of the wetland communities, the ash trees, will surely disappear, as did the American elm nearly a century ago.

Heading back toward the trailhead, you will soon pass a small pond off to the left and arrive at Station 8 and the spur trail to the observation blind. This trail-level structure, with slots through which to peer, offers a chance to observe all sorts of wildlife close up. Returning to the main trail, turn left to continue through the swamp forest. Shortly, there is a seating area in the middle of a stand of Phragmites. At Station 9, you'll find a repeat of the station welcome sign, as

VISITOR CENTER AT MAUMEE STATE PARK HONORS DOCTORS MILTON AND MARY TRAUTMAN

MAUMEE BAY BOARDWALK TAKES HIKERS TO A SMALL TOWER OVERLOOKING A POND

this is an entrance for the cabins-area vacationers. There are at least two large nesting boxes high in trees along the trail here, probably meant for barred owls or squirrels. Two additional rest areas provide for a respite as you continue toward the trailhead. As I passed this way one midsummer day, a wood-pewee was calling. It's one of the species that continues to sing long after the nuptial season.

Upon returning to Station 6, make the right turn to connect with the short loop. There, once again at Station 3, I suggest you turn right toward the lake. As the trail curves left to parallel the shore-line, it rises ever so slightly over a beach ridge. Station 4, the only station not at an intersection, is the place to stop and contemplate what role wetlands play in the ecosystem. From here, it's only a short way to Station 5, and another repeat of the welcome station. Take the right if you want to go to the lodge. The left fork will allow you to complete the short loop, and at Station 2 you can catch the connector back to the nature center.

Now that you have had an introduction to the Lake Erie wetland, return often to see what a new hour or season will hold for you in this wondrous shore-line environment.

Dutch Elm Disease

The American or white elm was once an important part of Ohio's forests. A component of the elm/ash/maple forests of poorly drained bottomlands, it was also part of the mesic woodlands in the northern part of the state. Forest-grown American elms had tall columnar trunks. For many years, the largest known white elm grew at Marietta. It was 26 feet, 6.5 inches in circumference at breast height. American elms, with their wineglass shape, once lined the streets of most Ohio cities and villages. The Dutch elm disease is a fungus, *Ceratocystis ulmi*, carried by the European bark beetle. It was first discovered to be affecting elms in Cleveland in 1930. By 1933, it was being seen at the port of New York, but by then no amount of quarantining could prevent its spread across eastern North America.

At the same time, a second disease was attacking the elms in Ohio. Originally called *phloem necrosis*, but now referred to as elm yellows, this phytoplasm-caused disease was first seen in Ironton, Ohio, in 1918. It was likely as devastating to Ohio's elms as Dutch elm disease. In any case, by the late 1940s Ohio towns had lost nearly all of their lawn and street shade trees, and the elm was gone from the swamp forests.

Today, an occasional young elm tree can be seen in places like Cedar Bog (where giant elms once stood), but they hardly ever make it past the 6-inch-diameter size. A few municipalities in the East still use the American elm as a street tree, but they have to use an aggressive spraying program to halt the spread of the two diseases that all but wiped out the species in the Ohio woods.

Oak Openings Preserve Metro Park

TOTAL DISTANCE: 16.6 miles (25.9 km)

HIKING TIME: 12 hours or 2 days

MAXIMUM ELEVATION: 690 feet

VERTICAL RISE: 50 feet

MAPS: USGS 7.5′ Swanton; USGS 7.5′ Whitehouse; MPDTA Oak Openings Preserve Metro Park map

Oak Openings is a sandy tract of land, about 130 square miles in area, that extends from western Lucas County into adjoining Fulton and Henry Counties. Though the area is mostly flat, there are sand dunes as high as 25 feet scattered throughout. Underlain by an impenetrable Wisconsinan-age clayey till, the land is covered with loose, permeable sand deposited on or near the shoreline of glacial Lake Warren, a precursor of present-day Lake Erie. The underlying glacial till is alkaline, but the sand is acidic. Rainwater that collects in low places and soaks into the soil becomes alkaline when it contacts the underlying limy till. The sand dunes and dry hills, however, remain acidic. In addition, the local accumulation of organic material in ancient swamps has led to locally acidic sites. Many native tree species that require rich soils or a neutral soil are thus absent from the area. On the other hand, small areas of wet prairie similar to those that occurred in pre-settlement days do remain, and the region is home to many rare and endangered species of plants and animals.

The incredible diversity of habitat and the presence of many species of plants and animals not commonly found elsewhere in the state make this trail especially attractive to naturalists. From mid-February, when the skunk cabbage comes into bloom, until late October, when heavy frost knocks down the last of the gentians, there is always an unusual flower in bloom somewhere in Oak Openings. Among them are at least a dozen species of native orchids. In the open areas where prairie and old field species occur, butterflies are common, and many species of mammals and birds reside in this vast park year-round. Reptiles with habitat requirements as different as those of the spotted turtle

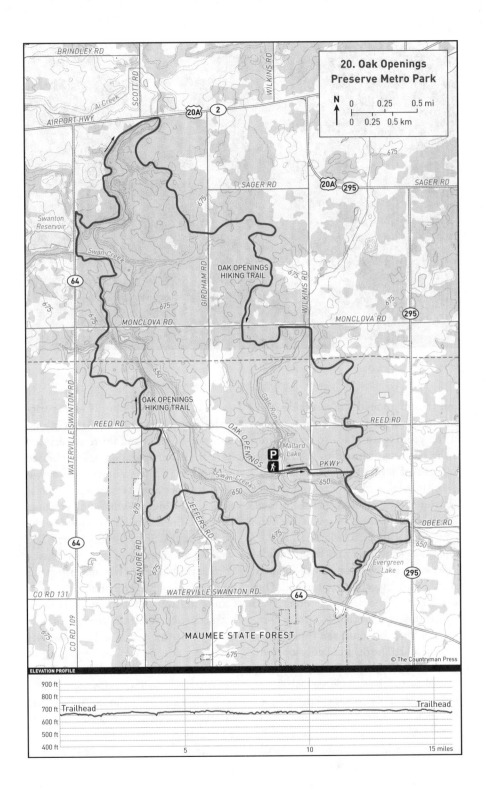

20. Oak Openings Preserve Metro Park

N

0   0.25   0.5 mi
0   0.25   0.5 km

BRINDLEY RD

SCOTT RD

Ai Creek

AIRPORT HWY

20A   2

WILKINS RD

SAGER RD

20A   295

SAGER RD

675

Swanton
Reservoir

Swan Creek

64

OAK OPENINGS
HIKING TRAIL

675

GIRDHAM RD

WILKINS RD

675

MONCLOVA RD

675

675

MONCLOVA RD

295

675

650

WATERVILLE SWANTON RD

OAK OPENINGS
HIKING TRAIL

REED RD

OAK OPENINGS

Gale Run

Mallard
Lake

P

REED RD

PKWY

650

Swan Creek

650

650

MANORE RD

675

JEFFERS RD

675

OBEE RD

64

650

295

Evergreen
Lake

CO RD 131

CO RD 109

WATERVILLE SWANTON RD.

64

675

675

MAUMEE STATE FOREST

675

© The Countryman Press

ELEVATION PROFILE

900 ft			
800 ft			
700 ft Trailhead		Trailhead
600 ft			
500 ft			
400 ft	5	10	15 miles

BUTTERFLY WEED

and the hog-nosed snake reside here. The rare lark sparrow is known to nest in the park. It's a place to come often with your senses tuned to the wonderful world of nature that abounds here.

In 1939, when the Metropolitan Park District of the Toledo Area was formed, plans were made to "revitalize" the sandy area west of Toledo. An initial 67 acres was acquired, and thousands of pines and other evergreens were planted in an attempt to stabilize the soil. One major sand dune area was conserved within the park so that future generations of visitors could see this type of Ohio habitat. The original development, known as Springbrook Park, is now only a small part of the 3,744-acre Oak Openings Preserve Metro Park. The complex includes a reservable lodge, picnic areas, and many miles of bicycle, horse, and foot trails, including a 16.2-mile loop trail (described below) that goes around the perimeter of the park.

Oak Openings Hiking Trail was originally developed as a Boy Scout hiking trail and is still used for that purpose. Its 50th year of operation was celebrated in 2005. It is said to have been developed by Max Shepherst, then commissioner of the Metro Parks, and Ben Long. They and the Scouts of Explorer Post 55 at Burroughs School did the original walking and blazing of what was then a 17-mile trail. It was a two-day hike with an overnight at the Springbrook Scout Camping Area. In the many years since it first opened, thousands of Scouts from throughout the region have walked its earthen path. Scout units wishing to walk the trail should contact the Trails Committee, Erie Shores Council, BSA, 1 Stranahan Square, Suite 226 Toledo, OH 43604, phone number 419-241-7293, for information on reservations, awards, and camping. The trail can be hiked as a single 16.2-mile loop or, by adding a 2.5-mile connector that utilizes public roads and the parkway, you can do it as two segments of close to 10 miles each. There are no campsites available to the general public, and camping is not permitted along the trail. There are, however, two privately operated campgrounds within a mile or two of the trailhead. There is a group camping area at the trailhead available to youth groups only, on a reservation basis.

Dogs are not allowed on the trails. This is a wet area, and during some seasons of the year insects will be bad. A prudent hiker will be prepared. Be especially careful about matches and cigarettes because of the flammability of the prairie grasses and pine needles. Water is available at pumps located at picnic areas along the trail. There are no concessions serving food anywhere within the park.

GETTING THERE

To reach the entrance to Oak Openings, take OH 2 west from I-475/US 23 at Exit 8 on the west side of Toledo. Travel 8.5 miles to Wilkins Road. Turn left (south) and travel 2.75 miles to the park entrance on the right side of the road. Park in the Mallard Lake Picnic Area lot on the right side of Oak Openings Parkway, 1.25 miles beyond the entrance.

THE TRAIL

There is a trailhead kiosk near the Buehner Center for Oak Openings at the parking lot on the west side of Mallard Lake. This serves all of the trails in the park. Oak Openings Hiking Trail is well signed and marked with yellow blazes. To begin the hike, walk east to the lake edge, then turn right to follow the trail around the southern end of the lake. Follow the trail along the left side

of the parkway to its intersection with the orange-blazed Evergreen Trail. Turn right and cross the parkway to a kiosk in front of the lodge. There, turn left (east) and begin following the yellow-blazed trail.

After 200 feet, the trail crosses the road and enters a deciduous forest. Here it passes the area designated for group camping. It is used by Scout groups that arrive on a Friday so they can camp near the trailhead and get on the trail early the next morning. After you have walked about a quarter mile, the trail divides into inbound and outbound forks. I suggest hiking the southern loop first, but the choice is yours.

Turning right, for three quarters of a mile the trail travels between Swan Creek and the parkway, soon reaching OH 295. After another right turn, walk the berm of the road across Swan Creek toward the entrance to the Evergreen Lake Picnic Area. About two-thirds of the way between the creek and park entrance, the trail turns right on a path through the woods. It soon joins the paved All-Purpose Trail just a few feet from the trailhead signs alongside the parkway. Turn right on the All-Purpose Trail and follow it across Evergreen Lake Dam. Don't miss the turn at the far end of the dam. The All-Purpose Trail goes straight, the hiking trail left.

Now tracing the shoreline, the trail passes a stand of hemlock where a horse trail comes in from the right and follows it along the lakeshore. Where the two trails enter a pine grove, a shelter house, horse stalls, and restrooms serve those using the bridle trail. Having almost reached the southern boundary of the park, the trail crosses the bridle trail to the left, and then makes a tight clockwise turn as it begins heading northwest. As it passes through a narrow pine plantation, it crosses an east-west-running fire lane. After leaving the pines and entering a woody wet area, it crosses a second fire lane. A quarter-mile later, the hiking trail turns west, crosses the All-Purpose/Wabash Cannonball Trail Connector, and then travels along the edge of a deciduous forest for another quarter mile. Next it crosses a horse trail and angles left, beginning a sweeping semicircular arc through pine and regenerating fields. A fire lane going straight ahead can be easily mistaken for the footpath. This is the Pine Ridge Area, where prairie forbs such as Carolina puccoon can be found in the grassy openings. A quarter-mile later, the path crosses the fire lane as it begins heading north through a nice deciduous woods.

Winding its way to the northwest, the trail stays among the hardwoods on high ground for about a half mile before passing through more pines and crossing two horse trails in quick succession. Now turning toward the north, the trail crosses another horse trail, then Evans Ditch, which drains into Swan Creek. This ditch is part of a large network of ditches in Oak Openings, built many decades ago in an attempt to make the land suitable for agriculture. After crossing the ditch, the hiking trail turns north, then west to cross another horse trail.

The trail now passes between regenerating fields on the right and older woods on the left. After a quarter mile, the trail reaches and crosses Jeffers Road near a picnic area. Beyond Jeffers Road is a good place to look for badgers, or at least for signs of badgers. Seventy-five yards past the road the trail turns south, crosses a small bridge, and makes a large loop through a wet woods, crossing two horse trails as it does so. It next heads north on slightly higher land, parallel-

ing the west boundary of the park. A fire lane enters from the right after a half mile, and several hundred feet beyond that the trail makes an abrupt right turn to follow another ditch toward Jeffers Road. After crossing another horse trail and turning left across the ditch, the trail travels the road's edge as it goes west to reach Reed Road near its intersection with Manore Road.

Your hike has now covered about 5 miles. This is a good place to return to the trailhead if you wish to reduce your mileage. To do so, turn right (east) on Reed Road and walk three quarters of a mile to Oak Openings Parkway. Turn right and follow the drive a half mile to the Mallard Lake parking lot, for a total walk of 7.5 miles.

Return to the trail another day by reversing the 1.25-mile cutoff described above. To continue walking the 16.2-mile trail, angle left across Reed Road and across a horse trail to where the yellow-marked trail leaves the road, headed north between a white pine plantation and regenerating old field. As pines blend to hardwoods, the trail angles slightly right for a couple hundred feet, turns north on the highest land in the park, then turns west, continuing through oak forest. At the edge of the older forest, you will cross a north-south horse trail just as the hiking trail turns north-northeast to cross the All-Purpose/Wabash Cannonball Trail on the former Norfolk & Western (N&W) Railroad right-of-way. The Springbrook Picnic Area and the Springbrook Lake Trail (formerly a part of the hiking trail) are located about a quarter mile west of this crossing beyond OH 64. They can be accessed via the All-Purpose Trail. There is also a restroom there.

As demonstrated here, many years ago the park district began experiment-

BLAZING STAR IN BLOOM AT OAK OPENINGS

ing with pines to stabilize the sand blow-outs of Oak Openings.

Beyond the railroad right-of-way crossing the hiking trail follows the yellow markings on a path to the north. It crosses an old service road that is now a horse trail leading to a horse resting area (at one time a group camping area that was used as a midpoint campsite for the hiking trail). This is the site of the original dedication monument for Oak Openings Scout Trail. On relatively high land above a creek, the woods has one of the largest red maples I have seen in Ohio. Beyond the horse trail, the hiking trail drops to the creek valley, traveling north. Just before the trail reaches Monclova Road, it turns left across a small stream before crossing the road at the west end of the Swan Creek Bridge.

For the next 3.25 miles, Oak Openings Hiking Trail follows the west bank of Swan Creek, with the exception of a single place where it moves nearly a quarter mile away to cross the stream coming in from Swanton Reservoir.

Crossing side ravines on small bridges, it passes through riverine forest and more white pine plantations. When the trail comes within sight of OH 2, it stays off the highway berm as it uses the right-of-way to get over Swan Creek. At the east end of the bridge, watch the utility poles and the end of the guardrail for blazes and arrows.

The return route from this point, the northernmost on the trail, provides a diversity of habitat. The trail passes through prairie openings, old fields, mixed black and white oak forest, pin oak swamp, sand dunes, and pine forest. The soil varies from alkaline in the wet prairie to very acidic in the pin oak swamp forest.

At the east end of the OH 2 Swan Creek crossing, the trail turns south into regenerating old fields and old mixed oak forest. After crossing some almost flat land, the trail begins to swing left as it drops toward Bushnell Ditch. Turning left at the ditch, the trail travels upstream (east) through more evergreen forest for a quarter mile. Near a property line corner it turns south again, traveling through deciduous woods, brush, and meadow. Where it reaches an east-west horse trail, the footpath turns left (east) to share the equestrian path for a couple hundred yards. Turning south once more, the trail next travels through dry, sandy terrain with prairie grasses and forbs between small stands of oaks. Here and there the mounds of harvester ants can be seen.

After traveling .3 mile through mostly open land, the trail enters a large stand of red pine, where it turns left (east) and soon reaches Girdham Road. Many of the pines are dying and being removed. After crossing the road, the trail skirts another evergreen planting and then continues east through swamp forest. The hiking trail crosses a fire lane and then makes a left turn and crosses a horse trail, turning right shortly thereafter. After another one-eighth of a mile traveling east, the trail swings south in a reverse S-curve. This is the flattest area of the preserve. The trail meets and then leaves the horse trail once more as it turns left to follow the edge of the woods.

South of Monclova Road, the trail crosses the All-Purpose/Wabash Cannonball Horse Trail connector, then turns left (east) on a fire lane along deciduous woods for a quarter mile. The trail next turns north until Monclova Road is visible through the trees; then it turns right (east), parallel to the road and connector trail. As it approaches Wilkins Road, it crosses the connector one last time and turns right (south). Traveling along the road and the connector trail, it crosses a small bridge, then passes a lovely stand of cinnamon fern before reaching the Wabash Cannonball Trail.

The hiking trail crosses the Wabash Cannonball Trail and Wilkins Road together, then shares an old track with a horse trail and the connector trail as together they head uphill to the southeast. Moving through oak woods, the trails split as they reach high land. The hiking trail takes the left fork through a wet area, and the connector trail continues east for a short way and then makes a half turn to the north parallel to the hiking trail. The horse trail swings to the right (south) toward a large evergreen forest. The hiking trail next swings south and crosses the bridle trail just prior to where it joins the Wabash Cannonball Trail to exit the park. Traveling through rough, very wet pin oak woodland, the hiking trail utilizes corduroy road and boardwalk to keep hikers dry. About a mile after the Wabash Cannonball crossing, Oak Openings Hiking Trail emerges from the swamp onto Reed Road amid a stand of black oaks.

After a direct road crossing, the trail goes a short distance into a spruce forest, and then turns left (east), then south to continue among the evergreens. When it reaches a fire lane coming in from the left, the trail turns right and soon leaves the spruce stand, headed south through more mixed oak forest. After two jogs to the right, it crosses a horse trail before curving right to cross Oak Openings Parkway. In the forest just beyond the road, the trail meets the outbound 16.2-mile trail, thus closing the loop. A turn toward the west takes the trail past the main Group Camp and Oak Openings Lodge. Turn right onto the orange-blazed Evergreen Trail, follow it across the road, and turn left to follow the path around the lakeshore to the trailhead and the Mallard Lake parking lot.

Flowers of the Air

Adult butterflies are considered to be creatures of the summer by most Ohioans, but I have encountered them in forest and field in every month of the year. As cold-blooded creatures, they need heat from an external source to allow them to move about. In nearly every case, that means an ambient air temperature above 60 degrees Fahrenheit and unfiltered sunlight in which to bask. Though the vast majority of the 144 species that are found in Ohio overwinter as pupae or eggs, a few make it through the winter as adults in a condition called reproductive diapause. Instead of breeding shortly after emerging from pupae in late summer or fall, they wait until warm weather the following spring. During one of those rare warm spells in January or February, one of these insects may take to the air. I once saw a Milbert's tortoise-shell along the boardwalk at Cedar Bog State Memorial in January, and I have seen mourning cloaks along the trails at Glen Helen in many February warm spells.

At least two species found in the summer in Ohio, the monarch and the painted lady, do not overwinter here. While some species, notably the cabbage white and the clouded and orange sulphurs, seem to breed continually, with overlapping broods from April through November, most species have only one, two, or three broods. When there is more than one brood, there is usually an overlap. If you are out and about much you will soon come to recognize the peak period of each hatch. To learn more about Ohio butterflies, look for *Butterflies and Skippers of Ohio*, by Iftner, Shuey, and Calhoun (Ohio Biological Survey, OSU, Columbus).

III.

NORTHEASTERN OHIO

21

Atwood Lake Park (Mingo Trail)

TOTAL DISTANCE: 3.75 miles (6 km)

HIKING TIME: 2.5 hours

MAXIMUM ELEVATION: 1,125 feet

VERTICAL RISE: 175 feet

MAPS: USGS 7.5' Mineral City; MWCD Atwood Lake brochure

At 8,038 square miles, the watershed of eastern Ohio's mighty Muskingum River is far and away the area's largest. The Muskingum Watershed Conservancy District (MWCD) was created in 1933 to protect the towns along the river and its many tributaries from suffering a repeat of the devastating flooding that occurred in the first third of the twentieth century. Independent from state or local government, the conservancy owns and manages 14 major flood-control reservoirs in that giant watershed, 10 with permanent lakes. Over the years the district has established multiple-use recreation facilities at many of the lakes. Such is the case at Atwood Lake, east of the city of New Philadelphia. There the conservancy has built a resort lodge, vacation cabins, campground, nature center, marina, and boat docks, as well as provided many fine facilities for walking and hiking.

Atwood Lake was named after the village nearest to the dam at the time of construction, in the tradition of the US Army Corps of Engineers in the era before congressmen began putting their own names on nearly every civil works. Atwood must have disappeared under the lake, because it is nowhere to be found on the modern topographical map of the area.

Though the district owns 3,000 acres of land at Atwood, the recreation facilities are concentrated at Atwood Lake Park on the northwest corner of the reservoir.

GETTING THERE

The area is reached by taking OH 800 and OH 212 northeast from New Philadelphia to New Cumberland, then County Road 93 north and east to the

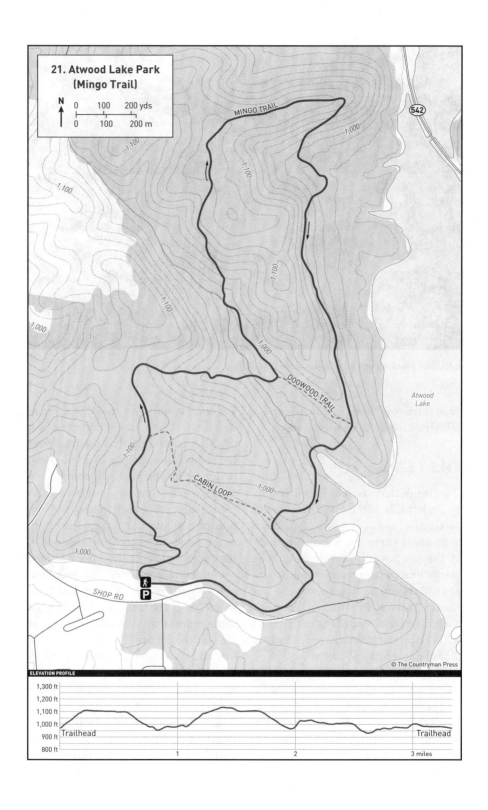

21. Atwood Lake Park (Mingo Trail)

N

| 0 | 100 | 200 yds |
| 0 | 100 | 200 m |

MINGO TRAIL

DOGWOOD TRAIL

CABIN LOOP

Atwood Lake

SHOP RD

542

1,100
1,000

© The Countryman Press

ELEVATION PROFILE

| 1,300 ft |
| 1,200 ft |
| 1,100 ft |
| 1,000 ft |
| 900 ft | Trailhead |
| 800 ft |

1   2   3 miles

Trailhead

BLACK-EYED SUSAN BLOOMS ALONGSIDE ATWOOD LAKE TRAIL

park entrance. There is a small fee for vehicles during the vacation season.

THE TRAIL

Once inside the park, look for a driveway on the left side of the road that leads to parking for the amphitheater. Park there to access the trail system. As you look up the hill toward the woods and the amphitheater, turn to your left, where you will see the trailhead about 100 feet distant. To the right of the trail entrance is a large colored map of the trails; to the left is a sign that gives distances and the times required to walk them.

The trail heads into the woods and starts uphill immediately, swinging first to the right (uphill from the amphitheater), then to the left to continue the steep climb through a pine plantation. As the trail nears the top of this rise you will see an observation tower. At the time of my visit, it was in disrepair

and was closed, surrounded by a chain-link fence. One foot beyond the tower is a sign indicating that the trail goes to the left. Directly ahead is the water reservoir for the park, which explains the wide trail thus far: It acts as a service road, too. The trail follows the contour of the land north from here, still in the woods. It passes the other end of the service road for the reservoir as it continues toward the well-marked intersection with the Cabin Loop and Dogwood Trails. The trail then passes under some especially tall white oak trees as it nears the corner of the MWCD property and rises to a high point. In a damp area, the papaw trees had fruit on them when I last passed by. A tiger swallowtail flew by my side as I crossed an open utility line that headed down the hill toward the cabin area. The trail next swings to the right, gently easing down a ravine. Passing under tall tuliptrees of the mixed mesophytic woods, and a lot of escaped multiflora rose, the trail enters a pine forest that is perhaps 25 years old.

After you reach the bottom of the ravine, cross a creek, and begin to climb, you'll arrive at the next intersection. Dogwood Trail goes to the right, continuing on down the ravine. The trail to the left, which is the one you want, is now Mingo Trail. Leaving pines behind, it climbs through young hardwood, then past older tuliptrees and a magnificent, tall, wild black cherry. It is headed almost due north now, climbing to reach a long stretch of nearly flat trail past beautiful pines. A sign on a service road that crosses the trail says NO ADMITTANCE. This is the highest point on the trail: 1,125 feet.

Beyond the pines, the trail begins its long sweeping curve to the right to turn toward the lake and the return leg. After dropping a bit, you make a hard turn to the right and continue to drop, hanging on the side of the hill below more pines. After crossing a usually dry creek bed, the trail follows the contour of the hill heading south. In the summer, both pale and spotted jewelweed—also known as touch-me-not—fill the forest floor. Initially the park service road is downhill from the trail, but soon they merge. To

WOODLAND TRAIL AT ATWOOD LAKE

the left is an oil-pump jack, and about 100 feet down the service road there is an intersection where Dogwood Trail exits hard right (a sign also directs hikers seeking the observation tower to take the hard right).

Follow the trail labeled CABINS straight ahead. This is a narrow footpath through tall pines—and poison ivy. After turning to the right, the trail levels off on the hillside through a patch of ground pine. The trail reaches a service road and follows it a short way to where a sign hidden in the brush directs you to the right for the nature center and to the left for the waterfowl observation area. Go right on the service road, where you will be almost at lake level. About 100 yards down this service road there is a vertical post labeled TRAIL, with an arrow pointing left. Head for that sign, and soon you will be at the intersection where the Cabin Loop, and Dogwood and Mingo Trails all go right, up the hill toward the defunct observation tower. Another sign directs you straight ahead to the amphitheater—the trail you follow to return to your vehicle. The trail follows the contour of the land as it winds its way around the base of the hill. A service road crosses it headed uphill. From here the trail follows an electric service line for a short way, then runs just inside a meadow, a few feet back from the mowed lawn, where the goldenrod greets you in the late summer. Your vehicle is in view.

When I revisited this area in the summer of 2006, the only real change I noticed was the size of the trees. This was especially true of areas of planted pines. It's hard to tell that a maple or an oak tree has grown taller, but when pines are growing in a nourishing environment, 10 or 20 years makes a real difference. Though this part of Ohio was not originally pine forest, through the years many pines have been planted on public lands as a way of controlling erosion and jump-starting reforestation. In most places, native hardwoods eventually invade the pine plantings, returning the area to its native cover. And that's good. As I revisit areas that I have known for many years, I'm always struck by the size of pines that I remember being planted or that were the size of Christmas trees the last time I saw them.

While you are in the area, why not visit some of the other nearby attractions? If you are interested in Ohio history, Zoar Village, Schoenbrunn, and Fort Laurens are not far from here. The New Philadelphia/Tuscarawas County Convention and Visitors Bureau (1-800-BUCKEYE) will be glad to provide brochures and maps.

22

Beaver Creek State Park

TOTAL DISTANCE: 5 miles (8 km)	

HIKING TIME: 3 hours	

MAXIMUM ELEVATION: 1,100 feet	

VERTICAL RISE: 140 feet	

MAPS: USGS 7.5' East Liverpool North and West Point; ODNR Beaver Creek State Park map

During the 1820s and 1830s, canal fever swept the Buckeye State, and it didn't miss Columbiana County in eastern Ohio. Finding themselves high and dry halfway between the Ohio River and the new Ohio and Erie Canal, the businessmen of New Lisbon were certain that prosperity would pass them by unless they found a water route to markets in the East. The state legislature did not look favorably upon another public works canal project, so a private stock company was formed—the Sandy and Beaver Canal Company—to construct a 73.5-mile canal from Bolivar, on the Ohio and Erie Canal, to Glascow, Pennsylvania, on the Ohio River. Under-funded and under-supported from the start, the canal project ran into one obstacle after another. Construction was started in 1835, but it was 1848 before the first boat, the *Thomas Fleming*, made its way from one end of the canal to the other. Traffic did not commence in earnest until 1851. Canal construction had taken 31 years from the chartering of the company, and the project had required construction of 90 locks, 30 dams, one aqueduct, one large and three small reservoirs, and two tunnels. In 1852, one reservoir gave way, causing the loss of local support, and by 1853 the canal company failed as great chunks of its land were sold to satisfy long overdue judgments. Parts of each end of the canal operated for a few more years, but floods in the early 1860s ruined whatever was left.

Beaver Creek State Park straddles Little Beaver Creek, the route of the eastern division of this ill-fated project. The stream is one of Ohio's most attractive and was the first to be named a State Wild River. It is also a federally designated Scenic River. The nearly intact remains of a number of Sandy and

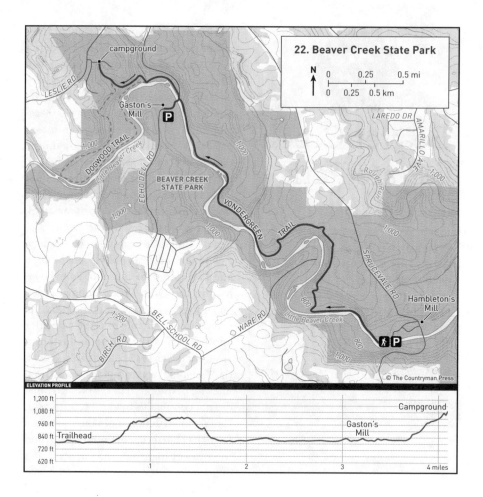

Beaver Canal locks are located within the 3038-acre park. For many years Boy Scout Troop 12 of East Liverpool has maintained the 21-mile Sandy Beaver Trail from Elkton, west of the park, to the Point of Beginning monument on the Ohio River. This hike is along the section known as Vondergreen Trail as it passes through the state park.

Since this is a linear hike, it is necessary to plan for the return trip. The trail is accessible from two road crossings and at the park campground. With two vehicles, a shuttle can be arranged between any two of these points.

GETTING THERE

Beaver Creek State Park is located off US 30 about 15 miles east of Lisbon. From US 30, turn north on OH 7. If you wish to hike the entire 5 miles, leave one car at the campground about 3 miles up OH 7. To cut a half mile off the hike, leave one car at the picnic area across Echo Dell Road from Gaston's Mill in the center of the park. To reach Gaston's Mill, travel 2 miles north from US 30 on OH 7 to Bell School Road and turn right (east).

To reach the parking area at Gaston's Mill, turn left (north) on Echo Dell Road and go about 1.4 miles. To reach the east trailhead, travel east on Bell School Road until you reach Sprucevale Road (County Road 428). Turn left here and travel north to the Sprucevale overlook, where you should stop for a good view of the stream and parklands to the west. Continue on County Road 428 to where the village of Sprucevale once stood along the banks of the river and, after crossing the river, turn left into the park. Leave your car at the picnic area parking lot. From the Columbus area, it is about a 4-hour drive; from Cleveland, 2.

THE TRAIL

Before beginning the hike, walk back to the picnic area entrance on County Road 428 to have a look at the ruins of Hambleton's Mill. Then explore Lock No. 42 (Hambleton's Lock) and the site of Dam No. 13 in the picnic area. A house, said to have been the lockkeeper's, stands next to the lock. The trail is marked with 2-by-6-inch white blazes on trees, posts, and occasionally large rocks. Pick up the trail at the far end of the primitive camping area, upstream from the lock and dam ruins.

Little Beaver Creek lies just south of the farthest advance of the glaciers in this part of Ohio. It is cut deeply into the bedrock, which dates from the Pennsylvanian epoch. Its side ravines contain trees such as hemlock, whose existence in this part of Ohio dates back to the colder era when the continental ice sheet lay only a few miles to the north. The wooded slopes are especially beautiful in the spring, when there is a grand display of wildflowers. A walk along this trail offers a special blend of natural and human history.

About three quarters of a mile upstream from Sprucevale the trail passes Lock No. 41, Gretchen's Lock, and the site of Dam No. 12. This well-preserved lock lies about 100 feet to the left of the trail. The timbers and planking of the dam can be seen in the stream in times of low water. Gretchen was the daughter of canal engineer E. H. Gill. Her mother died on the trip to America from their home in Europe. Gretchen died of malaria during canal construction, and her casket was entombed in this lock. When Gill left the project after the money ran out, he removed Gretchen's casket and took it with him on his return voyage to Europe. His boat sank, and both he and the casket were lost at sea. The ghost of Gretchen is said to haunt this lock still.

Less than a half mile beyond Gretchen's Lock is a cliff area where, in the past, the trail was difficult to travel in wet weather. It was very narrow and located on a shale bank. Stairs have now been built around the shale bank, but caution is still in order along this stretch of the trail.

About a quarter mile beyond the shale bank area lie Locks No. 40 and No. 39. The trail goes through Lock No. 40, which is in poor condition. Lock No. 39 is in very good shape and is unusual because of its 140-foot length, its gatework at different levels, and its steps. Shortly beyond the lock, near a fork in the trail, lies an old foundation, possibly that of the lock tender's home. Notice the mason's marks—his "signature," in the form of anchor and cross—on some of the stonework. Be careful to avoid poison ivy and snakes around this and all other stonework.

The trail continues upstream using the left fork. The footpath is blazed with white. A horse trail also traverses this

LARGE-FLOWERED TRILLIUM AMONG MANY WILDFLOWERS AT BEAVER CREEK STATE PARK

valley; it crosses and on some occasions uses the same path as the hiking trail. The bridle trail is easily discernible by the ruts made by horses' hooves.

Not far upstream stands Vondergreen's Lock, No. 38, and the earth embankment of Dam No. 11. This is a good place to contemplate the skill of the workmen who built this well-preserved lock perhaps 150 years ago. Gill is said to have been a perfectionist, and it shows in the workmanship here. Try to imagine the excitement of the arrival of a canal packet at the lock on its way to Philadelphia with a load of Ohio salt pork.

In the middle of the stream, a half mile beyond Vondergreen's Lock, sits a massive rock. The cliff face reveals

where this tremendous piece of rock came from. What a roar it must have made!

A foundation marking the remains of a home or storage building is seen along the trail about a half mile farther upstream. The rock in this formation probably originated at the next lock area, having been pirated away after the failure of the canal. Grey's Lock, No. 37, and the site of Dam No. 10, are just beyond. The trail now heads gently upslope, away from the river, to intersect a paved road. Upon reaching Echo Dell Road, turn left and go downhill, then cross the iron bridge to explore restored Gaston's Mill (built in 1837 to take advantage of the canal dam) and the pioneer village. At this point the canal has moved to the south side of the stream, where it will continue for many miles. Lock No. 36, located at the picnic area, is another well-preserved structure. It has been rebuilt with new wooden gates and lining to help visitors visualize its original appearance. Restrooms and drinking water are available at this area and the park office is only a short distance up the road beyond Gaston's Mill.

To continue hiking to the campground, re-cross the iron bridge and turn upstream (left) through another picnic area. The trail begins climbing the hillside beyond the last picnic site. The camping area is uphill about a quarter mile to the northwest. Signs along the trail can direct you to the Dogwood Trail through the old strip mine area, to add 1.5 miles to your 5-mile hike.

Little Beaver Creek offers good fishing and canoeing. The camping area is primitive, with few modern conveniences, but the rewards of the more than 15 miles of trails in the park are worth exploring while you are in the area.

23

Brecksville Reservation Metro Park (Deer Lick Cave Trail)

TOTAL DISTANCE: 4 miles (6.4 km)

HIKING TIME: 3 hours

MAXIMUM ELEVATION: 855 feet

VERTICAL RISE: 20 feet

MAPS: USGS 7.5' Northfield; USGS 7.5' Broadview Heights; CMPD Brecksville Reservation map

With 3,392 acres, Brecksville Reservation is the largest jewel in the Cleveland Metro Park Emerald Necklace. The wooded reservation is cut by seven distinct gorges. It has a spectacular native tallgrass prairie planting. And its nature center is probably the oldest structure built for that purpose in any park system, having been constructed by the Work Projects Administration (WPA) in 1939. For the hiker, it has an extensive system of well-labeled trails, including a section of the Buckeye Trail (BT).

GETTING THERE

To reach Brecksville Reservation, take I-77 or I-271 to OH 82. The entrance to the park is just east of the intersection of OH 82 and OH 21, to the south of OH 82. The park is open every day of the year during daylight hours.

THE TRAIL

The trailhead is located about 0.4 mile beyond the park entrance. The trailhead kiosk is on the right side of the road between two parking lots. This three-sided structure has a map of the park, photographs of interesting features, and announcements about seasonal activities. From the kiosk, follow the walkway into the forest and head directly toward the nature center. Throughout the park, trails are clearly marked by signposts with color-coded diamonds containing symbols and arrows. A green diamond marked "NC" above another diamond with an arrow points the way to the nature center. About halfway there, the Prairie Loop Trail to the right leads to a planted tallgrass prairie. If you are hiking anytime between the first of July and the first fall frost, you should stop

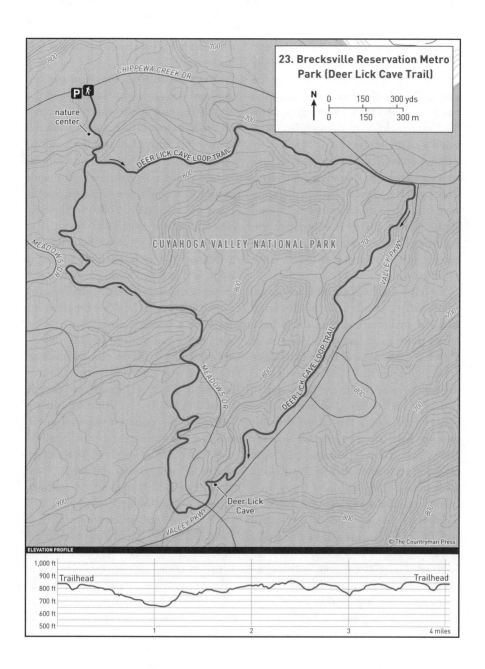

23. Brecksville Reservation Metro Park (Deer Lick Cave Trail)

CHIPPEWA CREEK DR

nature center

DEER LICK CAVE LOOP TRAIL

CUYAHOGA VALLEY NATIONAL PARK

MEADOWS DR

MEADOWS DR

VALLEY PKWY

DEER LICK CAVE LOOP TRAIL

Deer Lick Cave

VALLEY PKWY

© The Countryman Press

ELEVATION PROFILE

1,000 ft
900 ft Trailhead
800 ft
700 ft
600 ft
500 ft

Trailhead

1   2   3   4 miles

to visit the prairie on the way in or out of the park. There is a restroom at this trail intersection, probably the handiest one you will see on your hike.

Go inside the nature center to see exhibitions about the natural history of the park and to pick up a trail map. This is a good opportunity to chat with a naturalist and learn what in the way of seasonal phenomena you might want to watch for along the trail. Leaving through the front door, turn right to pass the bird-feeding area at the end of the building and begin following the tan oak leaf symbols that identify the 4-mile Deer Lick Cave Loop. Heading downslope, the trail passes an amphitheater on the left before dropping steeply on 55 wooden steps to where, in another 60 feet, the trail crosses a creek on a small bridge. There is a bench here where you may rest and enjoy the scenery, and other benches are scattered along the way. On the Halloween morning when I last walked the trail, the sun coming through the golden leaves was a sight to behold.

Beyond the bridge the trail splits. Angle left to climb a set of 59 stairs. Like the earlier steps, these also have heavy hawsers as handrails. Very soon the trail reaches a T. Deer Lick Cave Loop signs on the post indicate that the trail goes both left and right and, in fact, it does, for this is where the spur access trail meets the loop. Turn left to walk the loop clockwise. Hemlock Loop Trail utilizes the same tread and in a short distance, Bridle Trail No. 4 joins in too. The combined trails drop in and out of a small ravine, crossing a creek on a small bridge. The mixed mesophytic forest includes some really tall hardwood trees with an occasional hemlock. Exercise caution, as this is an earthen trail with many surface roots that can easily trip you. Granite boulders of all sizes, piled in the woods or lying in a row where there was once a fence, give away the glacial history of the area. An open field can be seen about 100 feet to the right, through the woods. When the trail reaches the corner of the open field, the combined loop trails are again joined by Bridle Trail No. 4 along a wider corridor with some gravel surface. After a couple hundred yards, the bridle trail turns left and the

two loop trails continue at a slight angle to the right.

The trail follows the high ground between two ravines, sometimes in the middle on the highest ground but often on the left rim of the tableland. It's relatively flat for quite a while, then dips up and down as it loses some altitude. Still to the left, the trail next descends at almost a 45-degree angle through a stand of beech trees. Following a steep downhill slope to the left and a long gentle downhill slope to the right, the combined foot trails reach the end of the ridge and make a downhill switchback toward Chippewa Creek. Bridle Trail No. 4 once again joins in. After crossing the creek on a bridge shared by a road at the Chippewa Picnic Area (where there are restrooms), the combined trails go their own way. Hemlock Loop Trail turns left, while Deer Lick Cave Trail travels parallel to Valley Parkway. You begin with a couple hundred yards of uphill walking on a rocky, rooty path, along a sharp spine between two fairly steep slopes. After a quarter mile or so, Deer Lick Cave Trail is joined by a connecting trail from Valley Parkway. This is the Buckeye Trail, which is coming from the Ohio & Erie Canal Towpath on the east side of the Cuyahoga River, a path it shares with Towpath Trail. Normally marked with blue paint blazes, in the park this trail is denoted by light blue diamonds with a backpacker symbol and a directional arrow. The Oak Grove Picnic Area, with restrooms, lies across the road just a short distance southwest of where the Buckeye Trail crosses.

Back in the woods, the combined Buckeye and Deer Lick Cave Trails drop down the hillside. For reasons only the trail builders know, the two trails separate for a short distance and then rejoin. The BT traces a "U" along the rim of a hill, while Deer Lick Cave Trail connects its top. Soon the combined trails arrive at the side trail to the right that goes to the Deer Lick Cave(s). A set of broad stone and gravel steps arc left as they carry the hiker to the caves and waterfalls. A light rain was falling when I visited the area on the last day of October. Enough leaves had fallen that I had to kick through them along the narrow trail, yet there were still enough on the trees to make it a special time to be there.

Returning to the main trail via a couple of bridges and another set of long, wide steps, it is time to begin closing the loop by heading north. After crossing Meadows Drive, the combined Buckeye and Deer Lick Cave Trails intersect with Bridle Trail No. 3, coming from the left. At this point, the Buckeye Trail continues straight ahead (west) along the north side of Valley Parkway, soon to leave public land. Deer Lick Cave Trail turns right to join Bridle Trail No. 3 heading north on a broad trail that looks like it might have been a township road at one time. Crossing streams on bridges built by the Ohio Civilian Conservation Program of the 1970s, the trail weaves through the hardwood forest and old pine plantings toward another crossing of Meadows Drive. This crossing is at an angle, so you will need to look down the road to the left to find the entry point for the continuing trail.

DEER LICK CAVE

Not far beyond this crossing, the hiking and horse trails part company for the last time. The bridle trail heads east through a ravine to where it earlier came north of Valley Parkway, essentially closing the loop. The hiking trail swings to the west, and after following high ground for nearly a quarter mile it drops into a ravine and makes two stream crossings. Here the streams have cut deeply into the black shale bedrock. After rising from the last ravine, the trail moves through more forested tableland before it reaches the Meadows Picnic Area and trailhead, crossing Bridle Trail No. 4 on the way. When Deer Lick Cave Trail reaches the driveway to the picnic area, you must look slightly to the right across the open area to find the signpost mark-ing the continuation of the trail. Again traveling on nearly level ground, the trail goes straight ahead for perhaps 250 yards before making a right turn and reaching a T. A left here puts you on the loop access path for Deer Lick Cave Trail. The nature center sign now joins Deer Lick Cave Trail sign in point-ing hikers toward the trail and the two flights of steps that lead back out to the nature center and the parking lot.

This is an extraordinary trail. It is within a short drive of bustling down-town Cleveland, yet it offers interesting terrain entirely within a forest. There are other trails to explore within the park's nearly 3,500 acres, and it adjoins the Cuyahoga Valley National Park, where there are many additional miles of hiking trails.

24

Cuyahoga Valley National Park– Ledges Trail

TOTAL DISTANCE: 2.5 miles (4 km)

HIKING TIME: 1.5 hours

MAXIMUM ELEVATION: 1,050 feet

VERTICAL RISE: 100 feet

MAPS: USGS 7.5' Series Peninsula; CVNP Trails of the Virginia Kendall Unit

Less than one month after the inauguration of Franklin Roosevelt as the nation's 32nd president, in March 1933, Congress established the Civilian Conservation Corps. From the following summer until the Corps disbanded at the beginning of World War II, more than 2.5 million young men and boys, mostly from America's cities, spent six-month tours of duty in the nation's forests. By the end of 1933 a camp had been established near Peninsula, probably along Truxell Road, where park district shops stood for many years. Over the course of its existence, the boys of the corps built shelters, restrooms, stairways, and miles of trails in what was then known as Virginia Kendall Park. In 1937, they completed the Ledges Shelter. Two years later, they finished the building known as the Happy Days Camp, 2 miles east of Peninsula along US 303. That structure was built to be operated as a day camp for children from the inner city. It replaced an old farmhouse near the same site that had previously served the same purpose.

The feature attraction of this area is the Ritchie Ledges, an outcrop of Sharon conglomerate dating back about 300 million years to the days when a large shallow sea covered this area. The conglomerate resulted from the fast movement of streams carrying sediment from the north. With time and pressure it was compacted into conglomerate rock made up of cemented sand and small quartz pebbles. Occurring here as cap rock at about 1,000 feet above sea level, it is exposed in a similar way at Nelson and Kennedy Ledges, Thompson Ledges, Cuyahoga Falls in northeastern Ohio, and Lake Katharine in southeastern Ohio's Jackson County. Here, as at other places where it is exposed, Sharon conglomerate is usually closely

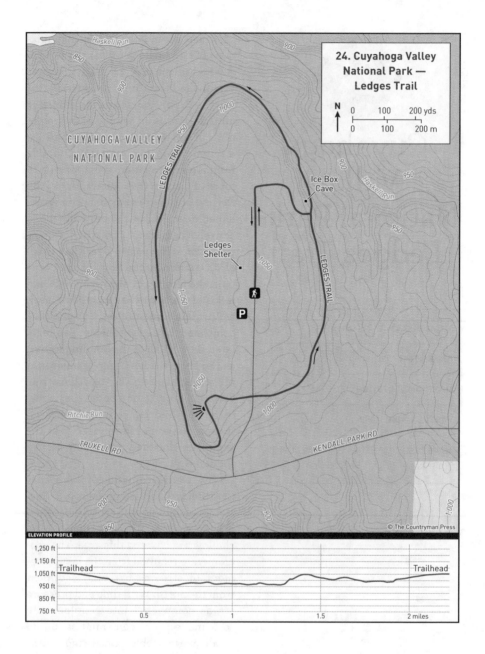

24. Cuyahoga Valley National Park — Ledges Trail

N

0	100	200 yds
0	100	200 m

Haskell Run

CUYAHOGA VALLEY NATIONAL PARK

LEDGES TRAIL

Ice Box Cave

Haskell Run

Ledges Shelter

LEDGES TRAIL

P

Ritchie Run

TRUXELL RD

KENDALL PARK RD

© The Countryman Press

ELEVATION PROFILE

1,250 ft				
1,150 ft	Trailhead			Trailhead
1,050 ft				
950 ft				
850 ft				
750 ft	0.5	1	1.5	2 miles

associated with hemlock, yellow birch, ferns, and bryophytes in the microclimate that the ledges create. Look for hardwoods of the mixed-mesophytic forest on the hillside below.

The land around the Richie Ledges known as Virginia Kendall Park had been owned by Hayward Kendall, a Clevelander who called himself a "coal peddler" because he was in the coal and oil business. He had named the area after his mother and maintained a retreat home there in a park-like setting. Before he died, he bequeathed it to the National Park Service, state of Ohio, city of Cleveland, or a trust at his bank, in that order. The federal government turned it down, but the old Division of Forestry of the Ohio Agricultural Extension Service—part of The Ohio State University—accepted it and began operating it as a park. The state of Ohio had no state park organization in those years and, even though there was an endowment to help pay for its operation, the area was a bit of a "stepchild." In 1933, Harold Wagner, director of the Akron Park District, is reported to have complained about what a poor job the state was doing in managing it as a park. In response, he was told, "If you can do a better job, you take it." Arrangements were made with the OSU Board of Trustees to transfer operation to the park district, along with an annual operating income, and the 1,600-acre tract was operated as Virginia Kendall Metro Park until the late 1970s. After the creation of the Cuyahoga National Recreation Area (now a national park) by Congress in 1974, 400 acres of the park, including the ledges, were turned over to the national park district.

The old day camp facility, where thousands of boys and girls had spent Friday nights on cots when it was run by the park district, is now the Happy Days Visitor Center. Here you will find exhibitions, program space, a sales area and offices, and, to the rear of the building, a historic cemetery. In 2000, a bronze statue of a corpsman was erected outside the entrance to the visitor center as a tribute to the work of the young men of the Civilian Conservation Corps, though the former Virginia Kendall CCC camp had not been at this site.

A half-mile loop trail, Haskell Trail, originates from and returns to the visitor center parking lot. From it, a spur connects to the other trails of the Virginia Kendall Unit, but the best way to reach the trails of the area is from the south.

GETTING THERE

To reach the 2.5-mile Ledges Trail that, as the name implies, circumnavigates the high land surrounded by the ledges, come in from the south by driving either west from SR 8 on Kendall Park Road or east from Akron–Peninsula Road on Truxell Road. In either case, you must watch for an easy-to-miss sign directing you to the Ledges Shelter. Drive as far north as you can and park along the road in any available space.

THE TRAIL

Begin hiking by walking north past the Ledges Shelter. Indoor and outdoor picnic facilities and restrooms are located there. Just beyond the building there is a trailhead bulletin board. Continue walking north on the wide service road, which quickly changes from blacktop to gravel. Ignore the assorted picnic tables that are scattered here and about in the woods. Traveling through oak–hickory forest, you will soon reach an intersection where a wayside interpretive sign illustrates the ledges area. Turn right on this trail as it leaves the oaks and hickories of the hilltop and enters a grove of hemlock. You have reached the top of the conglomerate in an area where tree roots both create and use the fissures in the rock. To prevent the accidental destruction of this spectacular area's vegetation, visitors are asked to remain

SANDSTONE OVERHANG AT THE LEDGES

on the trails. Rock climbing is strictly prohibited.

The trail drops cautiously over the ledges and soon reaches a level near the bottom of the conglomerate that it will use to carry you completely around the mesa-like formation. For no particular reason, I opted for the counterclockwise route. Begin hiking by turning left as you reach the bottom of the ledges. About 100 feet beyond the turn, the trail reaches Ice Box Cave. Not a true cave—it is not the result of solution of rock by water—Ice Box nevertheless reaches nearly 50 feet into the dark through this narrow slit in the rock. Just beyond the cave entrance there is a bridge over the flowage from a spring.

Ferns grow vigorously in this cooler, moist environment.

Beyond here, the trail crosses a bridge and climbs a set of steps. Several wild trails lead into a maze of ledges. Follow the trail along the cliff base. After about a quarter mile, the trail reaches a set of stone steps to the left that lead to the picnic area and playing fields above. These steps were built by the boys of the Civilian Conservation Corps nearly 70 years ago. The Berea sandstone was quarried at Deep Lock Quarry alongside the Ohio & Erie Canal on the west side of the Cuyahoga River, south of Peninsula. A trail in that area is described elsewhere in this book.

Follow Ledges Trail straight ahead

along the base of the ledges. Not far beyond the steps a trail to the right leads to the Happy Days Visitor Center. Can you imagine the voices of children of 60 years ago, here from the city for the day, running up the path to hike the trail or to go up to the play fields?

Continue around the north end of the exposed rock via boardwalk and steps. Another trail exits to the right to lead to the Ledges Shelter; shortly after, a trail leads downhill and to the right toward the Octagon Shelter in the valley to the west. To continue the Ledges Loop Trail, stay on the trail straight ahead at the base of the rock, along the towering rock face.

After about a half mile of southerly travel, you will notice that the ledges are beginning to diminish. At the next trail intersection, turn to the left and follow the trail uphill at an oblique angle as it heads toward the play fields and picnic areas. (If you follow the trail to the right at this intersection, it will take you to the Lake Shelter nearly a mile to the southwest.) When you reach the top of the ledges, watch for one of several trails to the left (west), along the edge of the woods on the west side of the play fields. One of these will lead you to an expansive area of exposed cliff top where you can enjoy a great view of the Cuyahoga Valley—a good photo point on a clear day. Don't get too close to the edge.

Back toward the play field from the overlook is a restroom. Look just beyond for a trail just inside the woods; it heads east, and soon makes a road crossing and reenters the deciduous forest. Still circling counterclockwise, the trail crosses a wooden bridge, then enters into a magical forest of hemlock trees as it turns north on the east-facing slope. Continue until you reach a trail to the left that returns you to the top of the trail you came out on. If you reach Ice Box Cave, you have gone too far; backtrack a short distance.

Once back on top, take advantage of one of the many picnic areas provided for a meal or a short break. It was a warm early-November day when I walked this trail the first time, kicking leaves ahead of me most of the way. I marked it on my list of parks to return to when I find myself in this Glaciated Allegheny Plateau area of northeastern Ohio in other seasons. It was hard for me to believe that this area—which looks so much like areas in unglaciated southeastern Ohio—had been under the Wisconsinan ice sheet not too many millennia ago.

While you are in the area, consider a 9.5-mile loop trail hike on the Ohio & Erie Canal Towpath and Buckeye Trail, originating from the trailhead at Boston Mills or the park headquarters area at Jaite. A description of that trail is provided in this book.

25

Cuyahoga Valley National Park–Ohio & Erie Canal Towpath Trail

---

TOTAL DISTANCE: 9.5 miles (15.3 km)

HIKING TIME: 5 hours

MAXIMUM ELEVATION: 850 feet

VERTICAL RISE: 200 feet

MAPS: USGS 7.5' Series, Northfield; BTA Akron Section map

Just as the Cuyahoga National Park is a study in contrasts, so too is this 9.25-mile trail. For 6.25 miles it traverses high hills and stands witness to tall timber and deep ravines. For the other 3 miles it travels open fields, roads, and a very level canal towpath.

Cuyahoga Valley National Park was created in 1974 as an urban park of the National Park System (NPS). It preserves 33,000 acres of pastoral valley along 22 miles of the Cuyahoga River between Cleveland and Akron. It is a diverse area, with some places of pristine beauty; others have been badly despoiled by the hand of man. The establishment of a national park has permitted the recovery of the natural values of the valley through active restoration projects and by passively allowing natural succession to occur. Preserving some of the artifacts of civilization has also been important: the company town, the railroad, and the canal, with its system of hand-operated locks.

Before the NPS came to the valley, both public and private agencies in Cuyahoga and Summit Counties protected many of the valley's special areas through the establishment of parks, preserves, and camps. Most of these have remained under the jurisdiction of the agencies that originally developed them, although the NPS works closely with them. The Buckeye Trail (BT) runs through the park on its way between Cincinnati and Mentor Headlands. Between Boston and Jaite it's routed on high land on the west side of the valley, making it possible to combine the trail with a section of the Ohio & Erie Canal Towpath Trail for a challenging and interesting loop walk.

Jaite, where one of several trailheads is located at a small parking lot east of

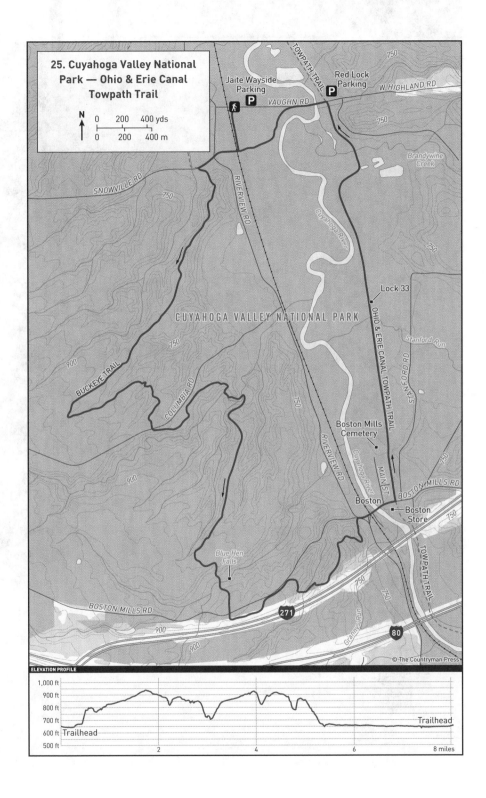

25. Cuyahoga Valley National Park — Ohio & Erie Canal Towpath Trail

N

| 0 | 200 | 400 yds |
| 0 | 200 | 400 m |

Jaite Wayside Parking

Red Lock Parking

P

P

VAUGHN RD

W. HIGHLAND RD

TOWPATH TRAIL

750

750

Brandywine Creek

SNOWVILLE RD

RIVERVIEW RD

750

750

Cuyahoga River

Lock 33

CUYAHOGA VALLEY NATIONAL PARK

750

750

Stanford Run

STANFORD RD

900

BUCKEYE TRAIL

COLUMBIA RD

750

OHIO & ERIE CANAL TOWPATH TRAIL

Boston Mills Cemetery

750

900

RIVERVIEW RD

Cuyahoga River

MAIN ST

Boston

Boston Store

BOSTON MILLS RD

750

Blue Hen Falls

TOWPATH TRAIL

BOSTON MILLS RD

900

271

750

750

80

Grant's Run

900

© The Countryman Press

ELEVATION PROFILE

1,000 ft				
900 ft				
800 ft				
700 ft				Trailhead
600 ft Trailhead				
500 ft	2	4	6	8 miles

OHIO & ERIE CANAL TOWPATH TRAIL NEAR RED LOCK

NPS headquarters, was once a company town for the Jaite Mill east of the river, adjacent to the canal. The buildings have been renovated for offices, and the town now looks much like it must have during its heyday. The Jaite paper mill has been razed, but many other properties of historic interest along the canal within the park have been restored. Only minimal restoration work has been done on the aging locks, but trees and vines have been removed to keep their roots from doing further damage to the old stone structures. The Canal Visitor Center is well worth a visit. It's located in a canal-era building at Lock No. 38, 7 miles north of Jaite, at the intersection of Hillside Road and the canal. You will also want to spend some time at the 1836 Boston Store located along this hike in Boston. It houses exhibitions on the craft of canal boat building. At Boston there is also a small store where snacks are sold. Drinking water is available there too, along with modern restrooms. There are vault toilets at the Red Lock trailhead. Be sure to carry ample drinking water on the trail.

GETTING THERE

To reach the Jaite trailhead, take US 271 to Exit 19, turn west on OH 82, and then travel 4.5 miles to Riverview Road. Turn left (south) and continue 3 miles to the intersection of Riverview and Vaughn Roads, where the park headquarters complex is located at the former community of Jaite. Turn east onto Vaughn Road. One trailhead is at the parking lot on the left (north) side of Vaughn Road, just beyond a railroad crossing, about 200 yards after the turn. Alternative parking is located at Red Lock, about a quarter mile east of Jaite, and east of the Cuyahoga River on the north side

of the road. Since the Red Lock lot is heavily used by bicyclists on weekends, the Jaite lot may be the better choice. Access to the trail is easy from either lot: Cross Jaite Road and pick up the trail. You could also arrive via I-77 and I-80. Watch for the signs.

THE TRAIL

From either trailhead parking lot, cross Vaughn Road and follow the blue blazes on posts to where the trail turns south beneath the power line. After a few hundred yards, you will reach a T in the trail. The outgoing trail turns west across the railroad tracks and comes out onto Riverview Road, where it intersects with Snowville Road. Cross Riverview and head up the left side of Snowville Road; after about 100 feet, watch out for the place where the trail enters the woods to the left. Upon leaving the road the trail immediately begins climbing a steep hill to a long northeast–southwest-aligned ridge. Over the next mile, as it climbs the ridge, the trail will gain more than 200 feet in elevation. Using a combination of old lanes and a newly created trail, it travels through mixed mesophytic forest of varying age and past occasional pine plantings. Eventually the trail makes an S-curve before crossing Columbia Road.

Once across Columbia Road, head northeast parallel to the road for several hundred yards beneath a stand of magnificent old white oaks. The trail then drops into a ravine where hemlocks grow in the cool environment along a beautiful shale-bottomed stream. An occasional glacial erratic on the upland is a reminder that, unlike the hills of southern Ohio, these have seen glaciation as recently as 10,000 years ago; yet the ravines cutting through the

RUINS OF RED LOCK AT JAITE

Mississippian-aged bedrock where hemlocks grow are reminiscent of Hocking County.

The trail begins to climb once more, crossing ridges and more ravines on its way toward Blue Hen Falls. Here the stream cascades over sandstone bedrock as it cuts its way east to the Cuyahoga River. The trail crosses the creek on a bridge just upstream from the falls, then turns upslope to emerge at a parking lot and Boston Mills Road.

Cross the road and head east, passing in front of a county road maintenance facility before turning right (south) to drop rapidly into a highly eroded valley close to I-271. The trail then climbs a set of steps to the top of the ridge, which it follows east as it descends to the intersection of Boston Mills and Riverview Roads. Cross Riverview and the Cuyahoga River on Boston Mills and head into Boston. You will pass an old Pure Oil/Union 76 station, now referred to as the "M.D. Garage." It serves as an events space for the park. The Boston Store, which has fine exhibitions on the building of canal boats, is just beyond the station. Behind it is the trailhead area where snacks and restrooms are available.

Across the road from the store, begin hiking north on the Ohio & Erie Canal Towpath Trail as it heads toward Boston

Lock (No. 32). A short way up the trail, on the left (west) side of the canal, is Boston Mills Cemetery. From this point back to the trailhead, the hike is level walking along the long-abandoned—but now restored—towpath. Be alert for bicyclers, walkers, and joggers. Lock No. 33, which the trail passes just north of the cemetery, has not been rebuilt, but trees along its banks have been removed. Because there are no plans to water this part of the canal, it's unlikely that it will ever be rebuilt.

As the trail reaches the Jaite Mill area, it moves to the left toward the hillside to make room for a section of the canal that carries water into the mill site, where it once was used in the milling process. In its heyday, in the 1920s and 1930s, the Jaite Mill was the 11th largest multi-wall paper producer in the nation. The paper went into strong paper bags such as those used for fertilizer and cement. All of the aboveground parts of the mill have now been demolished, although in the summer of 2006 there remained some and belowground cleanup to be done. Plans call for restoring natural habitat in this area and providing some interpretation of the mill. An impressive piece of paper-making machinery, a Fourdrinier machine, will also be left at the site.

The trail continues on the towpath as it approaches Highland Road. On the north side of Highland lies the Red Lock trailhead, an access point for people walking or riding the trail. The Canal Towpath Trail continues north through the park and on into the Ohio & Erie Canal Reservation of the Cleveland Metro Parks, ending at Harvard Avenue in Cleveland. It will continue to be extended in the future.

To complete this hike, turn left (west) along the south side of Highland Road (Vaughn Road on the Cuyahoga County side of the river) and cross the Cuyahoga River. Just beyond the bridge, a connecting trail to the Buckeye Trail drops off the left side of the road, then turns right to parallel the river before swinging toward the west. At a trail intersection beneath the power line turn right to head north to the parking lot.

There are many other fine facilities in this park. A special treat is an excursion trip on the Cuyahoga Valley Scenic Railroad that travels between Canton, Akron, and Rockside Road. Write or call the park for details on this and the many other public programs they offer.

Eagle Creek State Nature Preserve

TOTAL DISTANCE: 4.75 miles (7.5 km)

HIKING TIME: 3 hours

MAXIMUM ELEVATION: 960 feet

VERTICAL RISE: 20 feet

MAPS: USGS 7 1/2' Quad, Garrettsville; ODNR Eagle Creek State Nature Preserve brochure

A walk along the trail of Eagle Creek State Nature Preserve, a 442-acre area northeast of Garrettsville, in Portage County, can truly be a "walk with the wildlings." In addition to being one of the largest intact tracts of mature woodland in this area, it is home to many birds, mammals, reptiles, and amphibians infrequently seen in more intensely developed parks. Beaver, fox, white-tailed deer, raccoon, and skunk live here. Hundreds of Canada geese use the larger ponds as rest stops during migration, and the woods are full of songbirds during spring. Two species listed as rare and endangered in Ohio—the spotted turtle and the four-toed salamander—are known to live here.

There are more than 100 species of woody plants on the preserve, including many less common trees such as cucumber magnolia and yellow birch. The rich beech/maple forests on the north-facing slopes contain abundant spring wildflowers. The white oak forest communities more common on the drier, south-facing slopes have a sparser but equally interesting show of spring flowers. More than 70 species of wildflowers have been observed blooming in the preserve during May. Pin oaks are found in the swamp forest, and buttonbush swamps, small bogs, and marshlands dot the area.

Located on the eastern edge of an isolated area of terminal moraine, the preserve is mostly underlain by sandy glacial outwash. Eagle Creek meanders in a southerly direction through the middle of the preserve in multiple channels, and the manipulation of water levels by beavers has created more bottomland ponds.

A well-planned and well-maintained trail system allows the visitor to walk

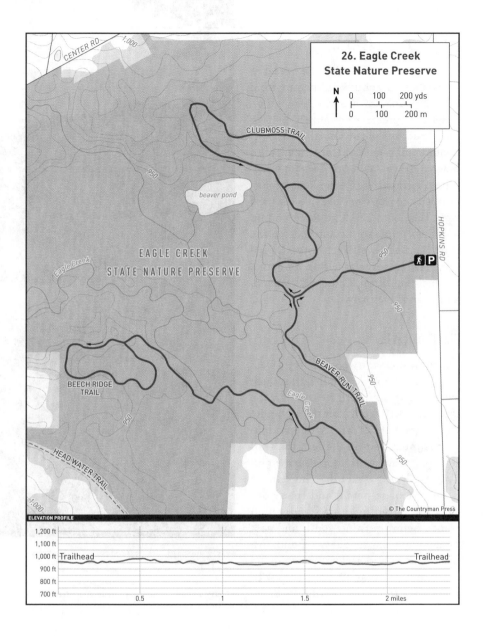

through the woods and fields past beaver ponds and beautiful wildflowers. Rather than a fast-paced recreational walk, this hike is better suited to a quiet stroll through nature's realm. The collection of any natural material is, of course, prohibited here, as are dogs, picnicking, alcoholic beverages, and camping. Bring water and other needed supplies, since nothing is available at the preserve.

This preserve, with its easily hiked trails, is one of those special places that can be visited throughout the seasons. It is open from dawn to dusk year-round.

GETTING THERE

Garrettsville, near which the preserve is located, is about equidistant from Akron, Youngstown, and Cleveland on OH 82. The preserve entrance is on Hopkins Road, which runs north and south about 2 miles east of Garrettsville. To reach it, travel OH 82 or OH 88 to Garrettsville, then take Center Road 3 miles northeast to Hopkins Road. Make a hard right turn onto Hopkins Road and go less than 1 mile to the entrance on the right, just north of Harrington Cemetery. The preserve is within an hour's drive of the Akron, Canton, Cleveland, and Youngstown areas.

THE TRAIL

The trail enters the woods directly from the parking lot. A small buttonbush swamp is to your left. At the T in the trail, go north (right) on the 1.25-mile Clubmoss Loop Trail. After passing a sphagnum bog on the left, the trail divides to make its loop. Turn right. This trail passes another bog and a skunk cabbage patch, and then goes through an old field area and young woods before turning south and east alongside a large beaver pond. An observation blind beckons you to spend a few minutes scanning the area with binoculars in search of wildlife. Since the blind faces southwest, great photographs can be taken shortly after sunrise or, for spectacular backlit pictures, just before sundown.

Now traveling south, the trail completes its loop. Continuing beyond the side trail to the parking lot, Beaver Run Trail stays on the high ground overlooking the east branch of Eagle Creek and

BEAVER POND AT EAGLE CREEK ATTRACTS A BOUNTY OF WATERFOWL

many small beaver ponds and dams. A half mile after passing the trail to the parking lot, Beaver Run Trail drops down the slope to cross both branches of the creek. A trail up the slope beyond the second bridge is the connection with the three-quarter-mile Beech Ridge Trail. Walk it in a counterclockwise direction. Tall beech trees provide shade for the vernal flora of the forest floor. The trail

circles, but does not pass through, a wetland. In this corner of the preserve, former agricultural fields are being allowed to return to woodland.

After completing the Beech Ridge Trail, return to the parking lot via Beaver Run Trail.

NOTE: As the fourth edition of *50 Hikes in Ohio* was being prepared for publication, I received word of the closing of the bridge over Eagle Creek, shutting off access to the three-quarter-mile loop trail known as Breech Ridge Trail. Beaver Run Trail now ends at the bridge. Efforts are underway to repair or replace the bridge, but no opening date has been projected. There remain four miles of great hiking, especially in the springtime. Enjoy!

Findley State Park

TOTAL DISTANCE: 3 miles (4.8 km)	
HIKING TIME: 2.5 hours	
MAXIMUM ELEVATION: 915 feet	
VERTICAL RISE: 24 feet	
MAPS: USGS 7.5' Wellington; ODNR Findley State Park map; BTA Norwalk Section map	

Findley State Park's origin as a state forest is evident from the moment you enter the area. Row after row of tall pine trees greet you. These trees were probably planted in open fields shortly after the area was purchased. Named for the late Judge Guy Findley, an early advocate of protection for the area, the original 890-acre tract was transferred to the Division of Parks and Recreation shortly after its creation in 1949. An additional 107 acres have been added since that time. Virtually all of the park's 9 miles of trails, which include about 1.3 miles of the Buckeye Trail, are within woods. The park includes a modern 275-site campground, several picnic areas, and a 93-acre lake with a public beach and boat ramps.

GETTING THERE

The park entrance is off OH 58, not quite 2 miles south of Wellington, in Lorain County. For this hike, turn right just after entering the park and follow Park Road No. 3 to the camp check-in station. If there is an attendant there, tell him/her that you want to hike, but not camp, and that you want to park on the lot inside the campground. You will be allowed to enter at no cost. Use the lot just northwest of the check-in station. If you want to stay overnight, make arrangements for a campsite as you come in.

Findley Lake is well stocked with fish, and only electric motors are permitted. It is a good place for some lake canoeing, perhaps "plugging" the shores for bass or using catalpa worms, red worms, or crickets for bluegill. It is a pleasant park for an outing within an hour's drive of Cleveland, Akron, or Mansfield.

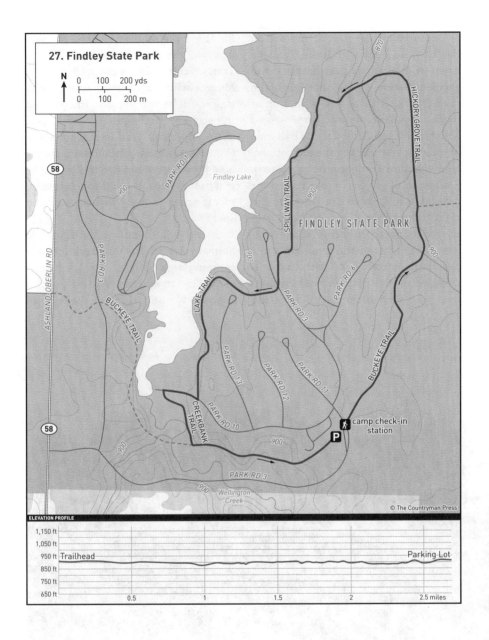

27. Findley State Park

N
| 0 | 100 | 200 yds |
| 0 | 100 | 200 m |

Findley Lake

FINDLEY STATE PARK

HICKORY GROVE TRAIL

SPILLWAY TRAIL

PARK RD 1

PARK RD 3

ASHLAND/OBERLIN RD

BUCKEYE TRAIL

LAKE TRAIL

PARK RD 6

PARK RD 3

PARK RD 13

PARK RD 12

PARK RD 11

BUCKEYE TRAIL

CREEKBANK TRAIL

PARK RD 10

camp check-in station

PARK RD 3

Wellington Creek

© The Countryman Press

ELEVATION PROFILE

| 1,150 ft |
| 1,050 ft |
| 950 ft Trailhead |
| 850 ft |
| 750 ft |
| 650 ft |

Parking Lot

0.5   1   1.5   2   2.5 miles

THE TRAIL

Nearly the entire hike at Findley State Park is within woods. At many times of the year the trails are damp, so be certain you have adequate footwear and are prepared for mosquitoes. The route suggested here is different than in earlier editions of this book. The change was made to avoid conflict with mountain bikers and to take the trail out of high-use recreation areas.

Begin your hike by starting out on the 1.1-mile Hickory Grove Trail as it enters the woods just north of the check-in station, on the right side of the road (No. 3). This is also a section of the Buckeye Trail, and as such is marked with blue blazes. After about a half mile of walking you will see the almost parallel Wyandot Trail join Hickory Grove Trail from the right. Ignore it. Not far beyond, the Buckeye Trail exits to the right to leave the park and head east toward its northern terminal at Headlands Beach State Park. Ignore this too, and the mountain bike path that will twice cross your path as you twist and turn your way to the east side of the

Findley Lake spillway. There you will intersect the Mountain Bike and Larch Trails coming across the spillway. The Mountain Bike is a one-way trail and any traffic will be coming toward you from the spillway. To continue hiking, turn left on Spillway Trail and head south. (You can, of course, circumnavigate the lake if you wish, but the trail will take you past the beach and through several picnic areas—not my favorite walking spots.)

About a half mile of walking on Spillway Trail takes you back into the camping area on Road No. 3, between campsite 112 and 113. At this point, I suggest turning right on Lake Trail

OLD PINE STAND AT FINDLEY STATE PARK

A PARK TRAIL SHARED BY THE STATEWIDE BUCKEYE TRAIL AT FINDLEY STATE PARK

located behind the campsite across the road. This half-mile woodland trail comes out on Road 10, just uphill from a boat-launching area near the upper reaches of the lake. Turn toward the lake and walk past the natural debris dump area on the right, watching for the entrance to Creekbank Trail on the left (south) side of the launching area parking lot. Take Creekbank Trail upstream through the woods for about a quarter mile, to where it intersects Mountain Bike Trail and the Buckeye Trail. Turn left on the shared foot and bike trail. After a few hundred yards a shortcut foot trail to the left goes to Road 10 inside the campground. Ignore it and continue uphill toward the amphitheater and naturalist program area. Mountain Bike Trail splits off to the right before you get there. Once at the naturalist building, you will see your vehicle in the distance across the mowed area. There is a small store in the check-in area. Enjoy a night at the campground or drive carefully on your way home.

28

French Creek Reservation

TOTAL DISTANCE: 2.5 miles (4 km)

HIKING TIME: 1.5 hours

MAXIMUM ELEVATION: 623 feet

VERTICAL RISE: 43 feet

MAPS: USGS 7.5' Series Avon; LCMP French Creek Reservation Trail Guide

French traders were probably the first whites to visit the area near the mouth of the Black River, in Lorain County, likely in the seventeenth century. They were here to explore and trade with the Native Americans of the area. Moravian missionaries came into the area in 1786, hoping to move south to the Moravian missions in the Tuscarawas Valley that had been burned out in 1782. After a warning of danger from local Delaware Indians they moved south, near the site of present-day Milan for five or six years, before moving on to the area near the River Thames, in Canada.

In 1795, agents for the Connecticut Land Company bought the land for a few dollars an acre, and the area became known as the Western Reserve. Settlement by folks from Connecticut and other New England states began in earnest.

As one of the best harbors on Lake Erie, the mouth of the Black River became the center of industrialization. Shipbuilding and steel making reached their peak with the all-out war effort in the middle of the twentieth century. French Creek, the meandering stream that passes through French Creek Reservation and joins the Black River about a mile to the west, became known as "the Ruhr of the West Side of Cleveland." Air and water pollution plagued the area for decades. The nature center at French River Reservation sits adjacent to an abandoned railbed, and a huge steel plant lies not more than a mile to the south, but the 428-acre wooded tract is a real gem in an otherwise urban/industrial area.

GETTING THERE

Reach the park by taking SR 611 northwest from I-90, the Sheffield exit. Travel west approximately 2 miles to the park

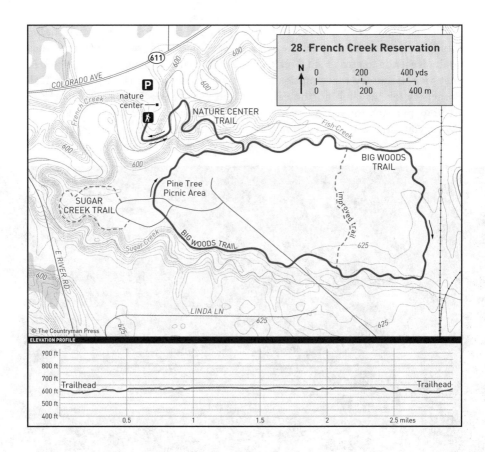

entrance on the south (left) side of the road. The nature center and trail entrances are at the far end of the lot. Begin your visit to French Creek Reservation with a visit to the center.

THE TRAIL

The hike begins when you step out the back door of the center, turn left, go down a set of steps, and cross French Creek. (There is an alternate route with a tarmac surface down the hill to the creek should you be in a wheelchair or using a walker.) The blacktop ends and the improved Nature Center Trail—with a limestone-screening surface and marked with blue Carsonite posts—begins beyond the bridge.

From the bridge, you can see exposed Devonian-age shale (perhaps Ohio shale) in one bank. In the streambed look for glacial erratics, the granite boulders characteristic of land that has been glaciated in past millennia.

The trail cuts across a meander so that almost immediately you can see French Creek, which you just crossed, below on the left. There is now elevation to be gained to return to the level of the old lake bottom that this creek is cutting its way through. The soil on top of the bedrock in the park is lacustrine (lake-deposited) sand, silt, and clay, and is easily eroded. Through nice woods, the trail ascends with a wide sweep to the right. A shorter, steeper route goes left up a ridge, but save this for the way back.

Surprisingly, once you're back to the elevation of the center, the trail again descends to cross Fish Creek, an east–west tributary that empties into French Creek just behind the center. As you approach the bridge over Fish Creek, you can see an observation platform that overlooks the creek from Big Woods Trail. If you need to rest, nice benches are provided along the trail. At the intersection of Nature Center Trail and Big Woods Trail, I suggest that—after a rest on another bench—you turn left and follow the yellow posts as you

FRENCH CREEK WOODLAND SCENE

walk east along the high ground south of Fish Creek. Early records suggest that the valley of French Creek along the northern edge of the park (where the trail system does not take you) was originally swamp forest but that the higher land where Big Woods Trail travels was

mixed-mesophytic forest. My observations of the current blend of hardwoods agrees—nice oaks, hickories, maples, and beech. The forest on the right is not very old, but the woods to the left along Fish Creek, which include some nice sycamores, are much more mature.

Soon, just beyond another bench, the trail enters an area of larger trees, with bur oaks, pin oaks, and red maples now in the mix, indicating a more poorly drained woods. Now, 150 feet into the "big woods," the improved trail makes a turn to the right and an unimproved but quite passable forest trail heads straight ahead. If you need the smooth surface, go right. Otherwise, take the trail straight ahead: it's the place to see more spring wildflowers. Orange markers identify this trail. Don't be alarmed if you find deadfall; you will be able to get around it. After a couple hundred feet, the trail leaves Fish Creek and swings left to head south. There are more beech trees here and consequently some roots to step over. A football field's distance to the left is the railroad right-of-way that marks the east border of the reservation. Speaking of football fields, on the autumn day that I walked the trail, along here was where I could hear a marching band rehearsing out-of-doors, doubtless for the following Friday night's gridiron battle.

In this corner of the woods is a large stand of nearly solid pin oak trees, causing me to think that this flat area probably has a clayey soil that drains poorly. As such, this is an area to which I would surely come armed with insect repellent during the warmer months. The trail next makes another sweeping 90-degree turn, this time into the valley of Sugar Creek, another French Creek tributary. The stream has not cut as deeply as Fish Creek.

Heading west now through nice woods following orange blazes, the trail soon travels close to the creek, where it makes a wide meander. Farther away from the creek again, the trail rises and, where the big trees run out, intersects with Big Tree Trail and its yellow blazes.

Continue your hike on this improved yellow-blazed trail. It shortly jogs right and crosses the park road that leads to the Pine Tree Picnic Area. According to the topographic map, this park road is a recycled former railroad right-of-way. During the winter you can see the US Steel plant to the south of the park. Among many young maple trees, both red and sugar, the trail continues west, winding its way more or less parallel to Sugar Creek. There is a drainage ditch alongside the trail here. The trail moves briefly closer to the creek, now rapidly cutting more deeply through the till to a spot where shale cliffs line both banks; there are still scattered glacial erratics in the streambed. At another area of old woods, a former road that descends into the stream valley is blocked by a rail fence.

The trail now turns northwest, leaving the woods to enter the Pine Tree Picnic Area. There is a restroom, some playground equipment, some picnic tables, and a water fountain. At the west end of the picnic area is the 0.55-mile improved Sugar Creek Trail, marked with red. It leads to an overlook above the now quite deep valley of Sugar Creek before looping right to return to the picnic area loop road. Sugar Creek turns to the northwest and enters French Creek just beyond the trail overlook.

Return to the blacktop-covered Big Tree Trail as it crosses a picnic area and the parking lot loop to pass a trailhead sign, then return to the woods, again on a stone surface. The woods are younger here, with crab apple trees left over from the thicket stage of succession still visible alongside the trail. After the leaves have fallen, you can see another picnic area through the trees to the right. This is just off the old railroad right-of-way. If you look carefully, you can see where the Big Woods Trail you are walking crosses the old rail bed.

Fish Creek is now down the hill through the woods to the left of the trail. A boardwalk comes in from the right connecting Big Woods Trail to the orphaned picnic area. Just before the boardwalk, steps leave to the left to the overlook above Fish Creek. In moments, the trail returns to the bench and an intersection with the Nature Center Trail. Turn left to follow the blue markers back to the bridge below the nature center. Or as an alternative, after you cross Fish Creek and start up the hill, catch the shortcut side trail to the right to climb back to Nature Center Trail on the ridge between Fish and French Creeks, enjoying another overlook on the way.

Once across French Creek on the bridge, turn left. Note the high banks of shale across the stream and the old foundation where the train came through here. The trail arcs widely to the left and climbs to the west end of the nature center, where it splits into a walk going to the center and one to the parking lot, using the old roadbed for part of the way.

Hinckley Reservation Metro Park

TOTAL DISTANCE: 5 miles (8 km)

HIKING TIME: 3.75 hours

MAXIMUM ELEVATION: 1,225 feet

VERTICAL RISE: 304 feet

MAPS: USGS 7.5' West Richfield; CMPD Hinckley Reservation Trails map

Like the swallows returning to Capistrano in California, the turkey vultures are said to return to Hinckley, Ohio, right on schedule each spring. On the first Sunday after March 15, the return of the buzzards is celebrated in this metro park and in the nearby community of Hinckley. The timely arrival of the large black scavengers is usually reported on the wire service news. People come from far and wide to see the birds ride the thermals as they pass over the high ridge that runs through the park.

The land for this southern anchor of Cleveland's Emerald Necklace park district was purchased in 1925, and 90-acre Hinckley Lake was built in 1926 by damming the East Branch of the Rocky River. Hinckley is the only reservation in the Cleveland Metro Parks System located entirely outside Cuyahoga County.

GETTING THERE

Located about 30 miles from downtown Cleveland in Medina County, 2,288-acre Hinckley Reservation is reached from north or south by traveling I-71 or I-271 to the OH 303 exit (Center Road). Head east 4.5 miles from I-71 or west from I-271 to OH 606 (Hinckley Hills Road). Turn south and drive a half mile to Bellus Road. Turn left (east), go a quarter mile, and enter the park by turning right (south) on West Drive. After about 1 mile on West Drive, you reach a road labeled Boat House and Johnson's Picnic Area. Enter to the left and drive to the boathouse parking lot. Park here and look for the trailhead kiosk. Though Hinckley Reservation is located within 50 miles of several million people, it offers good hiking in a natural setting. By virtue of being in park district ownership

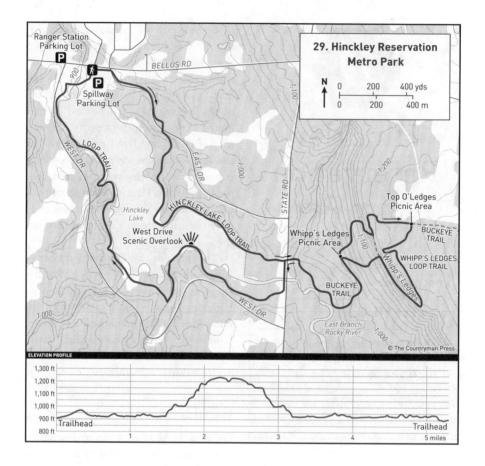

THE TRAIL

To begin walking Hinckley Lake Loop Trail, park in the lot adjoining the ranger station on the north side of Bellus Road, just east of Hinckley Hills Road, or at the lot at the spillway trailhead on the south side of Bellus Road, just east of the ranger station. If you want to carry a trail map, there is generally one available in a box on the front porch of the ranger station. The trailhead sign has a map of the area, a display about the park system and this park in particular, and announcements of upcoming activities. There are restrooms throughout the park, including one just west of the trailhead kiosk. Like other Cleveland metro parks, the trails are well marked with colored diamond-shape medallions and designs, usually with markers of the same shape and color and an arrow pointing in the direction of travel below the trail symbol. Most are located on meter-high posts along the trail at entry

for more than 60 years, those areas that were young secondary succession woods at the time of purchase are now mature forests. As an island of green in an increasingly urban area, it is a haven for wildlife.

points and intersections. The trails utilized on this hike include Hinckley Lake Loop Trail, identified with a great blue heron on a light blue diamond; Whipp's Ledges Loop Trail, which sports a white oak leaf on a tan diamond; and the Buckeye Trail, with a backpacker symbol on a light blue diamond. You will also interact with All-Purpose Trail, which is marked by a jogger on a maroon diamond. I have chosen to hike this trail clockwise, but it can be traveled in either direction.

Hike north on the sidewalk to where it makes a T with All-Purpose Trail. Turn right and follow this blacktopped trail with a green centerline through the spruce grove to East Drive. Turn right there, and join the combined All-Purpose and Lake Loop Trails as they begin climbing toward the southeast. Initially there is a ravine to the left of the trail, but soon the road and trail curve to the right, leaving the ravine behind. You will shortly see the East Drive Scenic Overlook through the woods, although it isn't shown on the map. At a point where the combined trails move left, away from the road, you will see an opening in the woods on the right side of East Drive where a trail angles off toward the lake. Though not marked as such, this is a shortcut to Hinckley Lake Loop Trail. You can walk under the spruce trees to cautiously cross the road and then join this trail to continue hiking. The alternative is to continue on the combined trails along the north and south ballfields, then out the drive and across East Drive to the Indian Point Picnic Area, where you will find a Hinckley Lake Loop Trail marker on a post at the head of a trail leading to the lake.

In either case you will soon find yourself hiking a shoreline trail. There are benches placed at good viewpoints, and short docks are set at convenient spots for the bank fishermen who use the lake quite heavily. Though the map would lead you to believe that Hinckley Lake is all open water, the presence of emergent vegetation reveals that it is actually the victim of heavy siltation and some industrious engineering by beavers. The hillside vegetation appears to be mixed mesophytic, with some nice oaks along the trail. Many specimen trees through here are identified with informative multicolored interpretive signs. Unfortunately, they have been placed high on the trees, evidently to prevent vandalism, so if you aren't looking for them you may miss them. The trail begins its drop to State Road after twisting and turning up the hillside, away from the lake, at a spot where it meets a labeled sugar maple tree. It reaches State Road directly opposite the roadway to the Whipp's Ledges Picnic Area and trailhead. Cross State Road and head up the entrance road to where you see a Buckeye Trail (BT) marker on the right. As an alternative to road walking, use the BT to work your way up the hill through the woods to the Whipp's Ledges Picnic Area.

The BT emerges next to the restroom opposite the trailhead kiosk at the upper end of the parking lot. A classic stone picnic shelter, probably built during the Great Depression, overlooks the hillside area. This is close to the halfway point on this hike, a great place to break out the sack lunch and take a bit of R&R. After filling your water bottle and using the facilities, it will be time to make an assault on Whipp's Ledges. Take the trail that begins on the steps near the shelter. Go easy and enjoy the special feeling of walking through the

A WELL-MAINTAINED TRAIL AT HINCKLEY RESERVATION

bedrock slump blocks and up and over the ledges. The trail gains more than 200 feet in elevation as it winds up the steep hillside. Once you are above the ledges and the Buckeye Trail has come in from the right, continue due east on the combined trails. At the Top O'Ledges Picnic Area there is another restroom.

Whipp's Ledges Loop Trail eventually makes a right turn, leaving the BT to continue east to exit the park and follow Parker Road. Whipp's Ledges Loop

Rocky River tributary. When it nears the restroom, you can opt to continue following the BT to State Road, or walk out on the blacktopped park road. Note that the National Audubon Society has designated the hollow through which the BT travels as an Important Bird Area.

In either case, when you reach State Road, cross it cautiously, then turn left on the All-Purpose/Hinckley Lake Loop/Buckeye Trails. As the merged trails approach the steel footbridge over the East Branch of Rocky River, there is a designated boat launch area on the right. If you are like me, you will make a mental note to return next spring with a kayak or canoe to explore the environment of the beaver impoundment. Once across the bridge, the Lake Loop/Buckeye Trail leave the paved All-Purpose Trail, turning right to closely follow the lakeshore.

The trail continues along the shoreline for a short distance, then climbs the hillside and passes along the bottom of a clearing beneath the deck at the West Drive Scenic Overlook. Dropping back to the lakeshore, the trail soon rounds a corner to the left and leaves the lake to pass between a hillside on the left and a picnic area across a creek on the right. As the combined foot trails approach the boathouse access road, the Buckeye Trail joins All-Purpose Trail to head south. Hinckley Lake Loop Trail takes a sharp right along All-Purpose Trail as it travels northwest toward the boathouse trailhead, the docks, a launching ramp, and the boathouse. Where All-Purpose Trail follows the road uphill, stay to the right and take the blacktopped path to the left of the boathouse. Just beyond it you will see the sign with a heron on a blue diamond, indicating that you are still on

Trail doubles back around and meets the incoming trail. Make a left turn on the combined trails, and when the BT quickly exits left, follow it to experience a different sensation as it drops into the upper end of the valley of another small

Hinckley Lake Loop Trail. The graveled path climbs the hillside among young hardwoods. Then it drops close to the lake as it crosses an area of swamp forest. As it leaves the wetland, it rises to the right about halfway up the hillside among young white oak trees, then returns to the shoreline.

There is a fork in the trail as the earthen dam comes into sight in the distance. Ignore the left fork that ascends the hillside. Lake Loop Trail continues along the shore. Again there are small fishing docks jutting out into the lake. Continuing the hike is now a matter of staying on the lakeshore trail as it approaches the west end of the spillway. Upon reaching the dam, take the 52 steps toward the swimming area and cross the tailwater on a footbridge. At the east end of the bridge the trail returns to sidewalk. The right sidewalk leads to the park concession building. The left one passes among some spruce trees and past a downed redwood tree to carry you back to the spillway trailhead and your vehicle.

THE LAKE AT HINCKLEY RESERVATION

30

Mohican State Park

TOTAL DISTANCE: 3.5 miles (5.6 km)

HIKING TIME: 2.5 hours

MAXIMUM ELEVATION: 1,240 feet

VERTICAL RISE: 265 feet

MAP: USGS 7.5' Jelloway; ODNR Mohican State Park map

Two waterfalls, tall hemlocks, and the sound of rushing water are in store for the hiker visiting Mohican State Park in southwestern Ashland County. Located along the gorge of the Clear Fork of the Mohican River, in the center of 60-year-old Mohican Memorial State Forest, the 1,294-acre park is best known for river canoeing. Even so, it boasts 9 miles of foot trails and 10 miles of bridle trails, and the adjacent state forest has multiple-use trails several times that distance. The most scenic hiking trail in the park originates in its center, to the west of the south end of the new bridge. The park is an area to avoid on holiday weekends, but it's beautiful year-round, and off-season visits reward you with peace and quiet. The Clear Fork has also become popular for fly-fishing since the Division of Wildlife began stocking it with golden trout.

GETTING THERE

The trailhead at Mohican State Park is about a 1.5-hour drive from the Columbus, Cleveland, and Akron areas via I-71 and OH 97. Travel east from Exit 165 for 18 miles, through Bellville and Butler, to the park and forest entrance located on the left, just after the Memorial Shrine on the right. Almost immediately after turning onto the park road, make a left to descend to the covered bridge river crossing, a distance of 1.5 miles. Park at the trailhead on the left side of the road just before the road reaches the covered bridge. During icy or snowy conditions, this road is impassable and will likely be closed. If in doubt, call the park office at 419-994-5125. Note: There is no drinking water and there are no restrooms along this trail, so come prepared.

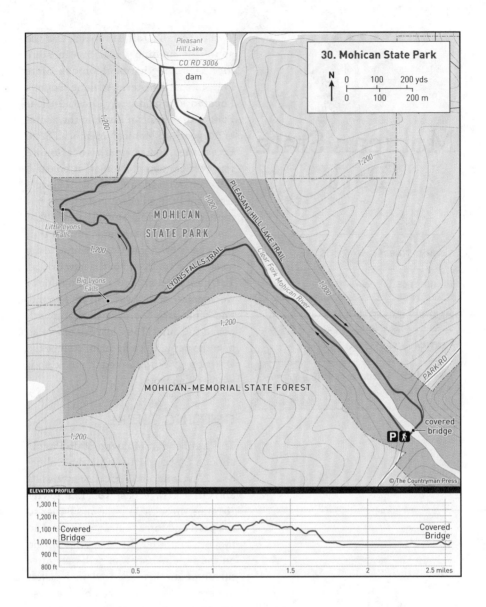

THE TRAIL

Clear Fork Gorge is a special place. The National Natural Landmark monument at the trailhead brings that message home. How did this deep gorge get carved out in this part of Ohio? It was a product of Pleistocene glacia- tion. The Wisconsinan Glacier, the last one to invade Ohio, stopped less than a mile north of this gorge. During the thousands of years when the ice sheet was advancing, then melting, millions of gallons of meltwater rushed through this valley daily on their way to the sea. Since the bedrock was a hard sandstone, the rush of water resulted in this steep-walled gorge. When the glacier melted and the climate warmed, it was still cool enough in this deep, east-west-running gorge for cool-climate plants like hemlock, yellow birch, purple raspberry, and yew to continue to thrive.

Start northwest from the monument and trail entrance sign, following Lyons Falls Trail. During the summer of 1988, park personnel spent many hours repairing and replacing the bridges beneath the towering hemlock trees, making the hiking easy. Just short of a half mile after leaving the road, the trail divides, with a riverside trail continuing straight ahead and a side trail going left to Big Lyons Falls. Follow the

THE LOVELY MOHICAN RIVER

A ROCK SHELTER AT MOHICAN STATE PARK

latter up the ravine to see the first of the two falls that tumble over the face of the sandstone. Follow the staircase up and over Big Lyons Falls to Little Lyons Falls. Continue on the wide trail, which requires some scrambling over bare rock, to arrive at a level trail that swings first right and then left near the rim of the gorge. Momentarily it comes out at the overlook area at the west end of Pleasant Hill Dam.

This earthen structure is 775 feet long and 113 feet high. It has a 199-square-mile drainage area. The permanent pool is at an elevation of 1,020 feet, and flood stage is at 1,065 feet. Like other dams in the Muskingum River Conservancy District system, it has no spillway over the top of the dam. There are steps down the front of the dam for access to tailwater fishing.

To continue a loop hike, cross the dam on the downstream side and, at the east end, turn to the right into the woods where the trail back to the park begins. The trail passes under pines, alongside skunk cabbage, past a patch of cup plant, and past a small cattail marsh before descending to the narrow gorge and the cool shade of more hemlock. After traveling downstream for three quarters of a mile, the trail emerges from the woods near the north end of the covered bridge. Cross the bridge to return to the trailhead parking area.

While in the area, consider hiking the trail at nearby Malabar Farm State Park (Hike 8).

IV.

SOUTHEASTERN OHIO

31

AEP ReCreation Land (Buckeye Trail)

TOTAL DISTANCE: 8 miles (12. 8 km)

HIKING TIME: 5 hours

MAXIMUM ELEVATION: 1,078 feet

VERTICAL RISE: 363 feet

MAPS: USGS 7.5' Reinersville; AEP ReCreation Land Map; BTA Buckeye Trail Belle Valley Section map

NOTE: PERMIT REQUIRED

Not long ago, the mention of coal mining brought visions of "yellow dog" seepage from worked-out hillside mines poisoning whole valleys for miles downstream. In the drift mines that operated in some areas of eastern Ohio in years gone by, that was often the true picture. Since the passage of Ohio's tough mining law in 1972, those mines are gone and many of the old mines have been cleaned up as much as possible.

In Morgan County, where the American Electric Power (AEP) Company has been mining coal since 1944, the story has been different. The AEP surface-mines coal on company-owned land to fuel its generators along the Muskingum River. From the beginning, the company has been concerned with what the land looked like after mining, so it constructed hundreds of ponds and planted 40 million trees as it went along. Current law now requires the land to be restored to close to original grade, but that was not the case before 1972. The power company owns thousands of acres of land where high walls from before 1972 still stand, and that are now covered with young forest. Thirty thousand acres of the "prelaw" land has been designated for use by the public as the AEP ReCreation Land. Eleven "park sites" have been built, with amenities for camping at nine of them. Miles and miles of old haul roads are open to hunters, hikers, and fishermen. There is no charge for use of the land, but a free family/individual permit must be carried at all times while in the ReCreation Land. These and a free map are obtainable from the Ohio Department of Natural Resources Publication Center in Columbus (see the Introduction for this address).

About 10 miles of the Buckeye Trail cross the ReCreation Land near its east-

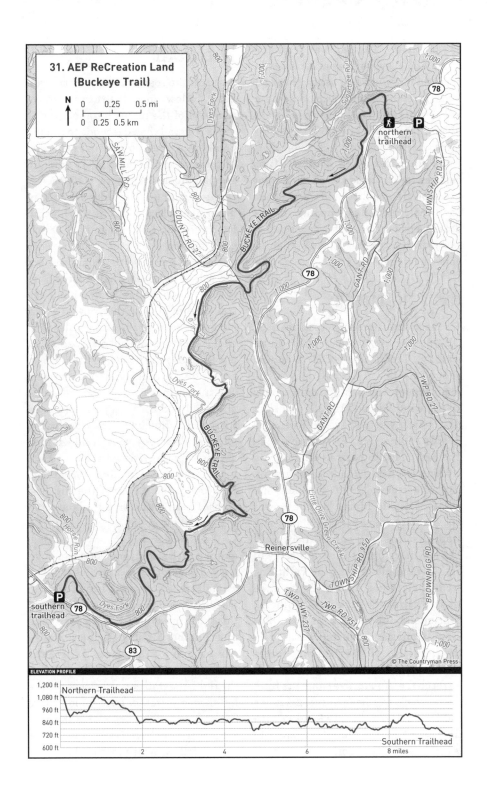

31. AEP ReCreation Land (Buckeye Trail)

N

0   0.25   0.5 mi

0   0.25 0.5 km

78

northern trailhead

P

800

1,000

1,000

Dyes Fork

SAWMILL RD.

COUNTY RD. 27

800

800

BUCKEYE TRAIL

1,000

78

Sugartree Rd.

TOWNSHIP RD. 27

GANT RD.

1,000

1,000

TWP. RD. 27

800

Dyes Fork

BUCKEYE TRAIL

800

800

GANT RD.

Little Olive Green Creek

78

Reinersville

TOWNSHIP RD. 950

BROWNRIGG RD.

1,000

P

southern trailhead

78

Horse Run

800

Dyes Fork

800

83

TWP. HWY 237

TWP. RD. 951

800

© The Countryman Press

ELEVATION PROFILE

1,200 ft	Northern Trailhead
1,080 ft	
960 ft	
840 ft	
720 ft	Southern Trailhead
600 ft	2 4 6 8 miles

ern boundary. The pathway is picturesque and easy walking and passes by
some ponds where the fishing is excellent. The 8-mile stretch around Reinersville along OH 78 is an easy day's walk,
given a drop-off and pickup arrangement. The Woodgrove park site, where
camping is allowed, is about halfway
between the trailheads, so an alternative
would be to camp there and walk out and
back one direction on one day and the
other way on the next. It is necessary to
carry drinking water because there is
none along the way.

GETTING THERE

To reach the northern trailhead on
OH 78, take I-77 to the Caldwell exit
(exit 27). Turn west on OH 78 and go
about 10 miles. The trail leaves the
road through an opening in the woods
on the west side of OH 78, a few hundred yards west of where Township
Road 27 joins OH 78 from the east.
The best place to park a car, however,
is along Township Road 27. After parking, walk back to OH 78, turn left, and
follow the blue blazes on the power
poles along the road. The blazes will
stop when the trail enters the woods.
The last blaze before the trailhead will
be a double blaze with the right one
set higher, indicating a right turn. To
leave a car at the southern trailhead,
continue about 7 miles on OH 78 to
where there is a gravel pull off area on
the right side of the road and where
there are blue blazes on the power poles.
To reach the Woodgrove campsite from
the northern trailhead, travel 2.3 miles
south on OH 78 to County Road 27, turn
right (west) and go .6 mile. The park site
is just beyond Dyes Fork on the left.

THE TRAIL

Once off the road at the northern trailhead, follow an old dirt road above
the level of the mines for about a half
mile. The trail then descends to a small
creek bed, goes up and over the end
of a small knoll, and travels down to
another creek. From here, you descend
to the first pond. I've seen a couple of
fishermen pull some mighty big bluegill
from this pond. In this part of Ohio's
coal country, limestone strata lie close
to the coal veins, so the ponds are not
too acidic to support fish (as they are
in other areas). From the first pond, the
trail goes uphill and then down to pass
along ponds for the next 2.5 miles. The
trail is mostly on an old dirt road about
25 feet above the ponds, but there is an
access trail to each pond for fishermen.
The trail swings east around the end of
one pond and across a pond drainage
that is a bit difficult to cross due to the
5-foot shale slopes on each side. It then
climbs a gentle grade with a switchback
to come out on County Road 27. Parksite
H, Woodgrove, is down the hill and
across Dyes Fork on the left, about a half
mile from this point.

The trail now crosses the road,
angling to the right, and enters an obvious old haul road. The first blue blaze on
a small tree to the right is quite invisi-
ble during the summer. The trail follows
this sometimes rutty road past one pond
after another for about 3 miles. Keep a
close watch for the blazes. Where the
road appears to be hooking hard to
the right, the trail abruptly leaves to the
left through a rather obscure low place
between two piles of spoil. For the next
2 miles, the Buckeye Trail is sometimes
hard to follow. Watch for the blazes and

for the narrow foot tread-way on the ground. In the summertime, the joe-pye weed gets tall and lops over the trail in places. There are no wet crossings, and, just as suddenly as it entered the brush, the trail emerges at a parking area near Dyes Fork on OH 78.

Although this is not pristine virgin forest, it is good hiking country. It is also country for big bucks, beaver, bluegills, and buckeye trees. On the spoil near the ponds, the trees are often black locust, planted here because they provide their own nitrogen and grow well on barren soil. But oak, hickory, maple, and other native hardwoods are returning to the hillsides, and in the autumn the golden glow across the valley is spectacular. At times you might hear the mining across the valley, but the noise is not overbearing. It's hard to get away from man-made noises anywhere in Ohio. Take advantage of Ohio Power's desire for a good public image and enjoy some recreation in the hills of Morgan County.

There is no charge for using the area but a permit is required. A permit can be obtained from the AEP office in McConnelsville, the AEP corporate offices, regional offices of the Ohio Division of Wildlife, or at any of the regional sporting goods or bait stores surrounding the Recreation Area.

BLACK-EYED SUSAN

32

Cooper Hollow Wildlife Area

TOTAL DISTANCE: 9 miles (14.4 km)

HIKING TIME: 5 hours

MAXIMUM ELEVATION: 875 feet

VERTICAL RISE: 186 feet

MAPS: USGS 7.5' Oak Hill; USGS 7W Rio Grande; ODNR Cooper Hollow Wildlife Area map

---

The gentle grade, sweeping curves, narrow cuts, and strange name (CH&D) of the road leading to the Cooper Hollow Wildlife Area give away its past as a railroad right-of-way. A hundred years ago, this eastern branch of the Cincinnati, Hamilton & Dayton Railroad wound its way through the hill country, serving the early industry of the area. Among these businesses was Ohio's once thriving charcoal iron industry. The Madison Furnace, located in the state wildlife area, was one of the most unique. Rather than being entirely made of cut stone blocks, it was partly carved out of solid sandstone. A mile north on the CH&D, now nearly lost among the vegetation, sat Limestone Furnace. Madison operated from 1854 to 1902, but Limestone was only in blast from 1855 to 1860. Both furnaces were the victims of exhausted supplies of iron ore and wood for charcoal and of newer processes and richer ores from other regions of the country. Not only are the railroads and iron industry gone now, but the subsistence farms of the nineteenth and first half of the twentieth centuries have almost completely disappeared as well. The hilly country of this part of Jackson County is now either being stripped for coal or largely left as old fields and forest, good country for hiking.

Remember, this is a wildlife area, paid for by hunting license and sporting goods tax monies, so it is managed for hunting and fishing as well as biological diversity. Avoid the area on weekdays during deer and turkey seasons, and at least wear a blaze orange cap or vest during squirrel season. The Division of Wildlife owns and/or manages hundreds of thousands of acres of land for wildlife throughout the state, but not many of them have good, interconnect-

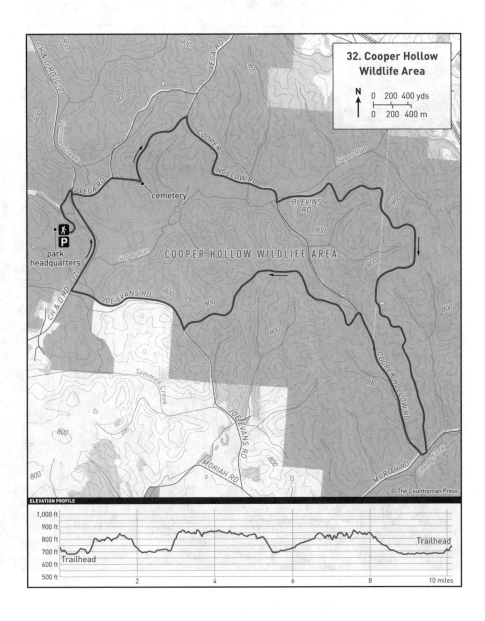

32. Cooper Hollow Wildlife Area

N
0 200 400 yds
0 200 400 m

ELEVATION PROFILE

1,000 ft
900 ft
800 ft
700 ft
600 ft
500 ft

Trailhead

Trailhead

2   4   6   8   10 miles

© The Countryman Press

ing foot trail systems. Parking lots and trails on most have been designed to provide the best access for hunters, but in recent years the division has begun constructing some observation towers and blinds. Most are good places for short exploratory walks and a number are especially good for watching wild-life. These are described in the *Ohio Wildlife Viewing Guide*, which can be purchased from the ODNR publications office. A free brochure listing all areas and maps of individual areas can be obtained from the same source. (See the introduction to this book for ordering information.)

WETLAND HABITAT

GETTING THERE

Cooper Hollow Wildlife Area is reached from the southern edge of Jackson, the county seat, via OH 32 east to US 35 south. Travel 5.5 miles on US 35 south to the OH 327 exit. The road to the right here, traveling south, is County Road 2, or CH&D Road. Take that road to the wildlife area entrance, a distance of 3.5 miles. The drive is on the right. Park at the pull-off just beyond the furnace, or .3 mile up the hill at the headquarters.

THE TRAIL

Start hiking by walking back out the drive, past the furnace, to CH&D Road. Turn right, then immediately left onto Vega Road. At a half mile on the

Hollow Road. Turn right on this lightly traveled gravel road, walking about 1 mile and crossing a small creek. You will pass a parking lot on the left before crossing the Sugar Run Bridge. A short distance beyond this small creek, there is a gated gravel road to the left (formerly OONR Road 4). Follow it several hundred yards to where there was once an active parking lot. In the late summer, as you walk this road, look to the bottomland beyond the creek, where (if the beavers have not flooded it) there may be a gorgeous display of summer wildflowers, including cardinal flower.

Hike beyond the old parking lot for 100 yards to where there is an opening that leads to the left toward a wetland. In the late summer, there is a large stand of joe-pye weed here. Now turn right and bushwhack up the hill past a pine planting to intersect another abandoned road, now a forest trail. Turn left and follow this lane through forest and field for better than 2 miles, until it comes to another parking lot and a pond. Turn left on the trail below the earthen dam. Walk the wide, grassy lane that heads south on a ridge paralleling Cooper Hollow Road for 1 mile. At Moriah Road, turn right, then immediately right again, and head back up the hill on Cooper Hollow Road. At the top of the rise, a road on the right leads to the pond and parking lot you passed 2 miles back. Directly opposite this road is a dirt track that heads up the hill through the woods. Take the latter, winding through the woods to the edge of a hayfield. The trail you want to take exits this hayfield diagonally from where you entered. To reach it, turn right just as you reach the field and walk two sides of the field until you locate the entrance of the trail into the woods. From experience, I know that missing this turn can lead to becoming

right, follow a recently reopened stone drive uphill to Madison Cemetery. The tombstones tell the tales of infant mortality, epidemics, and industrial accidents. From the cemetery, head north beneath tall oaks and hickories on a long-abandoned ridge road. After a few hundred feet the trail swings northeast, where it joins another old township road to go due east to Cooper

A GORGEOUS CARDINAL FLOWER IN FULL BLOOM

hopelessly lost (or at least temporarily off course).

After entering the woods, for the next 3 miles the trail follows ridge and saddle for some of the most delightful hiking anywhere. Old "wolf trees" (which grow in the open, producing large, low-growing branches) and patches of honeysuckle give away the locations of pioneer homesteads. The wolf trees will not yield even one 8-foot saw log, so they are often left standing by foresters as sources of seeds for natural regeneration. At one point the trail uses a deeply cut old road that has seen many a wagon pass its way. A gate at the end of the trail prevents off-road vehicles from entering the area from the parking lot.

Now turn right onto Joe Evans Road and follow it about 1 mile, first downhill, then across Symmes Creek to CH&D Road. Turn right, and another mile of road walking, this time heading north, will lead you back to the area entrance and the trailhead. Before leaving Cooper Hollow Wildlife Area, take time to explore the beaver ponds behind the furnace and pull-off. If you sit quietly, particularly in the evening, you might see beavers repairing their dam or storing vegetation for the cold season ahead; in the spring there is quite a cacophony of amphibian calls.

33

Dysart Woods

TOTAL DISTANCE: 2 miles (3.2 km)

HIKING TIME: 1.5 hours

MAXIMUM ELEVATION: 1,340 feet

VERTICAL RISE: 180 feet

MAPS: USGS 7.5' Armstrongs Mills and Hunter; Ohio University Dysart Woods Laboratory brochure

A walk through Dysart Woods is a walk among the giants; there is no other way to describe it. It is home to the largest number of 36-inch-diameter trees (at breast height) that I know of in Ohio. Acquired by Ohio University in 1962, with the assistance of The Nature Conservancy, it was one of the first natural areas in the state to be designated a National Natural Landmark by the federal government. Ohio University, whose Belmont campus is less than 12 miles to the north, uses the woods as an outdoor laboratory, with busloads of students and their teachers frequently visiting the area. There are no facilities here, but it is open to the public. Note that smoking is not permitted while in the preserve. Picnicking and camping facilities are available at Barkcamp State Park just a few miles to the north. Dysart Woods has experienced a number of severe storms in recent years and there are many downed trees, some lying across the trail. When I walked here in 2006, the bridges were in need of replacement, but I was able to use them. Exercise caution when you do so.

Dysart Woods has been the subject of much controversy during the first decade of this century. Like much property in mineral-rich Appalachia, the ownership of surface rights and the mineral rights have been separated. Ohio University does not own the mineral rights to Dysart Woods, and the people that do would like to extract coal from beneath the land. Several unsuccessful efforts have been made to prevent the mining, but mining is currently underway using a subsurface technique called long-wall mining. The hope is that no subsidence of the land and, hence, no disturbance to the forest, will take place. Only time will tell. This is an even more

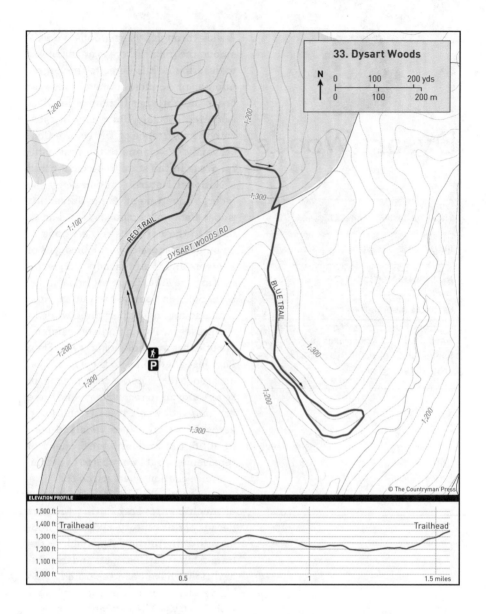

33. Dysart Woods

ELEVATION PROFILE

compelling reason to put Dysart Woods high on your list of places to visit soon.

GETTING THERE

Finding Dysart Woods is not difficult. Travel east of Cambridge on US 70 to Exit 208, OH 149. Take this road south for 3.5 miles into Belmont. There, take OH 147 out of the southeast corner of the community and travel 5 miles until you see the Dysart Woods sign on the right side of the road. Turn right onto Township Road 234, then immediately right again onto Township Road 194 (Dysart Woods Road). The preserve headquarters is at the farmhouse on the right (east) side of the road. A brochure that includes a map is usually available from a self-dispensing box there. The trailhead is at a grassy area labeled "Dysart Woods parking" on the left side of the road, about three quarters of a mile beyond the house.

THE TRAIL

There are two connected trails: the Red Trail on the west side of the road and the Blue Trail to the east. Their routes are marked with posts and/or blazes of the appropriate color. I prefer to begin to the west, crossing the gravel road to enter the woods past a red blaze, and then traveling downhill. You are soon struck by the size of the trees around you, including tall, forest-grown beeches and maples. The plaintive call of a woodpewee greeted me as I walked this way on a hot July afternoon. This is a dirt trail, with an occasional water bar to reduce erosion. The relatively wide track the trail starts on soon leaves to the left, and the red-post-marked trail becomes a narrow footpath and continues to wind around the hillside.

Once the larger trees begin to give way to much younger ones, you can look through the woods to the left to a large hillside pasture beyond the boundary fence. A well-kept barn stands out on the horizon uphill from the fence. As a red-tailed hawk screamed overhead, a female black rat snake appeared on the path in front of me. It was docile, as are most of its species, and it allowed me to lift it off the trail with my walking staff.

Beyond the view of the farm the trail enters a growth of much larger trees while moving gently downslope toward a small ravine. There the trail turns left

before hitting the bottom of the ravine, where it turns right. Stay left at a split in the trail, following the red posts. Here the large trees stand about 15 feet apart with small sugar maples in the understory and spicebush in the shrub layer. Beechdrops (parasitic plants that affect the roots of beech trees) can be seen beneath a large beech tree that appears to guard a narrow footbridge across a seasonal stream. Beyond the bridge, the trail turns upstream and winds its way up the hill, then turns right around the hillside to pass giant white oak trees, as well as a beautiful, straight, wild black cherry. It finally arrives at the fallen giant of the forest—a huge tuliptree that succumbed to a windstorm in the summer of 1995. Somewhere in my files is a slide of me standing in front of this tree in 1972. That was the first of many visits I made to Dysart Woods, and the tuliptree was magnificent to behold. I had to use binoculars to see the leaves on its lower limbs to identify its species. Even in death and returning to the earth, it is an impressive specimen.

The trail continues to make its way through the open forest of huge white oak and tuliptrees as it drops downslope to the creek. Down the valley, at a fork in the stream, the trail crosses the streambed on another picturesque but rather unsubstantial 2-foot-wide bridge with a single handrail. There is a small but photogenic waterfall downstream from the bridge. Fifty feet beyond is another footbridge that looks even less durable. The trail winds and dips, but mostly climbs as it makes its way toward the township road. As the trail makes an oblique approach to the road, multiflora rose begins to appear in the understory. At the road, a sign suggests crossing over to take Blue Trail, the entrance to

DYSART WOODS—A FOREST OF GIANTS

which is about 60 feet up the road to the left.

Blue Trail begins between a poison ivy-covered black walnut tree and a hawthorn tree, then heads toward the woods on a wide, grassy trail. The grass runs out as the trail enters a young wood of maple, ash, tuliptree, and other hardwoods. Soon the trail reaches an area of open forest with good-size trees. A wood thrush broke out in song as I passed through here in the summer of 1996. At a trail junction you have the option of exploring more deep woods by taking a short loop trail to the left or continuing straight to the parking lot on this trail. Take the loop trail, of course. A less-traveled trail, it winds among large beech and maple trees where spicebush makes up the shrub layer. It looks as if it would be a great spring wildflower trail. At a large blank sign, designed to tell you that this is as far as you can travel up this valley, turn right and hang onto the side of the hill as the trail returns to where it began.

Turning downhill and then downstream, the trail soon reaches a bridge over a small stream. At the far end of the bridge there are steps poorly carved into the hillside, and there was once a handrail here to help the hiker up a short steep place. Once over this hurdle, the trail climbs steeply up a ridge between two streams. The trees along here are of incredible dimensions. At the top of the slope, the trail turns left to follow a fairly level terrace for about 100 feet before breaking through the edge of the woods onto the parking lot.

This extraordinary woodland is a place to cherish, as are your memories of a walk along its trails. It strikes me as a place to return to—at different seasons of the year and at different times of the day. It's a place to share with the other living creatures whose presence makes it so very special.

TRAIL SIGNS AT DYSART WOODS

Storm Damage and Renewal

Severe storms can strike Ohio at any time of the year and are viewed with alarm by the public because of their potential damage to life and property. But to the naturalist, these storms are considered an important element of the ecosystem. Prairie fires set by lightning strikes from autumn storms contribute in many ways to the health and vigor of the prairie grasses and forbs. Heavy winter snowstorms effectively prune or even bring down dead, dying, or weak trees, allowing stronger, healthier trees to take their place in the canopy and creating openings where creatures that need brushy habitat can live. Springtime tornadoes or heavy wind and rainstorms likewise bring trees crashing down, allowing more light to reach the forest floor, thus creating new habitat. Untold numbers of species of invertebrates and vertebrates make their homes in, around, and under downed tree trunks and branches, and cavity-nesting creatures soon go to work on the dead snags left standing by such weather events.

34

Great Seal State Park

TOTAL DISTANCE: 4.75 miles (7.2 km)	
HIKING TIME: 3 hours	
MAXIMUM ELEVATION: 900 feet	
VERTICAL RISE: 170 feet	
MAPS: USGS 7.5' Series Kingston; ODNR Great Seal State Park brochure	

Only a few of the many trails that I have walked in Ohio have the aura that I felt when walking paths at Great Seal State Park. The magic of being on the land depicted on the Great Seal of the state of Ohio is in and of itself exciting to me. The story has been written many times. Here it is as told in Michael O'Bryant's *Ohio Almanac*: "It is said that when twenty-one-year-old William Creighton (who later became Ohio's first Secretary of State) was charged with designing the state seal, he rode from the temporary capital at Chillicothe to the nearby country estate Adena, where he consulted with the owner, Thomas Worthington, a future US Senator and one of Ohio's founding fathers. Creighton and some other guests enjoyed an all-night game of cards, and when the dawn broke, he stepped outside and was immediately taken with how the sun rising behind Mt. Logan cast a rosy glow upon the surrounding wheat fields. 'Gentlemen' Creighton proclaimed, 'there is our seal.'" Though the design has been modified in the interval since then, the low gap between Sugarloaf Mountain on the left and Bald Hill on the right is still central to the twenty-first-century iteration of the seal.

The feeling of the significance of walking on that hillside and in that gap has its origin much earlier than the first days of Ohio's statehood, however. There is credible evidence that long before white European settlers came into the Scioto Valley, prehistoric Indians, probably the culture of 2,200 years ago that we call Hopewell, passed through this low gap en route from their villages in the valleys of the Scioto and Paint Creeks to the major Hopewell center at the confluence of the Muskingum and Ohio Rivers. More than that, recent studies by Dr. Bradley T. Lepper, curator

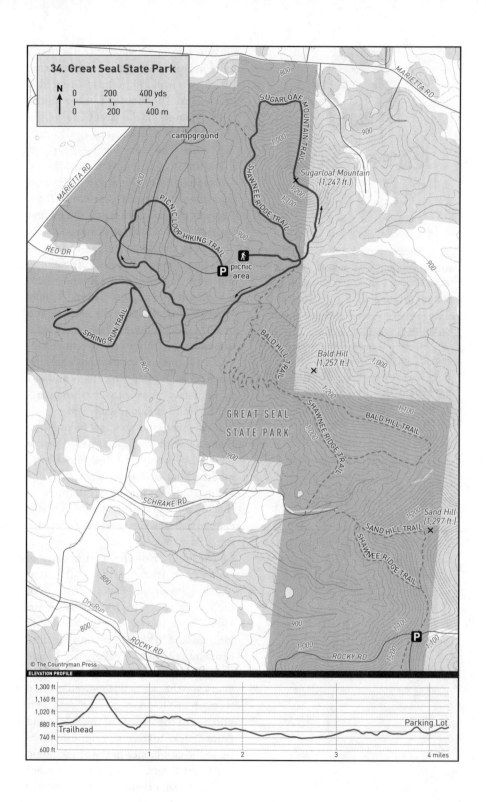

34. Great Seal State Park

N

| 0 | 200 | 400 yds |
| 0 | 200 | 400 m |

campground

MARIETTA RD

SUGARLOAF MOUNTAIN TRAIL

Sugarloaf Mountain
(1,247 ft.)

SHAWNEE RIDGE TRAIL

MARIETTA RD

PICNIC LOOP HIKING TRAIL

REO DR

picnic
area

SPRING RUN TRAIL

BALD HILL TRAIL

Bald Hill
(1,257 ft.)

GREAT SEAL
STATE PARK

SHAWNEE RIDGE TRAIL

BALD HILL TRAIL

SCHRAKE RD

Sand Hill
(1,297 ft.)

SAND HILL TRAIL

SHAWNEE RIDGE TRAIL

Dry Run

ROCKY RD

ROCKY RD

© The Countryman Press

ELEVATION PROFILE

| 1,300 ft |
| 1,160 ft |
| 1,020 ft |
| 880 ft |
| 740 ft |
| 600 ft |

Trailhead

Parking Lot

1   2   3   4 miles

of archaeology at the Ohio Historical Society, suggest that a "Great Hopewell Road" traversed the gap en route to the third great Ohio Hopewell culture center—the Octagon mound and other earthworks in the valley of Licking River and its tributaries in Licking County.

There is no doubt that one of the major foot trails of historic Native Americans heading east from Chillicothe followed this route. (Another probably followed close to present-day US 35 to reach the salt springs at Jackson.) And when Marietta, Cincinnati, and Chillicothe were in hot contention to serve as the capital of a still-undefined state to be carved from the Northwest Territory, Marietta Road left the Chillicothe area on the old road you can still travel in Great Seal State Park. Retired forester Emmett A. Conway of Chillicothe has spent many years tracing the old road on the land.

Marietta was settled in 1787, Chillicothe in 1796. Chillicothe was the headquarters for the Northwest Territory before statehood and was the first capital of Ohio, in 1803. A political map known as the Bourne map of 1820, and a government survey map of that period, referred to as the Hough map, both show that during the first 20 or 30 years of the nineteenth century Marietta Road stayed true to the ancient route. And why not? It was dry, level, and direct, serving travel on foot, horseback, and coach very well.

Also exciting is the setting of Great Seal Park as it relates to the Pleistocene glaciers that made their way across much of Ohio. Great Seal is located in one of the places where the last ice advance, the Wisconsinan, of 20,000 to 25,000 years ago, did not reach as far as its immediate predecessor, the Illinoian, of 125,000 years ago. It is a place at which the advancing glacier ran into the edge of the Appalachian Plateau, land that was considerably higher in elevation than western Ohio, bringing further southeasterly movement to a slow halt. At Great Seal you will find glacial moraine of Illinoian origin at the base of hills, glacial erratics brought to the area by the Illinoian glacier on the surface and in the creek beds, and, on the ridge, outcrops of Mississippian-age sandstone. The Illinoian glacier overran the tops of the hills here in its final advance, reaching almost to the Vinton County line, but more than 100,000 years later little evidence remains on the ridges and high hillsides.

When early settlers from Virginia and other mid-Atlantic coastal states began arriving in this part of Ohio, oak–sugar maple forests thrived on the rolling hills. In the broad valley of the Scioto River—really the valley of the pre-glacial northward-flowing Teays River—hardwood forests on that rich bottomland soil sometimes grew to huge proportions. According to early reports, many hollow sycamores were used for sheds or barns, and pioneers would occasionally live in them. One tree near Waverly, not many miles south of Great Seal Park, had a cavity more than 10 feet wide and was used as a blacksmith shop for a time. The river bottoms seen to the west of Great Seal soon yielded to the ax and plow to become great "corn bottoms," helping to feed—and incidentally quench the thirst of—a growing population in middle America. When, in the early nineteenth century, the Ohio & Erie Canal opened the Scioto Valley to the exporting of agricultural products, shipping corn liquor in barrels offered a real advantage over shipping grain, which was subject to spoilage, in the hold of a canal boat.

Great Seal offers 5 miles of exclusive foot trails and another 17 miles of trails that hikers share with equestrians and mountain bikers. The hiking trails are on moderately hilly terrain on the lower slopes of the park. The multiuse trails traverse rugged, steep terrain and are a challenge to hike, but they do afford access to the high terrain of the park. The multiuse trails are color blazed and easy to follow; still, you might want to pick up a park map as you enter the area if you are going to strike out on the Sugarloaf Mountain, Shawnee Ridge, or Mount Ives Trails.

GETTING THERE

To reach Great Seal State Park, take US 23 south from Circleville to SR 159. Turn right onto SR 159 and take it to Delano Road. Go east on Delano Road to Marietta Road and turn right. The entrance to the 1,682-acre park is on the east side of the road less than a mile after the turn.

THE TRAIL

Begin your hike from the main parking lot off Marietta Road (not the original road, but a straightened, much-improved version). I suggest you begin hiking at the upper end of the picnic area near the volleyball and horseshoe-pitching areas, where you will find the entrance to the multiuse trails. Sugarloaf Mountain Trail, blazed with yellow, 2.1 miles in length; Shawnee Ridge Trail, blazed with blue, 7.8 miles long; and Mount Ives Trail, orange blazed, 6.4 miles beyond Shawnee Ridge Trail, are all accessible from here. So too are Picnic Loop and Spring Run Trail, via a short walk on the multiuse trail that includes the ancient footpath-turned-road.

The trail begins climbing at once and after 100 yards reaches a junction where the yellow-blazed Sugarloaf Mountain Trail goes left or more or less straight. Sugarloaf Mountain Trail is a very strenuous trek, climbing 350 feet in less than a quarter mile, through dense, maple-dominated forest, to reach the crest of Sugarloaf Mountain. The trail returns to this parking lot or, via a spur, to the park campground, so you can hike it by going either direction at this junction and following the yellow blazes.

For a shorter hike using the footpaths, follow the yellow blazes straight as the trail winds its way through the woods to the right toward the gap. You will know when you reach Marietta Road. At a Carsonite post marked B the yellow trail continues ahead and Shawnee Ridge Trail, blazed blue, goes right to follow the ancient footpath downhill toward Chillicothe. If the rocks and the trees could talk, what tales they might tell about those who passed this way in earlier centuries. Old culverts are still visible.

A pileated woodpecker called as I walked through here on an early-November day, kicking oak leaves before me like I was a kid. Note here that granite boulders, those intrepid travelers of eons ago, are plentiful in the creek bed.

At another trail junction, the blue and orange trails go left and, following a sign that points to PARK, leave the multiuse trails to connect to Picnic Loop and Spring Run Trail. Hanging on the left side of the hill, the trail passes among red cedar and mound-building ant hills. Now traveling on wide mowed trails suitable for cross-country skiing, turn left onto Spring Run Trail to make a loop walk of a little more than 2 miles. The trail winds its way slowly downhill among young trees, fields, and thickets, soon splitting to make a loop. It loses

MOUNT LOGAN, THE HILL IN THE "GREAT SEAL OF OHIO"

around 100 feet in elevation. After making a wide swing to the south, it regains the elevation as it travels parallel to the park boundary before heading north to close the loop.

Back at the junction with the trail, turn left to drop into the valley of the stream you followed on Spring Run Loop. Beyond the bridge, a 100-foot climb brings you to a T where the trail splits once more. A sign identifies it as the hiking trail and tells you that traveling to the right will return you directly to the parking lot. Turn left to enjoy Picnic Loop as it winds among the red cedars and old field, on a wide trail among very young trees. The red cedars show evidence of deer browsing. The trail drops to a bridge across a chasm where sandstone bedrock is visible below the deep glacial drift. A straight-up-the-hill climb brings you via a winding path through thicket to a crossing of the park entrance road. Carsonite posts on each side of the road identify this as a hiking trail.

Beyond the road, the trail passes through a white pine planting as it circles right and climbs among young sassafras and Virginia pine to soon reach the road to the campground. There is a good view of Sugarloaf Mountain from this crossing.

Beyond the crossing, the trail drops down the hill and crosses the ravine on a wide bridge. After winding its way to the right and uphill the trail makes an abrupt left turn, when the road comes into view ahead, to climb to the parking lot.

If you want to assault Bald Hill, the hill on the south side of the gap, opt for the blue- and orange-labeled trail instead of the cutoff to the hiking trails as you descend from the gap on the old road. Along with the supplies you normally carry, tuck a park map in your pocket and plan your hike so you can get back well before nightfall. Know your limitations. Bald Hill is at 1,257 feet, more than 300 feet above the old road, and there are several very steep sections on the trail.

The blue-blazed Shawnee Ridge Trail also includes trail on the south side of Rocky Road, on Rocky Knob. As an alternative to approaching this area from the main parking lot, you may prefer to

SOME OF THE TRAILS OF MOUNT LOGAN ARE WELL WORN FROM YEARS OF USE

drive to the ridge by leaving the park and turning left to follow Marietta Road to Rocky Road, where you can turn left and drive to the ridge. There is room to park one or two cars there. The hike to the north to Sand Hill and the rock outcrops is a nice, fairly level walk along the ridge, about a mile round trip. To the south are the somewhat more strenuous trails of Rocky Knob and the connection to the many miles of Mount Ives Trail Loop with its several scenic vistas—also a strenuous trail.

Great Seal State Park has a small camping area located to the north off the main park entrance road. There are also two picnic shelters for day use as well as restrooms and drinking water. The park includes 1,864 acres and was established in the mid-1970s. There are 900 acres of public hunting land east of the park.

Sugarloaf Mountain Amphitheater borders the northeast corner of the park off Delano Road. The famous outdoor historical drama *Tecumseh* is presented there from late June through September.

The Chillicothe area is resplendent with historical and archaeological sites to visit. While in the area, be sure to stop at Adena, the historic home of Thomas Worthington, Ohio's first senator and sixth governor, who is considered the Father of Ohio Statehood. The National Park Service operates Hopewell Culture National Historical Park, which includes a prehistoric Indian complex with 23 burial mounds just north of Chillicothe on SR 104, well worth the visit. The Ross County Historical Society at 45 West Fifth Street in Chillicothe features exhibitions and programs during most of the year.

35

Lake Hope State Park

TOTAL DISTANCE: 1 to 4.2 miles (1.6–6.8 km)

HIKING TIME: 1 to 3 hours

MAXIMUM ELEVATION: 900 feet

VERTICAL RISE: 195 feet

MAPS: USGS 7.5' Series, Mineral

Count Peter Zaleski never saw the land in southeastern Ohio that bears his name. An exile from Poland, Zaleski was active in the Paris banking scene. Using investment monies largely received from Polish émigrés, he formed the Zaleski Mining Company to exploit the resources of Vinton County, Ohio. In 1856, the town of Zaleski was laid out, and two years later a charcoal-fired iron furnace, known as the Zaleski Furnace, was constructed just north of the settlement.

This was not the first furnace in the area. Hope Furnace on Sandy Run a few miles to the north had been "in blast" for two years, producing high-quality iron from the local ore and limestone and burning charcoal made from the abundant timber of the area.

Elsewhere in the county Eagle Furnace and Hamden Furnace were already producing iron. Nor was Zaleski's industrial enterprise the first to come to Vinton County since settlement by European whites. In the first half of the century, millstones had been produced from native rock at a site now under the waters of Lake Hope. By 1880, Madison Township, in which Zaleski was the only sizable community, had 2,217 residents, by far the most of any township in Vinton County.

Zaleski's town is still here but the furnace is gone, as are most of the people. Like most of the furnaces of the area, it survived long enough to flourish during the Civil War but was shut down within 10 years of the end of that bitter conflict. The operations had denuded the hills of timber for miles around, and the remains of the already thin iron-bearing veins were now so far under the hills that it was unprofitable to mine them. New sources of high-grade ore and

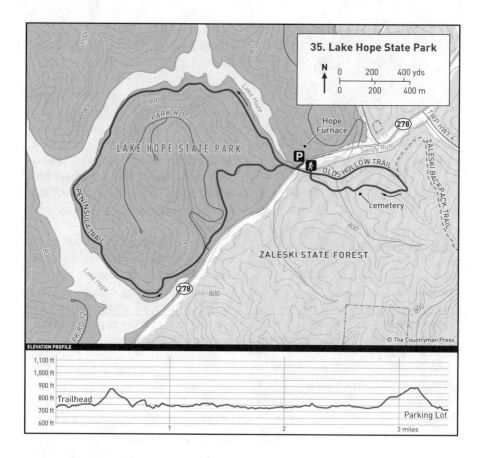

better smelting processes doomed the furnaces. The only remaining evidence of the iron industry here are Hope Furnace, preserved at Lake Hope State Park, and traces of haul roads along which ore, limestone, and wood were carted to the furnace.

Prosperity never really returned to Vinton County. In the mid-twentieth century the thin veins of high-sulfur coal were exploited, mostly by drift mining. Unfortunately, that left many of the small valleys of the area awash with "yellow boy" a yellowish deposit leached from mines that raised the acidity of the streams and rivers and made them inhospitable to life. Where there is yel-

low boy, the pH of the water will be very low—from sulfuric acid pollution—and that spells death to all creatures great and small. Today, strip-mining for coal, logging of secondary forests, blasting powder production, and tourism are the main industries of the area.

Established during the early 1930s, 26,827-acre Zaleski State Forest was the site of a Civilian Conservation Corps camp during the Depression. It also holds Ohio's first resort-type park development, Lake Hope Lodge and Cabins (the lodge was destroyed by fire during the winter of 2005–2006). Lake Hope State Park, now 3,223 acres, was carved from the state forest in 1949 when the

Department of Natural Resources came into being. It includes all the recreational facilities of the state-owned land except the backpack and bridle trails.

Many of the trails at Lake Hope were laid out by my lifelong friend, Bill Price, Ohio's first state park naturalist. Bill and I were friends at Ohio State, where we were together on many class field trips. A year ahead of me in school, he went to work as the first and, for many years, only state park naturalist shortly after the Division of Parks and Recreation was created, in August 1949. He, quite literally, built the state park nature interpretation program from the ground up. Based at Lake Hope State Park, the only park with vacation cabins, a dining lodge, campground, and thousands of acres of surrounding forest, he showed those of us who followed a couple of decades later how to be an interpretive naturalist. Bill loved to hike. Working with the park managers, he laid out hundreds of miles of the trails we know today in the parks of southeastern Ohio. When I walk these trails, I feel his presence.

The hand of Emmett Conway, known as "The Olde Forester" by many of his friends and colleagues, can also be seen at Lake Hope. He was the Zaleski forest ranger in the 1940s, before there was a Division of Parks and Recreation. He, too, loved to hike and especially to unearth the footpaths and wagon trails of our forebears. He could talk for hours about Ohio's ancient Indian trails and pioneer roads. He assured me that the first road from Marietta to Chillicothe traversed some of the same path you will walk on this hike. Before beginning your hike, explore Hope Furnace on the hillside above the parking area. Walk the paths, read the signs, and gaze at this work of human hands. Built in 1854, it was probably "in blast" nearly around the clock during the Civil War, producing "pig iron" for weapons and ammunition. Check "Hanging Rock Iron Region" websites for more information, and visit Buckeye Furnace State Memorial near Wellston to see restored furnaces.

GETTING THERE

The trailhead can be reached from the Columbus area by traveling southeast on US 33 past Logan. Turn right (south) on OH 328, then left (east) on US 56. At OH 278, turn right (south) and travel 4 miles to the upper end of Lake Hope. The trailhead is located at a parking lot on the east side of OH 278 opposite the Hope Furnace parking lot. An information kiosk at the trailhead has registration forms that must be completed. An alternative from Columbus is to take US 23 south to Circleville and then OH 56 east to OH 278, where you turn right. The trip takes two hours either way.

From western and southwestern Ohio, take US 35 east to Chillicothe from 1-71.

From Chillicothe, travel US 50 east through McArthur to OH 677. Turn left (north), and at OH 278 turn left (north) and drive to the parking lot about 1 mile north of the Lake Hope dam (a three-hour trip).

From Cleveland, the trip takes about 4.5 hours via the Columbus route.

THE TRAIL

This hike uses two Lake Hope State Park trails: the l-mile-long Olds Hollow Trail and the 2.9-mile Peninsula Trail. Both can be accessed from the same parking lot and together make a

WETLANDS AT UPPER REGIONS OF LAKE HOPE

good day hike. Neither are very difficult. Olds Hollow Trail takes the hiker into the forest to the village of Hope, where the Hope Furnace workers once lived. Peninsula Trail follows the shores of Sandy Creek and Lake Hope a short distance back from the water, and then returns to the parking lot on a trail parallel to the road. Together, with a few breaks, these two trails should require no more than three hours of hiking. Add some time to explore the furnace area and enjoy a picnic lunch and you have a four-hour outing at the park, plus your travel time.

The entrance to Olds Hollow Trail is on the east side of SR 278, across the road from the Hope Furnace parking lot,

nace and their families, or the residents of the nearby village of Hope that supported the iron-producing enterprise, a community of at least 300 persons. The furnace began production in 1854 and it surely wasn't built overnight, or without construction accidents and disease taking their toll.

After passing the cemetery, the trail goes through some lovely scenery, eventually dropping to creek level via a wooden stairway. I believe the village of Hope was located in this bottomland area, and that the iron workers walked to and from the furnace via the route you will follow alongside the wetland to return to the trailhead. Along that trail, you will pass the entrance to the Backpack Trail.

Now off to explore another part of this 2,983-acre hiker's paradise. Peninsula Trail, just shy of 3 miles in length, follows the inside shore of the D-shape lake between Lake Hope and SR 278. With a minimum of change in elevation, it should take no more than 1.5 hours to complete. Leaving your vehicle at the furnace lot, begin hiking by going south along the road berm, then immediately turning right onto the trail. Though this would seem on the map to be a streamside trail, it is not; it's a hillside trail through an oak-hickory forest. The hill to the left is the site of vacation cabins and the park's famous dining lodge, which has only recently re-opened following a devastating fire in 2006. Lake Hope, down the hill to the right, was created in the 1930s by the damming of Sandy Run. Expect to see woodland birds, mammals, and wildflowers along this trail. When you are close to Sandy Run or the lake you might even spot beaver. You will pass at least one trail forking to the left up the hill.

a site it shares with the well-known Zaleski Backpack Trail. Begin and end there. The two trails follow the same footpath for less than a quarter of a mile, then the Backpack Trail heads left. Stay to the right to begin Olds Hollow Trail. A climb of about .4 mile will take you to Hope Cemetery, the burying place for those who worked and died at Hope Fur-

HOPE IRON FURNACE, BUILT IN 1852

Ignore it and continue within sight of the lake. Here and there a fisherman's trail will lead right to a favorite bank fishing spot—explore or ignore. After about two miles of "unwinding the clock," the trail bends more sharply as it heads upstream along an embankment to begin closing the loop. It parallels SR 278 as it crosses the main park entrance road and a small creek. Moving up the side of the hill, Peninsula Trail then intersects with Greenbriar Trail. There, after about 3 miles of hiking, make a right turn and you will shortly be on the road headed toward the parking lot at Hope Furnace. If you caught the "iron furnace bug," as I have, your computer will set you on the road to exploring Ohio's and Kentucky's famous nineteenth-century Hanging Rock Iron Region.

Lake Katharine State Nature Preserve

TOTAL DISTANCE: 4.5 miles (7.2 km)

HIKING TIME: 3 hours

MAXIMUM ELEVATION: 800 feet

VERTICAL RISE: 170 feet

MAPS: USGS 7.5' Jackson; ODNR Lake Katharine State Nature Preserve map

More species of plants have been recorded in Jackson County than any other county in Ohio. This fact can most likely by attributed to the late Circleville farmer and botanist Floyd Bartley, who spent decades collecting in the area and depositing his specimens in university herbaria. The area also served as a refugium for plants of the Teays River Basin during Pleistocene glaciation. And, because of its deep, cool ravines, it retained relict communities of boreal plants after the last glacier melted. Big-leaf magnolia, a tree of the southern highlands whose northern limit is only a few miles to the north, is found on the preserve. The rare round-leafed catchfly grows on the slopes below the sandstone cliffs of the preserve, and the small, thorny tree known as Hercules' club can be found in the mixed mesophytic woods that dominate the area.

Though unusual plants and spectacular cliffs—reaching as high as 150 feet in places—are the main features of Lake Katharine Preserve, wildlife also abounds. Deer and wild turkey are seen often, and bobcats have been reported in years past. Needless to say, the spring wildflowers are spectacular, and for many years the Division of Natural Areas and Preserves has conducted a wildflower workshop here at the peak of the wildflower season. Information on this and other programs is available on the bulletin board at the main parking lot or from the division office in Columbus. There is a regional maintenance facility near the parking lot, but it offers no public services. There is also a private residence occupied by people who aren't ODNR employees. Please do not disturb them.

There are no facilities for picnicking or camping at Lake Katharine, but both are available at Lake Alma State Park,

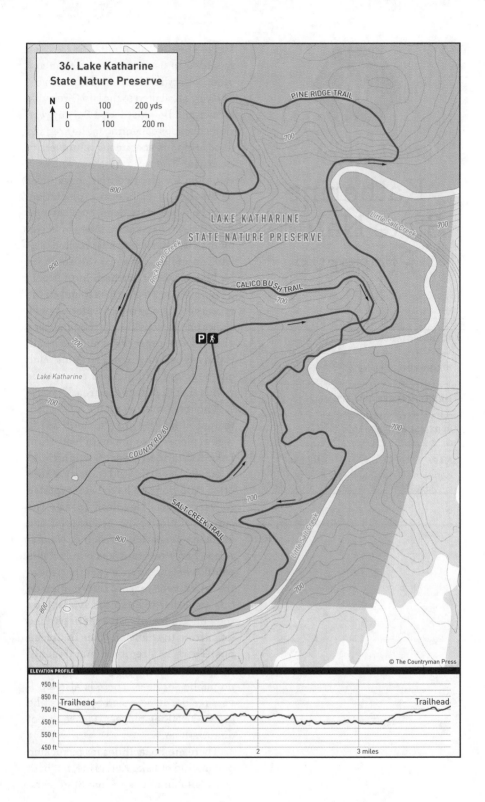

36. Lake Katharine State Nature Preserve

N

| 0 | 100 | 200 yds |
| 0 | 100 | 200 m |

PINE RIDGE TRAIL

800

700

LAKE KATHARINE
STATE NATURE PRESERVE

Rock Run Creek

Little Salt Creek

700

CALICO BUSH TRAIL

700

P

800

700

Lake Katharine

700

COUNTY RD 60

700

SALT CREEK TRAIL

800

700

Little Salt Creek

700

800

© The Countryman Press

ELEVATION PROFILE

| 950 ft |
| 850 ft | Trailhead | Trailhead |
| 750 ft |
| 650 ft |
| 550 ft |
| 450 ft | 1 | 2 | 3 miles |

UNDER THE SANDSTONE ON LAKE KATHARINE TRAIL

about 12 miles to the north, off OH 93, just above Wellston. For the person interested in industrial archaeology, there are a number of old charcoal-fired iron furnaces located in the area around Jackson. A map giving their locations is available from the Ohio Historical Society in Columbus.

There is a small impoundment known as Lake Katherine on the preserve that was created by the damming of Rock Run, when, during the Great Depression, the area was Camp Arrowhead, a summer youth camp for children of Jackson County. It offers good fishing for bass and panfish, but fishing requires a written reservation. Restricted to five boats per day, with no motors of any sort allowed, fishing is permitted Monday through Friday between April 1 and October 31. To obtain a permit, call 614-286-2487 during normal working hours on the last Friday of the month before the month for which fishing permission is desired. To reach the lake, you must haul your boat down a 110-foot slope, which, of course, you must clamber back up as you leave. As you drive into the preserve you will see another vestige of the area's youth camp days, a small blockhouse located to the right of the road, just before you reach the parking lot. The camp lodge that for many years sat just beyond the parking lot was removed after many years of deterioration.

GETTING THERE

The preserve can be reached from Chillicothe by traveling US 35 to Jackson. Turn right (east) onto County Road 84 and follow it for 3 miles into Jackson, until you reach State Street. Follow State Street out of town—it becomes CR 76—for about 2 miles, then turn right onto CR 60. After traveling a little more than 1 mile, this road ends at the location of old Camp Arrowhead, where the preserve office and trailheads are located. It takes about 2 hours to reach the preserve from the Columbus area.

From the Cincinnati area, travel OH 32 to the OH 93 exit on the south side of Jackson. Turn left and take OH 93 north past downtown Jackson to State Street, where it turns right. Instead of following it right, though, turn left and follow the directions above.

THE TRAIL

At the right end of the parking lot, three trails head toward the woods' edge: Calico Bush Trail, Pine Ridge Trail, and Salt Creek Trail. This hike uses all three in a figure-eight pattern. You will travel the top loop counterclockwise and the lower loop clockwise.

About 200 feet from the parking lot, the combined trail passes through a stand of young tuliptrees, then encounters Virginia pines before entering mature oak woods. The trail turns right when the old road it has been following continues straight. Rock outcroppings begin to appear on the right, with hemlock and mountain laurel now being seen. Not far down the trail you will see a sign for Salt Creek Trail pointing to the right. Fifty feet beyond is another sign that points to the right for Pine Ridge Trail, and one that points left for Calico

Bush Trail. Take Pine Ridge Trail. (After hiking Pine Ridge Trail you will arrive back at this point from the left on Calico Bush Trail. Then you will need to go up the hill a short way on the combined trails and leave to the left, or south, on Salt Creek Trail to complete the hike.)

Going right, Pine Ridge Trail heads down an old logging skid, with cliffs on the left. At the bottom of the slope the trail turns left, then right, then tra-

LAKE KATHARINE SEEN THROUGH WILDFLOWERS ON EARTHEN DAM

verses bottomland before crossing a bridge across Rock Run close to where it empties into Little Salt Creek. The latter gently curves to the right. Cliffs appear on the left, with tall hemlock at their base, and tuliptree, bigleaf magnolia, and wahoo on the talus slope. The cliffs seem to run out, then reappear. The trail heads up the valley. There is a good spicebush understory in this area. Large slump blocks of the Sharon conglomerate, the exposed rock of the preserve, lie between the trail and the overhanging cliff. A small arrow indicates a turn from the old road uphill to the left. In wintertime you can see US 35 traffic and a farmstead from here. The trail climbs on multiple switchbacks, reaching the Virginia pine-covered summit shortly. It then winds its way through young hardwood, with an occasional young white pine and ground pine on the

forest floor. The trail next drops to the hardwood-covered hillside above Rock Run, where it follows the hillside just above the steep, hemlock-covered slope. It then climbs back to the pine-topped ridge, for which the trail was named.

There is an interesting invasion of young hemlock under the pines in this area. The trail along here can be particularly lovely after a light snowfall. Two short boardwalks cross a wet area above the cliffs. The woods include a lot of red oak, white oak, and chestnut oak, with an occasional scarlet oak. Leaving the ridge, the trail drops into the hemlock-filled valley, to a small footbridge below a rock face. Moving along the cliff, it drops farther to the bridge over the Lake Katharine spillway before emerging from the woods to cross the lake's earthen dam.

Beyond the dam, the path enters a hemlock woods, heading uphill past a cliff on the right that shows evidence of having once been quarried. Bore holes for blasting charges are visible. About two-thirds of the way up the slope, a sign indicates that Pine Ridge Trail leaves the roadway to the left. Take the five wooden steps to the left and follow a lovely trail through young hemlock trees below low cliffs. After 100 feet, a sign indicates that Pine Ridge Trail goes upslope to the right, toward the road, that the parking lot is straight ahead, and that Calico Bush Trail goes left. Unless you need to cut your hike short by returning to the parking lot, continue hiking on Calico Bush Trail. (Calico Bush is an alternative common name for the late-spring-blooming mountain laurel, *Kalmia latifolia*, of Ohio's Allegheny Plateau.)

The trail travels among the calico bush and hemlock just downslope from rock outcroppings. Here you can easily see the layers of quartz pebbles in the Sharon conglomerate. In early summer you may be able to catch a glimpse of the uncommon, scarlet-flowered, round-leafed catchfly in bloom in the nooks and crannies of the cliffs above the trail. (This is one of only a half dozen or so bright red native Ohio wildflowers. Red flowering plants are, for some reason, much more common in the tropics. Hummingbirds have a special attraction to red flowers. They seem to show up in Ohio in the spring when the columbines begin to bloom, and they are known to be the principle pollinator of the royal catchfly of the west-central Ohio prairies.)

Shortly the trail meets up with Pine Ridge Trail, completing a loop. After a right turn, 50 feet up the combined trails Salt Creek Trail originates at a fork, going to the left down the hillside. Should you want to end your hike, the trail to the right leads up the hill to the parking lot. To continue hiking, follow Salt Creek Trail downhill on an old road to where it turns right up a set of wooden steps between a cliff and a slump block. There are lots of pebbles in the rock wall here. The trail next descends to the valley floor where it continues beneath the base of the 75-foot-tall cliffs along the bank of Little Salt Creek. Then it climbs another set of steps to travel along the middle level of the Sharon conglomerate. Where the cliff meets the stream, the trail climbs nearly to the cliff top via the stairs before returning to the valley floor on still more steps. The sheer cliff face shows centuries of erosion, as the stream cuts deeper into the valley. At a boardwalk beneath a cliff overhang, the layer of quartz pebbles in the conglomerate lies about 6 feet above the ground. There are usually antlion holes in the dry sand below the overhang. This is a good place to observe vertical fractures and

HILLSIDE TRAIL AT LAKE KATHARINE

horizontal bedding in the rock, a quartz pebble lens, and honeycomb erosion.

A sign points left to the long loop and straight ahead to the short loop. I suggest going left to where you cross a wet area on several hundred feet of boardwalk, passing beneath umbrella magnolia, sweet gum, red oak, black oak, spicebush, and hemlock. Reaching a nearly pure stand of hemlock, the trail goes up and then back down the slope, with the cliffs above disappearing and reappearing. It bears left to cross a Little Salt Creek tributary on a bridge, then swings right to once again follow the right bank of Little Salt Creek. Cliffs and hemlock are visible across the stream, and magnolia along the trail. Passing through another hemlock stand, this time on an old sandbar, the trail moves at floodplain level through sycamores, cottonwoods, and willows before passing more magnolia. As the stream moves back toward the cliff face on the right, an arrow on a post indicates

that the trail goes to the right and up an old road. After a steady climb of several hundred yards through hardwood forest, the trail turns right to cross streams on bridges at the heads of ravines. It then follows the hillside to the left, rising and falling as it crosses more small streams that parallel the hemlock/hardwood ecotone (an ecological community of mixed vegetation formed by the overlapping of adjoining plant communities). Moving back into hemlock and then uphill into the mixed mesophytic hardwood community, the trail continues to climb, passing an especially handsome shagbark hickory. A hard left turn and a gentle left curve take you just inside the edge of the woods. In a few hundred feet, the trail emerges from the woods just below the aging blockhouse that is about the only remains of the old youth camp. It then passes through a pine planting and an old meadow that is being rapidly overgrown with shrubs and trees, before returning to the parking lot.

Wildflowers

The common name "catchfly" is used for two of the most attractive wildflowers of the state: one a plant of the woods, the other of the prairies, although the two are closely related. There are only five native wildflowers that are scarlet in color: Oswego tea (*Monarda didyma*), a mint; cardinal flower (*Lobelia cardinalis*), of the bellflower family; and three members of the pink family, fire-pink (*Silene virginica*), round-leaved catchfly (*S. rotundifolia*), and royal catchfly (*S. regio*). The name catchfly is used for a number of other members of the genus *Silene*, including some from Europe. Where did that strange name come from? All three of these bright-red-flowered *Silenes* of our Ohio flora have what could best be described as sticky stems. They have a viscid sap that exudes from the stem.

If you touch them, they feel tacky, but it does not come off on your skin. Most botanists believe that this sap prevents crawling insects from stealing the nectar without pollinating the flower.

The Latin name is also derived from this sticky characteristic. Most sources say it comes from the Greek word *sialon*, which means "saliva." Another opinion is that it is named for Silenus, who was Bacchus's foster father in Greek mythology and was said to have been found with sticky beer all over his face. Believe what you wish, but do gently touch the stem of the next fire-pink or round-leaved catchfly you come across on a southeastern Ohio hillside, or the next royal catchfly you encounter in a prairie preserve in Madison County. Don't pick it, though. Let it live in your memory, not die in your hand.

Wayne National Forest– Archers Fork Trail

TOTAL DISTANCE: 9.5 miles (15.2 km)

HIKING TIME: 7 hours (day hike) to 2 days (backpack trip)

MAXIMUM ELEVATION: 1,125 feet

VERTICAL RISE: 375 feet

MAPS: USGS 7.5' Rinard Mills, OH, and Raven Rock, WV; USFS Wayne National

On a warm spring morning I made the long drive from my home in the Columbus area to eastern Washington County to walk my last un-walked section of Archers Fork Trail. The hike could not have been nicer. Though the trees were still bare, spring peepers were calling, mourning cloak butterflies (which overwinter as adults) were on the wing, and a dozen wild turkeys crossed the trail about 75 feet in front of me. I saw not another soul the entire time I was in the forest. It was a wonderful wilderness retreat for me. I returned to Columbus late in the evening, buoyant after my walk on this forest path. As in other Wayne National Forest areas, I could have camped overnight along the trail if I so chose.

Archers Fork Trail is a loop trail in an Appalachian oak forest area of southeastern Ohio. Along the route there is a beautiful natural rock arch, many rock shelters, early oil-pumping rigs, and lots of tall timber. The North Country Trail (NCT) uses part of Archers Fork Trail as it crosses the state; there are connecting trails to Ohio View Trail to the east and Covered Bridge Trail to the west, should you want to make an extended backpacking trek.

GETTING THERE

To reach an Archers Fork trailhead—there are two other parking sites—travel east from Cambridge on I-70 to Exit 202 (OH 800). Turn south on OH 800 and follow it through Barnesville and Woodsfield to its intersection with OH 26. Go south on OH 26 to the OH 260 intersection. Turn east and drive approximately 4 miles to Hohman Ridge Road (Township Road 34). The road goes to the right

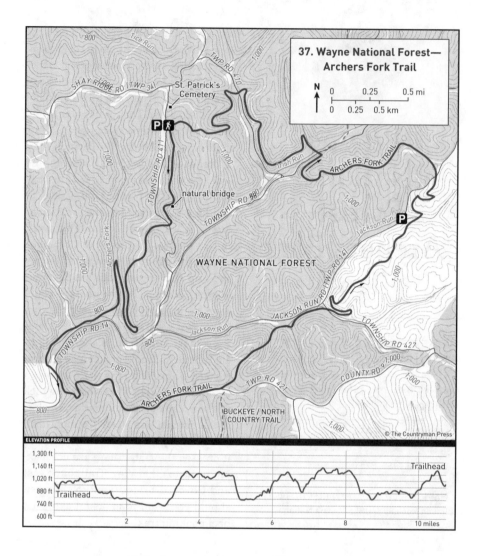

THE TRAIL

just as OH 260 turns sharply left, so it is easy to miss. Turn right (south) and follow this gravel road 1.3 miles until you see a North Country Trail parking sign on the left side of the road. Enter here and drive past the front of St. Patrick's Cemetery to the parking area. A sign directs you down an abandoned road to where you pick up the Archers Fork and North Country Trails. If you started in the Columbus area, you will have driven about 165 miles.

The trail begins just a few hundred feet due south from the parking lot. Blue diamonds with arrows on them indicate you are headed toward the NCT. The combined NCT/Archers Fork Trail will come in from the left and continue straight ahead, and will be blazed with two different signs: a white diamond with a blue disk for Archers Fork Trail, and a solid blue diamond for the NCT.

Archers Fork is the name of the principal stream that drains this area, along with two small tributaries: Irish Run and Jackson Run. Archers Fork empties into the Little Muskingum River and thence to the Ohio. It is also the name of a small community downstream, a little more than a mile from where the trail crosses the stream.

The bedrock nearest the surface in this part of Ohio is Permian, the youngest in the state, thought to date from 280 million years ago. As you walk the rutty old road toward the trail, the fine-grained Permian sandstone is visible underfoot and the cliffs and rock shelters of the area are of this same stone. The presence of oil in the deeper bedrock of the area is indicated by the number of wells you will pass along these trails, including one to the right as you walk toward the juncture of the trails.

Turn left at a sign on a tree on the left side of the old road that reads "hiker." Just down the trail is the corner where the combined trails go both east and south. There is a sizable cave (really a rock shelter) located near here. To visit it, walk east across the dip in the trail and scramble down the east side of the ravine. The cave is virtually under the trail you just traveled.

You can, of course, hike either direction on Archers Fork Loop Trail. Since the day I was walking was "cloudy-bright"—a good day for taking photographs without hard shadows—I wanted to get to the natural bridge, and so I began walking south, counterclockwise on the loop. The trail travels at a fairly constant elevation on the hillside above the ravine for three quarters of a mile before rising to the right, then turning left to where a sign reads "bridge." There is an open area along the trail just prior to the bridge that would make a good campsite. The natural bridge, or arch, is up against the hillside, and it takes a bit of scrambling to get into position to take a picture. (Though the forest service map calls it a natural bridge, most geologists save that term for a feature that water flows under, or has in the past. The preferred term for a structure such as this one is "arch.") This one has been called by two names: Irish Run Natural Bridge and Independence Arch: take your pick. When the forest service map was created, the authors knew of only four natural bridges in Ohio. Since then, Tim Snyder, formerly of the Ohio Division of Natural Areas and Preserves, has scoured the state looking for such features. He now has a list of 87 confirmed locations of arches and natural bridges, and he is still looking. Tim's book, *Rainbows of Rock, Tables of Stone: The Natural Arches and Pillars of Ohio*, should be on the "must read" list of every Buckeye outdoorsperson.

The forest is not what anyone would call old growth, the area having been logged many times since settlement. Nevertheless, it has been more than half a century since it was last clearcut, and it provides a nice environment for walking. Beyond the arch, the trail turns west and rises more than 100 feet before crossing a hilltop, making a downhill arc to the right, and then crossing the ridge to begin its descent to Archers Fork. Over the next half mile the trail drops about 300 feet on a path that angles gently down the hillside. After crossing a small side stream, the trail stays above the valley floor on the right side of Archers Fork for another quarter mile before crossing an old farm lane and dropping to the floodplain. This bottomland is subject to periodic flooding, which sometimes leaves debris or washes out a bit of the

IRISH RUN NATURAL BRIDGE NEAR ARCHERS FORK TRAIL

trail. There is a trail junction here where a connecting spur goes to the right toward Covered Bridge Trail along the Little Muskingum River.

Continuing this hike requires fording the stream (many township roads of the area do that, too) before leaving the floodplain to cross Township Road 14 and heading on a right oblique up the hillside. The rise over the next .3 mile is from the 740-foot elevation of the road to 1,100 feet. An uninterrupted climb of short steps with a slow pace brings you alongside a small old hilltop field. From there, the trail heads southeast to drop into a saddle, then rises again to the same elevation before turning east to follow a winding ridge for a half mile and passing another 1,100-foot knob. This is the country of ancient oil wells and pipelines. Lots of Ohio crude oil from this Washington County well field helped fuel an oil-hungry nation before low prices for foreign oil made further development here uneconomical, although it never gushed from Ohio wells as it did from wells in the American Southwest or the Middle East. Some oil is still pumped from the area, but not nearly as much as in the past. (The Macksburg oil and gas field, one of the earliest in the nation, was in the northwestern corner of the county.)

After about a mile of ridgetop travel

no sign. If you want to make an over-night trip using camping gear that you don't want to carry, this might be a good place to cache your supplies. However, during hunting seasons, especially those for turkey and deer, there will likely be hunters in pickup-truck campers parked here.

Beyond this access point the trail heads northeast and makes a steep climb, gaining 300 feet in a half mile. After reaching the 1,100-foot level it hangs on the hillside to drop gently, and then more steeply, to the upper reaches of Jackson Run. (Another connector trail exits the loop, headed right (east) to carry you to Ohio View Trail.) From here it is a short climb on Archers Fork Trail to reach a nearly flat section of trail and the crossing of TR 14. The third forest service parking area that serves this trail is but a couple hundred feet up the road to the right (east). Continue hiking by climbing the steps across the road and following the trail through the woods. It soon joins a wide old service road to head northwest, rising and falling along a ridge for less than a half mile. The trail crosses gas lines that may confuse you—watch for the blazes. This is where I saw the 12 wild turkeys I mentioned above. Just beyond a point where the trail stays on high ground and the road (or gas line) that the trail was following falls off the left side, the old road turns left and the trail goes a short distance straight ahead. Where the gas line/road heads steeply downhill ahead, the trail ducks through a hole in the woods to the left, remaining on high ground. This is an easy turn to miss. Again, look for the blazes. The trail then begins to drop off the point of the ridge, soon catching an old logging skid to head down a valley to Irish Run. There are very

on an old well service road, the trail reaches a junction where the NCT goes straight ahead and Archers Fork Trail heads through a gap between two hills to the left. Follow the white diamonds with blue dots as the trail arcs right and begins its slow descent toward the 800-foot elevation of the valley of Archers Fork. Once in the valley, the trail stays a couple hundred feet back from the road, crossing first one stream, then another. It is at this second side stream's valley that a gas-well road connects the trail to a forest service parking lot along Township Road 14. This is a grassy parking area cut in among young trees and, unlike the other two parking lots, has

AUTUMN COMES TO ARCHERS FORK TRAIL

picturesque small rock shelters above the trail here, and a wonderful carpet of moss underfoot. One of these rock shelters would surely protect a lone hiker from a sudden thundershower and might even provide cover for a night's sleep.

The trail reaches the road and, although the North Country Trail (NCT) map makes it appear to go directly across, it does not. Turn right and go the length of a football field, then look for a trail dropping off the left side of the road. On the floodplain next to the creek there is a sign marking another juncture with the NCT, which goes to the right, back up onto the road to head northeast, then north, eventually crossing OH 260 a couple miles to the east of Hohman Ridge Road. Archers Fork Trail, combined once again with the NCT, heads across the creek. Be prepared to wade.

The trail is now about a mile from closing the loop. After crossing the creek, it heads uphill about 150 feet, curving left to follow the hillside. Next it drops gently down to cross Township Road 40. There are wonderful tall trees up this valley, and the forest service has considered designating this a Special Interest Area. Across the road, the trail drops down to ford a small unnamed headwater creek of Irish Run. Heading up a small ravine, the trail curves right, then left to head almost due west toward the cave and the service road to the parking lot at St. Patrick's Cemetery. May the luck of the Irish, who pioneered this area many years ago, travel with you on the trail, and may your years of hiking be many.

Wayne National Forest

Wayne National Forest has its roots in the Weeks Law of 1911, which allowed the federal government, with the concurrence of state legislatures, to purchase land to create national forests. Ohio approved such action in November 1934, and between 1935 and 1942 approximately 77,000 acres were acquired in the five purchase units in southeastern Ohio. During the 1930s, the Civilian Conservation Corps planted trees, halted erosion, and built much of the infrastructure of what, in 1951, officially became Wayne National Forest. In 1983, it was targeted for disposal, but strong public reaction saved it. In the late 1980s and early 1990s, the Wayne (as it is generally referred to) received strong support from Congress and Ohio's citizens.

Though scaled back in the number of purchase units, the forest service has worked hard to consolidate its holdings and reduce the checkerboard pattern of ownership. As of the last accounting, it comprised 237,529 acres in 12 Ohio counties. There has been a steady increase in the number and mileage of high-quality hiking trails in the Wayne during the past decade, to the benefit of those of us who enjoy the deep woods of southeastern Ohio's hill country.

Wayne National Forest– Vesuvius Recreation Area, Lakeshore Trail

TOTAL DISTANCE: 8 miles (12.8 km)

HIKING TIME: 6 hours

MAXIMUM ELEVATION: 710 feet

VERTICAL RISE: 104 feet

MAPS: USGS 7.5' Kitts Hill; USGS 7.5' Sherrits; USGS 7.5' Ironton; USGS 7.5' Pedro; USGS 15' Ironton (OH and KY); USFS Wayne National Forest Lake Vesuvius Trail guide, Wayne National Forest hiking and backpacking trails map guide

The production of iron in the area that became known as the Hanging Rock Iron Region began in 1826 with the construction of Union Furnace, in western Lawrence County. Before the whistle signaling the last cast of charcoal iron sounded at Jefferson Furnace, near Oak Hill, in December 1916, a total of 46 furnaces had been built in this area of Ohio, 24 on the Kentucky side of the river. Each furnace was capable of producing 2,000 to 3,000 tons of iron per year. They helped arm the Union forces during the Civil War and were an important segment of the early years of America's industrial revolution. Now, a century after their heyday, only 17 of the old furnaces still stand in the region, surrounded by the crumbling ghosts of what were once thriving communities, with the houses, stores, rail spurs, schools, churches, and cemeteries needed to keep the enterprises going. A map detailing the locations of the Ohio furnaces is available from the Ohio History Connection in Columbus. The restored Buckeye Furnace in Jackson County is maintained by the Friends of Buckeye Furnace and is well worth a visit.

Vesuvius Furnace, at the heart of the Lake Vesuvius Recreation Area, within Wayne National Forest, is one of the best preserved. Though it looks like the other furnaces, it has a special claim to fame: It was supposedly the first hot-blast furnace erected in America. John Campbell, who along with Robert Hamilton built the nearby Mount Vernon Furnace (later known only as Vernon), had experimented with his cold-blast operation by placing the boilers and blast over the tunnel head to provide a hot blast. In 1837, Campbell and three other ironmasters agreed to cover any loss incurred if William Firmstone would test the hot-blast principle on his new Vesuvius

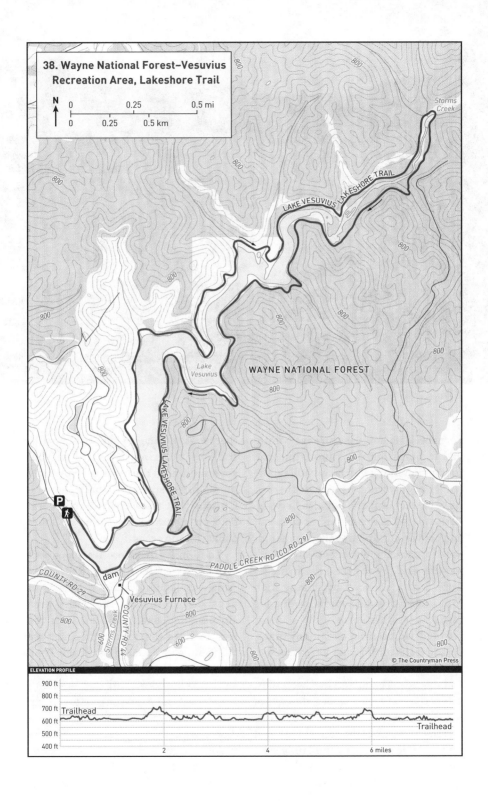

38. Wayne National Forest–Vesuvius Recreation Area, Lakeshore Trail

N

| 0 | | 0.25 | | 0.5 mi |
| 0 | 0.25 | | 0.5 km | |

800

800

Storms Creek

LAKE VESUVIUS LAKESHORE TRAIL

800

800

800

800

WAYNE NATIONAL FOREST

800

Lake Vesuvius

800

LAKE VESUVIUS LAKESHORE TRAIL

800

800

800

P

800

PADDLE CREEK RD (CO.RD 291)

800

COUNTY RD 29

dam

Vesuvius Furnace

800

COUNTY RD 44

800

600

Storms Creek

600

600

800

© The Countryman Press

ELEVATION PROFILE

900 ft	
800 ft	
700 ft	Trailhead
600 ft	Trailhead
500 ft	
400 ft	2 4 6 miles

LAKE VESUVIUS

Furnace. This hot-blast furnace continued in operation until 1906, but iron production inflicted a heavy toll on the land. Not only were the hillsides carved up to extract iron ore, but also between 300 and 350 acres of timber were cut and converted to charcoal each year for each furnace, thereby effectively denuding the land. By the time the furnaces were finally silenced by competition from richer ores and more productive furnaces in other parts of the country, the land had been cut over many times.

The trails of the Lake Vesuvius Recreation Area take you through beautiful countryside. The mixed hardwood forests of the east-facing slopes, the oaks of the ridgetops and southern exposures, and the hemlock of the sandstone-lined ravines give variety to the landscape. Ruins of old roads, homes, industries, and early park development turn back the pages of time for the visitor. With trails that are well designed without severe climbs, the area is especially good for beginning backpackers. Options that allow for one to several days on the trail make it one of Ohio's choice hiking areas.

The 8-mile Lakeshore Trail is perfect for a day hike. The Vesuvius Recreation Area—no camping allowed—has been expanded to include the entire area surrounding Lakeshore Trail. So if you want to do a backpack trip, you must use the 16-mile designated Backpack Trail. It begins and ends at the same trailhead as the Lakeshore Trail and is one of Ohio's best trails for a one- or two-night trek. Both are laid out using gentle gradients, with no really hard climbs. Like the other units within the Wayne Forest complex, camping is allowed anywhere along the trail. There are no convenient sources of drinking water, so you need to carry water or cache your supply at a road crossing. Open fires are discouraged, and prohibited at times of high fire danger, so be prepared to use stoves for cooking. Human waste must be buried properly, and all trash must be carried out. Lake Vesuvius and the shoreline facilities underwent a multimillion-dollar renovation in the opening years of the century. The lake was drained and dredged, the dam and spillway rebuilt, and a new shoreline walkway constructed. It was reopened with a gala celebration on Presidents' Day weekend, February 15–16, 2003. There are two forest service public campgrounds close by. I generally use Iron Ridge Campground when I visit the area.

GETTING THERE

To reach the Vesuvius Recreation Area, travel US 23 from Columbus, or OH 32 and US 23 from Cincinnati, to Portsmouth. Take US 52 east to OH 93 in Ironton—about 120 miles from Columbus and 130 from Cincinnati. At Ironton, travel in a little more than 6 miles north on OH 93 to where highway and forest service signs direct you right onto County Road 29. (Note that the U.S. Forest Service Ironton Ranger District office is located just north of this intersection on the right, or east, side of the highway, so stop there before going to the trailhead if you need information, maps, or other literature.) After about 1 mile on County Road 29, turn left on a forest service road just before reaching the dam and furnace. Travel this road not quite a half mile to the dock area and trailhead parking lot on the right. Park here and lock your car.

THE TRAIL

The trail begins from a trailhead kiosk at the lake end of the parking lot. Lakeshore Trail is marked with white diamond blazes with a blue dot, Backpack Trail with the diamonds and a yellow dot. Mileage is marked on both trails. The combined trail leaves the boathouse to climb a short distance into the woods and into what is the first of many pine plantings encountered along the way. The views along the first mile of this trail are extraordinary, especially in autumn. A large sandstone promontory across the lake creates a picture-postcard scene.

Following the shore of the lake, the trail passes a now-abandoned beach left from Civilian Conservation Corps days, and then goes by a building and intake structure from a water system abandoned in 1980. Moving slightly away from the shore, the trail follows an old road for a short way before crossing a side stream. About 100 feet beyond this crossing the trail splits, with the yellow-dotted Backpack Trail leaving to

AUTHOR'S CAMPSITE ABOVE LAKE VESUVIUS

SUNSET FROM LAKE VESUVIUS TRAIL

the left. There should be a sign pointing out the trails, but if it has been vandalized, be alert for the fork in the trail, as it is easy to miss.

Continuing straight ahead, Lakeshore Trail soon passes mile marker 1. It continues along the shore until just before the Big Bend Beach area, where it cuts left. Next it crosses a wooden bridge and follows the fence around the bathhouse. Restrooms and water are available here during the warm part of the year. The trail soon passes a 50-foot-long sandstone outcrop before climbing the side of the ridge at a moderate angle. At one point along this section of trail it is possible to see the lake on both sides of the peninsula. Past mile marker 2, the trail doubles back to drop toward

the shoreline. It then passes a wetland area between it and the lake and turns left up a small hollow. After crossing a creek, the trail turns right to travel again near the shoreline. A small pond lies between the trail and the lake. Climbing away from the lake on the slope, the trail passes through more stands of planted pines and then above a rock exposure with a 25-foot cliff below. Just beyond is mile marker 3. The trail next turns right as it climbs a ridge that goes toward the lake. There is a footpath out to the point overlooking the lake, but the trail turns left to drop down to the shoreline. From here, it stays at lake level until it begins its return route on the opposite shore (the lake is quite narrow at this point). The trail uses a service road to continue upstream. Just after crossing a small side stream, signs identify the junction with Backpack Trail ahead and the trails join together to cross Storms Creek.

This crossing is usually no problem, but in periods of high water it can be difficult. Beyond the crossing, the trail turns right through an old field and reenters the woods. At a fork in the trail, the combined Lakeshore/Backpack Trail stays along the forest edge, soon passing mile marker 4. It then leaves the lakeshore to travel up the left side of a side ravine. The two trails split, with Lakeshore Trail making a right turn across the creek bed before climbing the hillside. Lakeshore Trail next descends to cross another stream before making a fairly steep climb to once again overlook the lake. Past mile marker 5, it turns left to go around yet another inlet. After dropping once more to near lake level to cross two streambeds, the trail takes you to one of the nicest viewpoints of the hike.

Following a clockwise swing around a much longer inlet, there is an intersection with the half-mile Whiskey Run Trail. This trail goes past abandoned charcoal pits and at one time you could see remnants of a whiskey still and barrels, which gave the trail its name. It makes a loop that begins at Iron Ridge Campground. A short, steep climb up Whiskey Run Trail will lead you to a rock shelter where moonshine is said to have been made. The campground is beyond and uphill from the shelter.

The combined Lakeshore/Whiskey Run Trail travels north to round a point nearly opposite Big Bend Beach before heading due south for the next .6 mile. After it enters another pine stand, the trail splits as Whiskey Run Trail departs to the left. The old beach and water intake become visible across the lake on the right, and there are sandstone outcroppings on the hill above the trail on the left. After passing mile marker 7, the trail comes to another rock shelter, this one vandalized with spray-paint graffiti. The trail then drops closer to the lake and rounds the sandstone cliff face that was visible in the early part of the hike.

Now rounding the last inlet before the dam, the trail stays close to the lake and crosses two small streambeds. After rising slightly, it returns to near lake level and passes below a rock cliff with nearly square slump blocks on the hillside below. One cannot help but wonder if the sandstone used to build Vesuvius Furnace was quarried here. The trail follows the lake edge and arrives shortly at the dam spillway. There it makes a left turn, to be joined by Backpack Trail. You descend concrete steps along a chain-link fence to arrive at the lawn and road within sight of Vesuvius Furnace.

The trail then follows Storms Creek through pine plantings to the County Road 29 bridge, which it crosses. Turning right beyond the bridge, it climbs to the top of the dam and then heads toward the shoreline boardwalk, which it uses to return to the trailhead. My father grew up in Lawrence County, not far from this area. There is no place nicer to be on an Ohio autumn afternoon than on Shoreline Trail at Lake Vesuvius.

Note: Wayne National Forest earnestly solicits volunteers to assist in trail maintenance. If you or your group would like to help, please contact the Ironton Ranger District office at 704-534-6500.

39

Wayne National Forest– Lamping Homestead Trail

TOTAL DISTANCE: 5 miles (8 km)

HIKING TIME: 4 hours

MAXIMUM ELEVATION: 1,010 feet

VERTICAL RISE: 290 feet

MAPS: USGS 7.5' Graysville and Rinard Mills; USFS Wayne National Forest hiking and backpacking trails map

It is hard to say why the Lamping family chose to settle in the valley between Pleasant and Haney Ridges, near the Clear Fork of the Little Muskingum River, but they did. As far as we know, they were the first to put down roots and build a cabin on the land this trail traverses. The land had been part of the first seven ranges surveyed in 1786 in what was later to become the state of Ohio, in 1803. Though initially part of Washington County, in 1813 it became part of Monroe County. There was a land office to file patents on unclaimed land as close as Marietta. During those first two decades of the nineteenth century, a steady flow of Americans, mostly from the Mid-Atlantic states, headed to Ohio, Indiana, and Illinois. In 1816, on just one turnpike in Pennsylvania, 16,000 wagons rolled past a tollbooth on their way west, carrying families eager to carve new homes from the wilderness. Even so, by 1840 there were only 533 people living in Washington Township, where the Lampings had settled. One of my great, great, great-grandfathers, Thomas Farson, an Irishman, settled only a few miles to the west of here in the 1820s in what was then Washington County.

No one seems to know where the Lampings came from—or, for that matter, where they went when they left here—but they did not stay long. We will never know why they left, but perhaps the graves in Lamping Cemetery, located on a knoll along this trail a couple hundred yards from the site of their home, might provide a clue. At least two young Lamping children are buried there, victims of who knows what sort of malady. In moving on, the Lampings would not be the first family, nor the last, to uproot themselves to leave behind sad times. In any case, the house and barn of

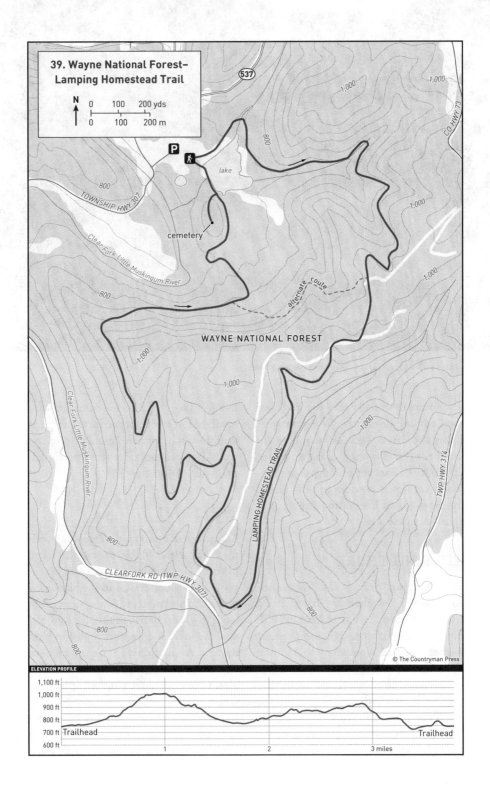

39. Wayne National Forest–Lamping Homestead Trail

N

| 0 | 100 | 200 yds |
| 0 | 100 | 200 m |

537

1,000

1,000

CO HWY 73

800

P

lake

TOWNSHIP HWY 307

800

Clear Fork Little Muskingum River

cemetery

1,000

1,000

800

alternate route

WAYNE NATIONAL FOREST

Clear Fork Little Muskingum River

1,000

1,000

1,000

LAMPING HOMESTEAD TRAIL

TWP HWY 314

800

CLEARFORK RD (TWP HWY 307)

800

800

800

800

© The Countryman Press

ELEVATION PROFILE

| 1,100 ft |
| 1,000 ft |
| 900 ft |
| 800 ft |
| 700 ft | Trailhead | | | Trailhead |
| 600 ft | | 1 | 2 | 3 miles |

LAMPING HOMESTEAD TRAIL SKIRTS SMALL UPLAND POND

what more than 100 years ago had been the Lamping homestead were removed when the forest service acquired the land in 1971. Over the next two years, the Youth Conservation Corps aided the forest service in developing the Lamping Homestead Recreation Area on the shore of a new lake.

GETTING THERE

The Lamping Homestead Recreation Area can be reached by driving east from Cambridge on I-70 to Exit 202 (OH 800). Turn south on OH 800 through Barnesville and Woodsfield to its intersection with OH 26. Turn south again on OH 26. One mile beyond Graysville, turn west on winding OH 537 and follow it about 1.5 miles to Township Road 307. Turn left onto this gravel road, and then almost immediately left again into the parking lot. There are picnic shelters and restrooms overlooking Kenton

Lake and several lakeside campsites are available. As with other forest service land in Ohio, you can camp along the trail after you get away from the developed recreation area.

THE TRAIL

Lamping Homestead Trail is well marked with white diamond-shape plastic blazes nailed on trees and fenceposts. It is a loop trail, and the blazes for outbound and inbound routes are visible from the lawn between the dry hydrant and the lake. Before I began hiking, on a warm August day, I took my camera and a 100 mm macro lens and walked along the expansive patches of joe-pye weed, milkweed, and ironweed, taking pictures of tiger swallowtails, red-spotted purples, and other scale-winged beauties sucking up nectar with their proboscises.

To begin walking, head to the left of

the lake through the pines that shade picnickers. There is a white diamond with a hiker on it and another with an arrow pointing toward the trail. At the far end of the picnic area the trail passes more pines, these planted too close together for good growth. The trail turns left to cross a bridge over one of the very small tributaries of the Clear Fork of the Little Muskingum River that was dammed to create the lake. Beyond the bridge the trail goes around the lake past more pines, then makes a left oblique turn to climb the hillside and head up the other headwater valley. Leaving pines behind, it hangs on the side of the hill as it enters a stand of young hardwoods and follows the creek upstream. It then continues around the hillside clockwise before climbing the hill at an oblique angle headed almost due south. After a half mile or so of travel, the trail reaches 1,000 feet in elevation and the edge of the forest service land. When it reaches an old road, it makes a right turn, then a second right to travel gently downhill before nearly reversing itself to head south-southeast back to the same old road. Just before reaching that road, there is a very short side trail to the right that goes due west to connect with the return route of the trail, allowing for a 1.2-mile loop hike.

Unless you need to cut your hike short, ignore the crossover trail and continue on the main Lamping Homestead Trail, keeping watch for the white-diamond trail markers. A hundred or so feet beyond the cutoff the main trail turns to the right, heading due southwest out and over a ridge at the 1,100-foot level. Turning now to the south, the trail has left the Lamping Homestead Lake watershed behind. From an overlook, you see the steep-sloped valley with drainage directly into the Clear

Fork of the Little Muskingum River. Now heading just a bit west of straight south, the trail drops nearly 200 feet in the course of .3 mile. Next, it turns to the right to drop again in and out of the heads of two small ravines, prior to circling right around the end of a promontory to begin its return trip to the homestead area. Traveling the hillside to the north, the trail gains 120 feet in 0.4 mile. Turning right (east), it follows a nearly level path for a half mile before turning north, then east to its junction with the crossover trail.

At one point you will find yourself in really nice Appalachian oak woods, much like it might have been when the Lampings roamed these parts. After meeting up with the short-loop crossover trail, the main white-diamond-blazed trail turns northwest and begins its descent to the floodplain below the dam. The trail's gradient is about as steep as you can comfortably walk on. Now back in boneset, ironweed, and wing-stem country, the trail emerges from weeds and woods at the east end of the dam. As you walk along the dam toward the picnic area, watch for the path that leads to the left (uphill) to Lamping Cemetery. Inside a vandalized iron fence are the badly weathered, moss-covered tombstones of the Lamping children, who did not survive the harsh reality of the Ohio frontier. It is a short walk from there back to the parking area. Before you depart from this early homestead site, try to imagine the hardships suffered by those who came into this country nearly 200 years ago to carve from the wilderness the civilization we are enjoying in this new century. We owe a great debt to all those who lie beneath the decayed wooden crosses in the unknown family burying grounds of Ohio's hill country.

Wayne National Forest–Wildcat Hollow Trail

TOTAL DISTANCE: 5 or 15 miles (7.25 or 21 km)

HIKING TIME: 4 hours or 12 hours to 2 days

MAXIMUM ELEVATION: 1,080 feet

VERTICAL RISE: 350 feet

MAPS: USGS 7.5' Corning; USGS 7.5' Beavertown; USFS Wildcat Hollow brochure, WNF hiking and backpacking trail map

In recent years sightings of wildcat are once again being reported from around Ohio. At one time these secretive felines were found in most of the state, especially in the rocky hollows of the southeast. History does not record how Wildcat Hollow on the Morgan/Perry County line got its name, but it would probably be safe to guess that a den of the elusive cats was thought to have been in the area.

Located in what is now Wayne National Forest, Wildcat Hollow is the site of one of Ohio's best hiking trails. The 15-mile route is laid out entirely on national forest land, mostly on high ground between drainage systems. The trail is typical of those developed by the forest service. It is well designed, with gentle grades and switchbacks as needed. It is also well marked with square Carsonite posts and white-diamond blazes nailed to trees. The miles are marked most of the way, and the standard federal agency backpacker signs are used in many places. A connecting trail of a little more than a quarter mile allows the trail to be shortened to 5 miles for a nice day hike. There are no designated campsites along the trail, but you may camp anywhere. There are neither fire rings nor latrines. The only restrooms are at the trailhead parking area. Portable stoves are suggested as an alternative to open fires. Because there are no water sources along the trail, water must be carried in. Human waste must be buried, and trash carried out. No permit is required. A map that includes rules for use can be obtained from Wayne National Forest (see the introduction for the complete address).

Since Wildcat Hollow Trail is located adjacent to Burr Oak State Park, this hike can be combined with Burr Oak

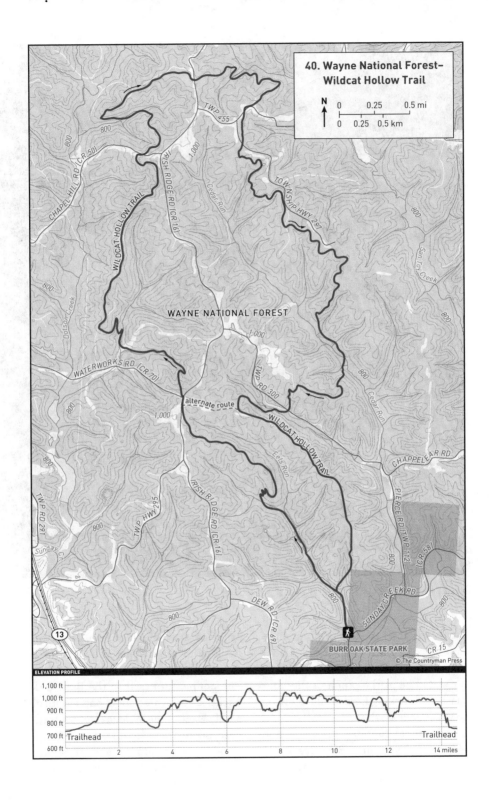

A PAINT BLAZE DIRECTS HIKERS INTO DEEP WOODS

Backpack Trail for a trek of about 34 miles. Such a hike would form an hourglass route: The Wildcat Hollow parking lot would be at the pinch of the hourglass, and parking here would allow you to stash your trash in your car and pick up additional supplies and water midway through your hike. Burr Oak Trail is laid out differently than Wildcat Hollow Trail, so extra planning considerations are necessary. Much of Burr Oak Trail is close to the water's edge and lake conditions must be taken into account. The connecting trail to the Burr Oak Backpack is located about one-eighth of a mile west of the Wildcat Hollow trailhead, on the south side of the road. There are also steeper climbs on the state park trail. Contact the Burr Oak park office for a map of their Backpack Trail.

GETTING THERE

To reach Wildcat Hollow from the central Ohio area, travel US 33 southeast to Nelsonville. Take OH 78 east to Glouster, and then turn left (north) onto OH 13 and travel 5 miles to Township Road 289. Turn right (east) there and follow the forest service signs for 3 miles to the trailhead, using Irish Ridge and Dew Roads. The drive takes about 2 hours from Columbus.

From Cleveland, travel I-77 south to I-70. Take I-70 west to Exit 154 in Zanesville. Turn south on OH 60, then turn south onto OH 93 in Zanesville. When OH 93 intersects OH 13, 21 miles south of Zanesville, turn left (south) on OH 13. Take it 13.5 miles to Township Road 289, turn left, and follow the signs noted above for drivers coming from Columbus. The distance from Cleveland is about 180 miles.

From Cincinnati, travel OH 32 east to Athens. Take US 33 north to Nelsonville, OH 78 east to Glouster, and OH 13 north to Township Road 289, also a trip distance of about 180 miles.

THE TRAIL

Departing the open area around the parking lot from the left rear corner, the trail immediately enters a lovely pine grove, crosses a short bridge, and then heads up the Eels Run valley. Remember to carry ample water; none is available on the trail. For the next mile, the trail goes in and out of these pines and back and forth across the stream several times. Just beyond the first creek crossing, a sign points both ahead and to the left. This is where the return trail completes the loop. The trail seems to be designed for a clockwise route, with the outbound trail going left at this juncture.

Wildcat Hollow Trail is an excellent choice for the fledgling backpacker or for a weekend trek. It is not heavily used, so crowding is not a problem. It is, however, within an area designated for hunting with primitive weapons, so it is probably best to avoid the trail in deer and turkey season. During small-game season, some hunter-orange apparel would seem appropriate.

When Eels Run splits, the trail follows the left branch. Mile marker 1 is just beyond this point. A few yards after the mile marker, the trail heads up the right slope to move counterclockwise around the end of the ridge. It hangs on the left slope of the valley, gently climbing toward Irish Ridge. Beech/maple and mixed mesophytic forest cover these hillsides, along with a healthy shrub layer of bush honeysuckle, evidence of a former homestead. Apple trees not surrounded by the secondary succession forest give further evidence of human activity in the area. As the trail moves higher up the hillside heading toward the ridge, it enters an open area where it passes mile marker 2. There, at an elevation of 1,000 feet, the trail has risen almost exactly 200 feet in 2 miles—a nice, gentle gradient for backpacking.

As the trail swings to the right toward its intersection with Irish Ridge Road, it passes more tall white pines, here with ground cedar covering the forest floor. Just after the trail joins Irish Ridge Road, a dirt road enters from the right. Obviously built for some other purpose, the quarter-mile track is the connector to the returning trail, creating a short loop of about 5 miles. The connector needs no description since it is an almost straight, level trail through brush and successional forest.

The main trail continues on Irish Ridge Road to its intersection with County Road 70, or Waterworks Road. Watch for an old wooden schoolhouse that sits near here, almost hidden from view by the encroaching forest. The trail turns left to travel very briefly on Waterworks Road, shortly to drop off the right side into white pines and young successional hardwood. The trail turns left to parallel the road for a short distance. It

MATURE TREES LINE THE TRAIL IN WILDCAT HOLLOW

then turns right, passes directly under a power line, and uses switchbacks to drop into the head of a ravine, which it follows downstream. As you pass mile marker 3, more whispery white pines appear alongside the trail. When I backpacked this trail a number of years ago, carrying only a bivy sack for a night's

rest, I sought out the white pine stands for my overnight stops.

Where the ravine widens and becomes a hollow, a large number of old oil-well shacks and collection pipes can be seen. The trail is not easy to follow as it turns to the right up the hollow. It ducks under a cable, and then joins an oil-well service road to cross the creek. Then it passes under an overhead collection pipe before turning left to reenter the forest. A sign for Wildcat Hollow Backpack Trail reassures you that you're on the correct route. The trail next curves to the left on the hillside as it climbs, using switchbacks, to reach the ridge. Passing through more pines as it swings right, the trail eventually hits an old dirt road that it follows to the right. Still climbing, the trail ignores another dirt road leaving to the left and continues to the top, where it turns left to follow the ridge. Less than 1 mile beyond, you pass mile marker 4.

The trail continues on this narrow ridge for another half mile, passing an area on the left that had at one time been clear-cut. At this point the trail becomes a haul road, providing access to Irish Ridge Road. The trail makes an easily missed left turn several hundred yards before this sometimes-muddy road reaches the gravel road. After leaving the haul road, the path circles to the left above a hollow, passes an oil well, and then climbs to Chapel Hill Road. There it turns right, going up the road about 100 feet to where, just before the road curves left, it exits left into the woods. Mile marker 5 is but a short way beyond.

Following the hillside to the right, the trail crosses several washes and then turns left on an old track. As you head downslope, there is a good view of the Perry County countryside. Leaving the old road, the trail winds past a series of white pipes that denote the presence of a gas transmission line. Using switchbacks, it drops to the valley floor and heads downstream. Still within sight of gas-line markers, the path curves right to begin climbing the hillside beside more pipeline markers. After it passes mile marker 6, it makes a single curving switchback to the right before gaining the ridge top. Eventually the trail reaches 1,060 feet and curves right to meet Irish Ridge Road for the last time. This is another crossing where there is an offset to the continuation of the trail. Turn right onto the road and walk about 100 feet to where a backpacker sign indicates that the trail exits the road to the left. Still following the ridge top, it passes the 7-mile marker about 250 feet after leaving Irish Ridge Road.

The trail next leaves the ridge, swinging right as it drops into a hollow. At a split, the blazed Wildcat Hollow Trail takes the right fork. It then goes in and out of a side hollow before turning right and starting to climb again to higher ground. The ascent begins with a short, fairly steep climb, and then continues at a gentler grade, passing through another white pine planting and close to a wildlife watering hole. Where the trail reaches Township Road 13 it cuts diagonally to the right to climb some log steps. Soon it crosses a gas-line right-of-way before emerging onto another gravel road. This road—Township Road 297 in Perry County and Township Road 113 in Morgan County—that follows the ridges southeast through national forest land is closed less than 1 mile to the left of this crossing. It is now used as a bridle trail and footpath.

Across the road from where the trail emerges, a dirt track enters. Wildcat Hollow Trail does not take this track, but instead exits the road just to its left. Shortly it passes another wildlife watering hole. For the next 1.5 miles, the trail stays high on the hillside east of Cedar Run, passing by or through four areas where timber was clear-cut. Because regrowth from live tree stumps is rapid during the growing season, many blazes are obscured by vegetation and difficult to find. Keep a constant watch for markings. At one point the trail uses another old roadbed for a short distance but soon leaves it, turning to the left. Not all the woods along this ridge have been logged, and in the area of mile marker 9 there is a very nice stand of mature mixed oak forest. Here the trail swings around the heads of ravines as it approaches another area that was clear-cut recently. With the timber-harvest area on the right, the trail descends to Cedar Run Hollow using a single switchback. Once in the valley, the trail crosses the main stem and then a small side stream of Cedar Run on log bridges. The last crossing is close to the 10-mile mark.

The trail turns downstream on the low hillside, but after crossing a dry wash in a side ravine, it makes a sharp right turn to begin ascending the ridge. Using only one switchback, the path swings gently to the right as it climbs. As it approaches a fence between national forest land and an inholding still being farmed, the trail turns left and begins descending into a small side ravine of Wildcat Hollow. As it leaves the forest it crosses Township Road 300, then turns right to move upstream parallel to the road. The path next passes a swampy area and another old oil collection area. After crossing the creek, the trail rises up the side of the valley wall, still headed upstream. It then makes a left turn to climb 100 feet to the ridge in less than 1,000 feet. The trail has come over 11 miles and now meets the connecting track for the shorter day hike. There are blazes on the trails going left and right.

To complete the 15-mile loop trail, turn left at this intersection. The dirt road soon divides, with Wildcat Hollow Trail taking the left fork. A fairly open area on the right affords a view back into Wildcat Hollow. The trail continues along the left side of the ridge, eventually reaching a brushy area where it crosses an old cement floor. This spot is near the 12-mile point of the trail. For a brief time the trail returns to the woodlands, but it soon enters another open area. Once again the trail uses the tracks of an early road as it traverses the left side of the ridge top for a little less than half a mile. After turning right off the old road, the trail passes through the middle of another formerly open area now closing in. Then it reenters the woodlands as it drops gently off the right side of the ridge to the valley floor. Following a dry wash downstream for a few hundred feet, it meets the outbound trail about 500 feet up Eels Run from the trailhead parking lot. There could hardly be a more fitting finish to a hike on Wildcat Hollow Trail than the grove of pines through which the trail passes as it comes to an end. Check out the boot-cleaning station and learn why thoroughly cleaning your footwear after every hike is important in the fight against the spread of invasive alien plants.

V.

SOUTHWESTERN OHIO

41

Caesar Creek Gorge State Nature Preserve

TOTAL DISTANCE: 2.5 miles

HIKING TIME: 2 hours

MAXIMUM ELEVATION: 892 feet

VERTICAL RISE: 140 feet

MAPS: USGS 7.5' Oregonia

ACCESSIBILITY: Because of the steep terrain, not wheelchair accessible.

FACILITIES: Restroom only. Picnic tables, grills, swimming beach, boating, campground, additional restrooms, and bridle trails are available at nearby Caesar Creek State Park

Imposing, 108-feet cliffs of Ordovician limestone and shale line the gorge of Caesar Creek where it flows through this 463-acre state nature preserve. Formed by great volumes of glacial meltwater cutting through the bedrock, the gorge provided the outlet for water from the retreating Wisconsinan Glacier lying to the northeast.

Though dammed to create Caesar Creek Lake—an Army Corps of Engineers impoundment located just east of the preserve—Caesar Creek supports a rich aquatic animal life and, on its banks, a wide variety of plant life. Now heavily wooded with beech, maple, hickory, and oak, even the steep slopes of the valley were probably heavily timbered during the nineteenth century. The uplands show evidence of having at one time been completely cleared for use as pasture and crop fields. Except for power line easement, natural succession has been allowed to occur since 1975 when the Department of Natural Resources acquired the land.

Old roadways, foundation stones, fruit trees, and other plantings betray the occupancy of the area by settlers. Earlier occupancy by successive cultures of Native Americans is well documented. Many earthworks thought to be of Hopewell origin are found within a few miles of Caesar Creek.

The preserve extends to the east bank of the Little Miami State and National Scenic River area, where a river access point is provided. A portion of Little Miami Scenic Park Trail passes through the area close to the parking lot on the former Penn-Central (nineteenth-century Little Miami) Railroad right-of-way.

The spring flora on the sweet soil of the wooded hillsides on both sides of the

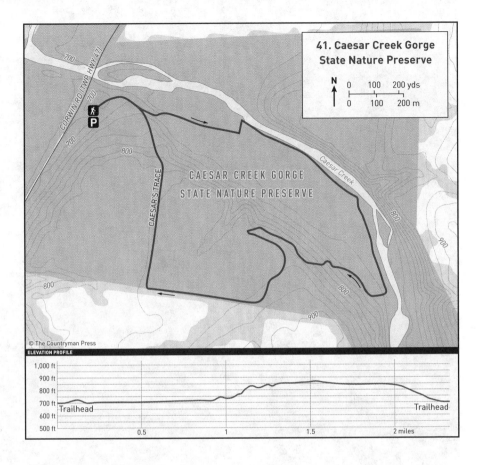

river is luxuriant. Among the less common species growing on the preserve is shooting star, a plant often associated with prairies but also found in open situations on thin soils above limestone or dolomite cliffs. Although the flowers are pink in color farther west, the species is white-flowered here and was, in earlier times, known as "Pride-of-Ohio." On the moist hillsides, the brilliant red-fire pink blooms about the same time as the white-blooming, large-flowered trillium fades. The floral show begins in mid-April and lasts into early June. Butterfly-weed, New England aster, and goldenrod are along the flowers in the meadows as summer progresses.

Unfortunately, like many natural areas in western Ohio, Caesar Creek Preserve has been invaded by bush honeysuckle and garlic mustard, but they detract only a little from the beauty of the place.

GETTING THERE

Located in Wayne Township in northwestern Warren County, Caesar Creek Gorge State Nature Preserve is 3 miles north of the village of Oregonia and about 2 miles south of the village of Corwin, on Corwin Road. To reach it from the north, take US 42 to OH 73 at Waynesville, then travel east about a half mile on OH 73 to the access to

GOOD WILDFLOWER HABITAT ALONG CAESAR CREEK GORGE TRAIL

Corwin Road. Turn left to travel south on Corwin Road about 2 miles to the preserve parking lot, just beyond a bridge over Caesar Creek on the left hand side of the road.

THE TRAIL

The long-abandoned road that forms the basis of the main trail of the preserve is known as Caesar's Trace. As the story is told, in 1776 a Shawnee party attacked a flatboat on the Ohio River and took captive a black slave called "Cizar." He reportedly was adopted into the tribe and spent much time hunting near a stream he liked so well he named it after himself. When the Kentucky frontiersmen Simon Kenton—who was being held captive at Oldtown, farther up the Little Miami—was planning to make his escape, Cizar supposedly advised him to follow "his" creek down to its confluence with the Little Miami, thereby avoiding

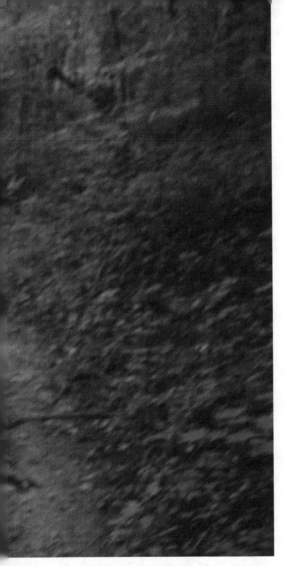

headed coneflower bloom along here in midsummer. Soon the trail moves closer to the river, where there are side trails to the river's edge made by bank fishermen. After passing through a long bed of scouring rushes, the trail comes out on a gravel bar on the stream. There are nice riffles in the stream here, and there is a spectacular view on the high banks of the gorge.

Traveling through floodplain forest, the trail first leaves the river, then returns to it alongside some rapids. It leaves the river for good as it moves toward the hillside. Here it turns right to move diagonally up the hillside on an old track. As the trail emerges from the woods, it passes through a huge patch of cup plant and alongside basswood, hackberry, cedar, and other calciphiles (plants that thrive on a limey substrate). The old fields of the high ground contain a number of prairie plants, such as Canada wild rye, and lots of red cedars. With black locust groves to the right, the trail winds its way near the rim of the gorge. Near the juncture with the old road, it passes a huge black locust. Turn right on the old track and begin the descent toward the parking lot. Shortly after the hillside forest reemerges on the right, the opening for the outgoing trail appears, and the sound of rushing water returns. In a few moments, the parking lot and privies come into view, marking the end of this hike. On a sunny summer day when I last walked this trail, butterflies of many species were my nearly constant companions. It is easy to see why, since many of the plants that sustain butterfly larvae are found along the trail and the flowers that provide adults with nectar are in the old fields nearby. The diverse habitats of this preserve make it an interesting one to explore at any season.

the well-traveled Indian trail along the west bank of the Little Miami; hence, the name, Caesar's Trace.

About 150 yards up the trace, leave the track, following a narrow foot trail toward the creek. Be aware that there are several wild trails before the real trail is reached, made by fishermen and sightseers. After a drop of 75 feet or so, the trail levels out on a terrace before dropping to a bridge and the floodplain. Escaped garden phlox and green-

42

Clifton Gorge State Nature Preserve and John Bryan State Park

TOTAL DISTANCE: 5 miles (8.8 km)

HIKING TIME: 3 hours

MAXIMUM ELEVATION: 990 feet

VERTICAL RISE: 150 feet

MAPS: USGS 7.5' W Clifton; ODNR Clifton Gorge State Nature Preserve brochure and map; ODNR John Bryan State Park map

The Clifton Gorge/John Bryan complex is rich in early Ohio history. As a year-round flowing river, the Little Miami powered the wheels of frontier industry. Dozens of mills running all sorts of industrial operations sprang up along the Little Miami, from Clifton to Cincinnati. Because of the narrow gorge at Clifton, those located there were among the best. A stagecoach road running from Pittsburgh to Cincinnati came through Clifton, dropped into the gorge, and returned to higher ground to head downriver. Its purpose was to pick up goods from the mills along the way. All the mill industries have now vanished, except for the long-lived Clifton Mill. The ruins of these structures and the road that served them can still be seen in the preserve and the park.

Considered one of Ohio's premier nature preserves, Clifton Gorge and the adjoining John Bryan State Park should be visited at all seasons to enjoy their full beauty. No visit to the area is complete without a stop at the historic Clifton Mill, located one block east of the trailhead in Clifton on the bank of the Little Miami River. Antioch University's Glen Helen Nature Preserve is located 5 miles west, in the village of Yellow Springs. Its 20 miles of trails, including Glen Helen Scout Trail, offer additional hiking opportunities in this area.

GETTING THERE

The main entrance to Clifton Gorge State Nature Preserve is located along OH 343, a half mile west of Clifton and OH 72; however, a secondary parking lot located at the corner of Jackson and Water Streets on the edge of the village offers a better starting point and is where this 5.5 mile hike begins.

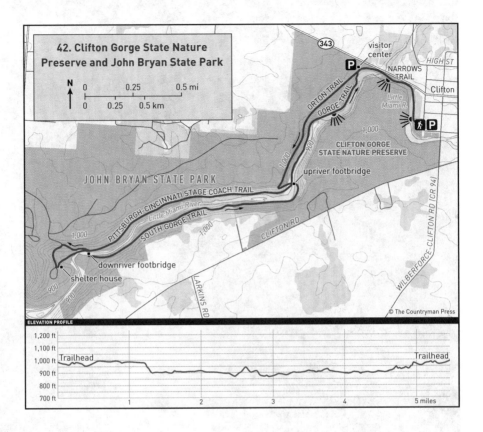

To reach the trailhead from Columbus, travel 1-70 about 50 miles west to OH 72, then travel 8 miles south to OH 343 in Clifton, and turn right (west). Jackson is the second street to the left. It meets Water Street in two blocks. From Cincinnati, travel north on 1-71, and then north on OH 72 to Clifton. From Dayton, travel east on US 35, north on 1-675, east (right) on Dayton-Yellow Springs Road, shortly north (left) on US 68, and then east (right) on OH 343.

THE TRAIL

The trail begins just to the right of the information kiosk. To the left of the kiosk is a glacial erratic bearing

a bronze plaque that commemorates Clifton Gorge as a National Natural Landmark. The trail heads directly to the gorge, about 100 feet from the parking lot. There, an overlook allows a first glance of the river, and an interpretive sign tells of the creation of the gorge by meltwater from the last glacier. The gravel-filled bed of this ancient river, known as the Kennard outwash, has been traced 33 miles from Logan County to the head of Clifton Gorge.

The trail immediately turns to the right to follow the rim of the gorge downstream. Passing between old "wolf trees" along the gorge and regenerating fields, the trail soon comes to two bridges built by workers from the present-day Ohio

CLIFTON GORGE

Division of Civilian Conservation. The tops of northern white cedar (arborvitae) trees growing in the gorge are visible, and on the upland red cedars (eastern junipers) grow. Just beyond, at a bend in the river, is an overlook at the site of the old Patterson Mill. This mill site was not the first in the area. Owen Davis and Benjamin Whiteman built a gristmill and inn on the present site of Clifton in about 1803. By 1809, however, Robert Patterson, the founder of Lexington, Kentucky, cofounder of Cincinnati, and an early settler of Dayton, had built this mill to make cotton and wool cloth. The four-story mill spanned the gorge like a bridge. Its 22-foot overshot wheel nestled in an alcove in the rock. During the War of 1812, the mill provided cloth for the uniforms of American soldiers fighting in Ohio. In 1870, a flood demolished the mill. Another flood in 1876 destroyed the dam. All that can be seen today are the square holes in the rock at the bottom of the gorge that held the beams that supported the mill.

This overlook provides an excellent view of the narrows of the gorge just downstream, and the trail continues downstream to follow the rim of the gorge. Several ancient arborvitae lean out from the gorge wall and reach for the sky along here. At the "pool overlook," a sign tells the story of Darnell's leap. In 1778, a party of men led by Daniel Boone was captured at Blue Licks, Kentucky, by a band of Shawnee Indians and taken to the principal Shawnee town of Chillicothe (now Oldtown, Ohio) on the Little Miami River. A few months later Boone managed to escape and returned to Boonesborough in time to warn of an impending Indian attack. Cornelius Darnell, another member of Boone's party, escaped some time later, but the Indians soon discovered his flight and

gave chase. They caught up with him at this spot on the north bank of the "narrows." Facing certain death by torture, Darnell chose instead to leap the chasm. Although he fell short of the far side, he managed to grasp hold of the trees that mantled the cliffs and so halt his fall. From there he was able to climb to the cliff top and escape.

The trail soon swings to the right, headed toward the highway. At a fork in the trail, take the left fork, which leads to the Cedar Garden overlook. A sign tells of the varied habitats visible from there, each supporting its own collection of plants. In the thin soil along the cliff tops, prairie plants such as whorled milkweed can be found. On the vertical cliff faces grow white cedars, a northern species brought here by the last glacier. The riverbanks below encourage tree species, such as sycamore and cottonwood, that do well in moist situations. The shaded cliffs across the river harbor several plant species rare to the state, including mountain maple, Canada yew, and red baneberry. The trail follows the cliff edge to the road and crosses a side stream on a walkway on the river side of the highway bridge. It then returns to the woods and immediately crosses another side stream on a wood-and-steel bridge parallel to a stone-arch bridge on OH 343. The highway department wanted to replace the stone bridge with a more modern one but was prevented from doing so by local outcry.

The trail now rises slightly to arrive at a grassy area that was once a parking lot for the Clifton Gorge refreshment stand operated by the Grindall family. The site at one time also contained a cage that for 55 years held Muggins, a black bear captured as a cub in Canada and brought to this place as a tourist attraction. The cage, store, and home are gone, but one outbuilding, formerly used as a shop by the Division of Natural Areas and Preserves, has been remodeled into a splendid new visitor center. Volunteer naturalists are on hand from the first weekend of April until the first weekend of October and there are many exhibitions about the preserve to be seen.

At this point, a set of steps lead into the gorge. Do not take them—you will return that way. Instead, go straight on the North Rim Trail. This is probably the route used by the old Cincinnati-to-Pittsburgh stagecoach road as it approached its drop into the valley of the Little Miami a few hundred yards west of here. At the right of the trail is an alcove called the Bear's Den, a place to gather for conducted walks. Near the information kiosk is a slice of a white oak tree that began growing in 1691 and died in 1985 in what is now the state park campground. Its annual rings have been labeled with the natural and historical events that occurred during the tree's lifetime. Just beyond on the right is a gravel trail that leads to the main parking lot on OH 343, where there are restrooms.

The trail passes through a gate and continues on the stage road, now called Orton Trail. Immediately thereafter, a trail goes to the left, following closely along the cliff edge. Take this trail along the top of the cliffs. Until early 1990, this was a favorite area for rock climbers and rappellers, but that activity has now been banned to preserve the plants and rock features of the gorge. Hardwoods and white cedars line the rim to the left of our trail. Old fields with invading sumac and red cedar are on the right. From one of the overlooks, Steamboat Rock, a large slump block

that originated along the cliffs is visible in the river below. A cut in the cliff once held a switchbacked road that led to a strawboard mill below. A hundred feet beyond, a grassy side trail comes in from the right. As you continue on the rim trail, the stage road soon appears in the woods to the right. The hiking trail moves on and off the stagecoach track several times before finally merging with it. About 100 feet beyond that point, the trail swings left toward the rim of the gorge. A newer side trail exits right to continue into the park on the upland. Still following close to the rim, the trail soon passes two overlooks, then reaches a junction with a side trail that goes to the right toward the Orton Picnic Area. Your path soon reaches the point where the stagecoach road descends to the valley (this is where you cross the boundary between the park and the preserve). A narrower trail, which you do not take, leaves to the right to continue along the rim. After crossing a new wooden foot bridge, the stagecoach road you are following travels over cobblestone paving as it drops rapidly to the gorge. It uses only one switchback on its route through the opening in the cliff and down the talus slope. What a rough ride it must have been in a stagecoach!

The trail coming off the hillside meets the river at an open area where the upriver Little Miami footbridge is located. Here, it turns right to continue following the Cincinnati-to-Pittsburgh stage road along the north side of the river. For the next mile it stays at a fairly level elevation at the bottom of the talus slope, sometimes passing between large slump blocks and occasionally fording a spring-fed side stream. Though the forest is mature now, the dead red cedars in the woods indicate that this flat land

NODDING TRILLIUM

was once cleared. The red cedars were the pioneering species that invaded the area when agriculture was halted.

Eventually the trail arrives at the downriver footbridge. The path labeled CAMP TRAIL close to the river will be your return route. Continue your hike by following the stage road as it angles uphill toward the blacktopped road that leads from the main park area to the lower picnic area. The break in the cliff face where the stagecoach road climbed out of the gorge is visible ahead. After a left turn onto the road the trail runs past a pond on the right (created by the diking effect of the road) and then to the picnic area. Restrooms are up the

slope to the right of the road, and drinking fountains to the left are on during the frost-free months. A beautiful stone shelter house is a heritage of the Civilian Conservation Corps (CCC) days at John Bryan State Park.

The trail then follows a set of 57 steps to the left of the shelter house that lead to a grassy area along the river. There stands a glacial erratic on which a National Scenic River plaque was erected in August 1973. This spot in the river is known as Kutler's Hole. It was once the location of Brewer's Mill and Distillery. The trail follows the left bank of the river upstream along the river's edge, rejoining the stagecoach road about 25 feet before the downriver footbridge across the Little Miami. Originally built by the CCC in the 1930s, this bridge and the one a mile upstream were rebuilt in the mid-1960s. This one has poured concrete abutments and piers, while the one upstream uses laid-up stone.

The hike continues by following the trail across the bridge, then turning left along the talus slope on the south side of the river. Shortly, the trail splits, with one branch going close to the river through a white cedar grove. The other branch angles gently up the slope. This hike follows the right fork, passing close to huge slump blocks and across ravines with lovely waterfalls. Though there are lovely vernal wildflowers on the north side of the river, the north-facing slope here is where the real show takes place in April and May. Walking fern is common on the blocks of dolomite. Where the trail drops to the valley floor, two sections of boardwalk keep the trail from becoming mired in mud. Many of the trees on the slope are chinquapin oak, a species especially well adapted to the calcareous soils of the area. Most of the way, a high cliff stands at the top of the talus slope. At one point, however, a road comes through a break in the cliff to a house on a piece of private property almost at the trail's edge. Just before the trail reaches the upper bridge, an interpretive sign on the right tells us that the land upstream on the south side has been designated a Scientific Preserve. The sign lists some of the rare plants to be found in this area.

The trail crosses the bridge to return to the north side of the Little Miami. There, it immediately turns right upriver. Soon another sign tells of the origin of the slump blocks on the rim of the gorge and of their slow descent down the shale slope below the cliffs. It also tells of the need for woodland spring flowers to bloom and set seed before canopy trees leaf out.

Using wooden steps and walkways to get over and around the slump blocks, the trail winds its way between the river's edge and the base of the talus slope. An exceptionally beautiful spot on the river is known as the Blue Hole. In 1851, this view of the Little Miami River inspired a young Cincinnati artist named Robert S. Duncanson. Born in New York in 1821 to an African American mother and a Scottish Canadian father, Duncanson spent his childhood in Canada. By 1842, he had settled in Cincinnati, where his paintings caught the attention of Nicolas Longworth, a prominent citizen. Longworth's commissions aided the young artist's success, and Duncanson traveled widely to find subjects for his paintings. The one he did of this spot is called *Blue Hole Little Miami River*; it now hangs in the Cincinnati Museum of Art.

The trail next climbs to the site of the Nixon-Hagar Paper Mill, operated during the mid-nineteenth century. Straw gathered from nearby farms was boiled and beaten into pulp, rolled, and drained to form cardboard and brown butcher paper. A dam upstream across the river near Amphitheater Falls created the head to drive the millwheel. Refuse was dumped into the river. A service road down the cliff face is still visible to the left. The mill was abandoned by 1899, and its chimney came down in 1912. Bricks from the latter can still be seen in the trail. Beyond the two mill overlooks, a sign on the left of the trail tells of the origin of a small cave. It is not a true solution cave (a cavern formed when rock dissolves) but a slump-block cave. It is the only cave in the preserve that is a part of the trail system and, as such, is open for exploration. The trail climbs to the base of the Cedarville dolomite cliff and passes the former rock-climbing area. The land is now being allowed to rest in the hope that native vegetation will eventually return to the nooks and crannies of the rock face.

The trail drops toward the river between two huge slump blocks, then climbs toward Amphitheater Falls on stairs and decking. The block-like, 7-foot-thick Euphemia dolomite that underlies the massive Cedarville dolo-mite and the layered Springfield dolomite gives the impression that these are carefully laid-up steps at the base of the falls. The trail heads upriver, passing Steamboat Rock. Soon moving uphill to the cliff base, the trail passes another formerly popular climbing area. Rising about halfway up the Cedarville dolomite, the trail reaches a set of 23 wooden steps that take it back to the rim trail near the Bear's Den gathering place. The trail to the right returns you to the trailhead at the Jackson Street parking lot for a total distance of about 5.5 miles.

East Fork State Park

TOTAL DISTANCE: 14 miles (21.2 km)

HIKING TIME: 8 hours or 2, 3, or 4 days

MAXIMUM ELEVATION: 860 feet

VERTICAL RISE: 125 feet

MAPS: USGS 7.5' Batavia; USGS 7.5' Bethel; USGS 7.5' Williamsburg; ODNR East Fork State Park map; USACE William H. Harsha Lake, Ohio, map

William H. Harsha Lake on the East Fork of the Little Miami River was one of the last Army Corps of Engineers flood-control reservoirs built in Ohio. Completed in 1978, the 2,160-acre impoundment established water-based recreation within 25 miles of Cincinnati. It was named in honor of the former congressman from Portsmouth, whose 21 years in the US House of Representatives included 11 as the ranking Republican on the Public Works and Transportation Committee. The East Fork of the Little Miami River drains 362 square miles of flat, relatively continuous Illinoian ground moraine in the middle of Clermont County. Of the project land area, the corps maintains 660 acres, the Ohio Division of Wildlife manages 2,248 acres for hunting, and the Division of Parks and Recreation manages 5,618 acres as East Fork State Park. State park literature calls the impoundment East Fork Lake, while the Corps of Engineers brochure refers to it as William H. Harsha Lake.

There are two major hiking trails in the park. The one I describe here is East Fork Backpack Trail, a 14-mile route where 5.5 miles of trail are hiked in two directions and the remaining 3 miles as a loop at the far end. It is located entirely on the south side of Harsha Lake and can be walked as a day hike or as a backpack trip using the two campsites it shares with a longer trail for one, two, or three overnights. The first campsite is just over 3 miles from the trailhead. The second is about 4 miles beyond, at the farthest point on the trail.

Though admittedly less scenic than some other backpacking trails in Ohio and nearby states, this trail is an excellent introduction to backpacking. The climbs are easy, the distances short and flexible, and the camping facilities good.

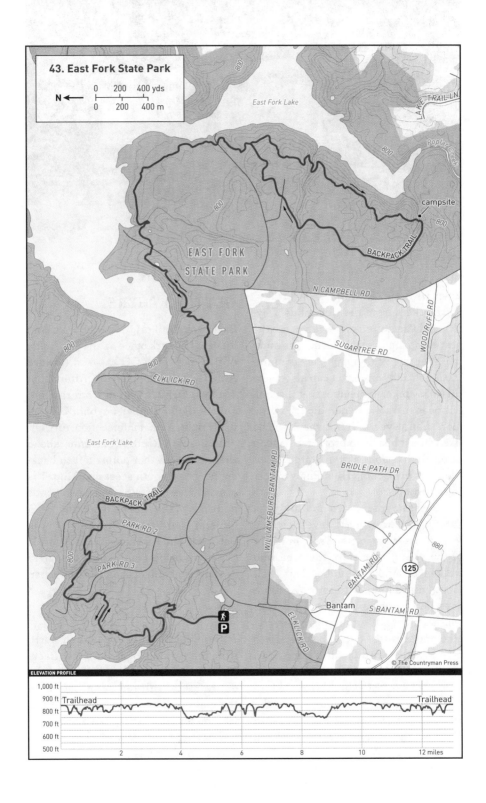

43. East Fork State Park

N ←

0   200   400 yds
0   200   400 m

East Fork Lake

LAKE TRAIL LN

Poplar Creek

800

campsite

800

BACKPACK TRAIL

EAST FORK
STATE PARK

800

N CAMPBELL RD

WOODRUFF RD

SUGARTREE RD

800

ELKLICK RD

800

East Fork Lake

WILLIAMSBURG-BANTAM RD

BRIDLE PATH DR

880

BACKPACK TRAIL

800

PARK RD 2

PARK RD 3

125

BANTAM RD

Bantam   S BANTAM RD

ELKLICK RD

© The Countryman Press

ELEVATION PROFILE

1,000 ft
900 ft Trailhead   Trailhead
800 ft
700 ft
600 ft
500 ft

2   4   6   8   10   12 miles

HIKERS' INFORMATION KIOSK

Even with an "after work on Friday" start, hikers from the Columbus, Dayton, and Cincinnati areas can make the first campsite by dark during the summer months. With a day pack containing lunch and water, you can also make this a day hike. Remember that the area has been in public ownership for a little more than 38 years. Think what it will be like when it has been protected as long as places like John Bryan State Park or the parks in Hocking Hills. Enjoy watching it grow.

The state park also maintains a second trail known as Steve Newman Worldwalker Perimeter Trail, in honor of the young man from the area who walked around the globe. This trail is 31.5 miles long, with four overnight sites, and is open to horseback riders as well as hikers. It circumnavigates the lake and requires two unbridged river crossings that are difficult at some times of the year. It is not shown on the map. If you are interested in this hike, a brochure with a map is available from the Department of Natural Resources. In addition, the combined Buckeye Trail, North Country Trail, and American Discovery Trail pass through the park on the north side of East Fork Lake.

GETTING THERE

Backpack Trail originates at a parking lot near the park office on the south side of the lake. Take OH 125 east (toward Amelia) from I-275, Exit 65. After about 8 miles, OH 222 enters from the left. One-and-a-half miles beyond, OH 222 turns right. At that intersection, turn left onto Bantam Road. A half mile ahead there is a sign that points left to backcountry trail south access parking. The gravel drive passes between two ponds and ends at the trailhead parking lot. A bulletin board shows the route of both Backpack and Perimeter Trails. There is no fee for using the trail, but for safety reasons every hiker should self-register.

THE TRAIL

A sign identifies the trail going north from the parking lot as East Fork Backpack Trail. It is well marked along the entire route with red paint blazes on the main trail and white on side trails. (Perimeter Trail uses green blazes.)

Leaving the trailhead, the natural-surface path winds its way through an area rapidly succeeding from shrubs to woodland. It soon transitions into older woodlands, heading toward the lake about 1 mile away. At a ravine, it descends downstream to the left on log steps before crossing the stream on stepping-stones. Turning right, it climbs to high ground and then heads left toward the lake. Footbridges span two smaller streams before the trail makes a sweeping U-turn, staying on the high ground. A bench for the weary or contemplative sits along the trail. After crossing a series of smaller ravines on steps and bridges, the trail splits. The first mile marker is in this area. Take the left fork along the edge of the woods. Before dropping to the picnic area, the trail crosses an open area where there is a grand view of the lake.

Beyond the road, the trail descends on another set of log steps, then, after about 50 feet, it turns right along an old field before entering the woods. This turn is easy to miss during the growing season. Two wooden bridges span small ravines, and then the trail climbs to an open field. It swings right alongside the woods, enters, and then drops to a deep ravine. Going upstream to cross without a bridge, the trail turns left and climbs to another fork. Now turning right, it travels between forest on the right and brambles on the left. In about 100 feet it enters the woods, turning to the right. The second mile marker is in this vicinity.

When it emerges from the woods, it crosses the beach entrance road. Water is available here during the warmer months, public toilets are present, and there is a picnic area just ahead on the right.

The trail now curves to the right just inside the woods from the picnic area. Pay no attention to the many side trails coming from that area. Staying on the contour around the curve, it intersects another trail, goes left, and proceeds down a set of steps. It turns right to intersect another trail before a bridge, and then turns left to cross the bridge before turning right again. Fortunately, these turns are all well marked with blazes. After crossing a small wash, the trail drops to a bridge. It then climbs back to the edge of the high ground, which it follows to another bridge. Steeply climbing away from that bridge, the trail returns to level ground, where you will find mile marker 3. Soon it intersects a side trail to the right where a sign reads OVERNIGHT AREA.

A white-blazed trail leads across the boat-ramp road, along an old fencerow, and into a woods to the camping area shared with Perimeter Trail. Facilities there include toilets, picnic tables, and two low, floorless bunkhouses that will each accommodate two campers. There is no drinking water at the site. Tents are welcome.

Back at the intersection of the main trail and white-blazed side trail, Backpack Trail soon emerges from the woods to cross the boat-ramp road and reenter the woods, continuing eastward. This is the last public road the trail crosses, although the next overnight area is within a short walk of one. Beyond this point the trail crosses a narrow, paved, abandoned road. The trail through here is sometimes difficult to follow. Keep checking for red blazes. Crossing ravines and washouts and moving up and down the slope, the trail passes mile marker 4. Eventually it swings south near mile marker 5 to follow the rim of the now-impounded valleys of Cloverlick and Poplar Creeks.

All along the trail the successional woods are full of alien "nuisance plants." Japanese honeysuckle, multiflora rose, bush honeysuckle, and *Euonymus*

WILLIAM H. HARSHA RESERVOIR AT EAST FORK STATE PARK

fortunei are ever-present. Add native brambles such as blackberries, and traveling along the edge of the abandoned fields can sometimes be difficult. But the trail is blazed well and can be followed if you watch carefully for marks. If the blazes do disappear, you have probably missed a turn. Just backtrack and you'll locate the proper route.

The trail crosses two more abandoned paved roads. Bantam Road—the northern extension of the still-open North Campbell Road—is crossed before the trail begins to swing southeast. From that crossing, the distance to the second campsite is just a little more than 2 miles. About a half mile farther down

the trail, after it turns to the south, you cross Anti-bantam Road. Next, the trail climbs slightly, passes an old fence line, then drops steeply to the left to cross a wooden bridge. Beyond the bridge, the trail rises gently to a shrubby area in the direction of the lake and then reenters the woods. Just beyond here your outbound trail goes straight ahead while the return route comes in from the right. The 6-mile marker is approximately a half mile beyond here.

There are many ravine crossings ahead, and the trail almost gets lost in tall grass a time or two. The blazes can be difficult to see where the trail passes through a peaceful pine planting, but the

The trail then drops to near lake level and crosses a bridge. When it intersects an old dirt road that comes downhill to the lake's edge from the southwest, the campsite is just ahead. The site is under large oak trees at the top of the hill beyond the road. White blazes lead to it. The two bunkhouses here are larger than at the other campsite and will house four people each on plywood bunks. There are also toilets and tables, but no water. Again, this area is shared with folks using Perimeter Trail, so there may be horses and trail riders as well as long-distance hikers. In case of an emergency, North Campbell Road is less than a half mile away; you can reach it by walking up the abandoned road below the campsite.

The entrance to the red-blazed return route isn't difficult to find if you know where to look. Return to the wooden bridge—sometimes washed out—that the trail came in on. A short distance after crossing a bridge, the trail goes left, not across the creek but following it upstream for about 50 feet before turning left up a steep diagonal climb. The hike now becomes easier than the outbound trail since the ravine crossings are farther from the lake. Even the power-line crossing is easier—go directly across the right-of-way. The trail passes through a nice grove of tall, well-spaced trees. There was a dump of old tires here when I walked the trail in 1989, and they were still here in 1996. Mile marker 8 is located nearby. After about 1 mile of walking, you will reach a familiar T. A left turn leads you back to the trailhead via the outbound trail. If you want to remain on the trail a third night, turn left at the white-blazed side trail 3 miles before reaching the trailhead.

most difficult place to follow the trail is where it crosses under a high-tension power line. After coming into the right-of-way, go uphill, angling left. There are a couple of very small footbridges across the wash that are obviously part of the trail. Look uphill to the next tower, where there is a blaze. After passing the tower, follow the left edge of the woods to a blaze indicating that the trail is exiting the right-of-way. Mile marker 7 is about 400 yards ahead. The campsite and the end of the loop are only minutes from here. The power line actually lies farther south than shown on the USGS map, having been moved during construction of the lake.

The North Country Trail in Ohio

Federal legislation authorized the establishment of North Country National Scenic Trail (NCNST) in March 1980 as a component of the National Trails System. Planned primarily as a route for pleasure walking and hiking, when completed it will extend from the vicinity of Crown Point, New York, to Lake Sakakawea State Park on the Missouri River in North Dakota, where it joins the route of Lewis and Clark National Historic Trail. It crosses seven states, including Ohio, and when done it will be the longest continuous hiking trail in the country. The best estimate is that the final length will be near 4,200 miles. The development and management of the trail is being accomplished in cooperation with many federal, state, and local agencies, as well as private trail groups and individuals. It is being built and maintained primarily by volunteers, mostly members or associates of the North Country Trail Association. As sections of trail are finished, they are inspected by, and receive certification from, the National Park Service.

Thanks to the many years of trail building by the Buckeye Trail Association, the Ohio NCNST is the most completely usable part of the trail. Statewide, 24 segments totaling 287 miles have been certified. Much, but not all, of the NCNST utilizes the path of the Buckeye Trail. And like the BT, much of the marked trail is located on secondary roads. The trail is marked with vertical painted blue blazes, much the same as the BT. Blazes are on trees, or on posts in treeless areas. At intersections with roads and other trails, small blue and gold North Country Trail emblems are used.

From the east, the trail enters Ohio near Negley on the former Montour railroad right-of-way. The first state park land it encounters is Beaver Creek State Park. At last writing, the route was still not clearly defined in this part of the state, but the proposed general route parallels US 30 and SR 183 to Zoar. At that historic village it meets up with the Buckeye Trail, which it follows more or less for 600 miles around Ohio, heading first southwest through conservancy district, state park, state and national forest, and Ohio State Memorial lands toward the Ohio River. From there, it parallels the river for stretches out toward the Cincinnati area. Turning north toward Michigan, it uses a State Scenic Trail that parallels a National Scenic River, a park district, municipal parklands, and old canal towpaths to reach the Maumee River. In many places, by necessity and with the owners' permission, it uses private lands or occasionally resorts to lightly used roads. At Napoleon, the NCNST and the BT separate. From there to the Michigan line it utilizes the Cannonball Trail. It exits the state north of West Unity. Information about volunteering to help build and maintain the trail and the most recent information about its route is available at www.northcountry trail.org/trails/states/ohio. If you are exploring the hikes in this book, you will encounter the NCNST at Atwood Park in the Muskingum Watershed

Conservancy District and at Archers Fork in Wayne National Forest, Fort Hill Earthworks and Nature Preserve, Shawnee State Forest, East Fork State Park, Lockington Reserve, and Oak Openings Metro Park. Look for the symbols where it joins and leaves the trail you are on and dream about trekking east to Crown Point, New York, to the site of what was once a French, then English, fort, and the setting for several of Kenneth Roberts's novels, including *Northwest Passage* and *Rabble in Arms*. Or the best of all dreams for a hiker, walk west to hit Lewis and Clark Trail to the Pacific Ocean.

44

Edge of Appalachia Preserve– Buzzardroost Rock Trail

TOTAL DISTANCE: 4.4 miles (7 km)

MAXIMUM ELEVATION: 1,040 feet

VERTICAL RISE: 400 feet

MAPS: USGS 7.5' Lynx; Edge of Appalachia Preserve map

On the back cover of *Walks and Rambles in Southwestern Ohio*, which I wrote in 1994, I am pictured standing on the platform atop Buzzardroost Rock. I was 65 when I last made that climb and took that picture. I never thought that I would again reach Buzzardroost Rock to marvel at the prairie plants that rim the platform and scan the beautiful valley of Ohio Brush Creek before me. But when I was considering which new trails to add to this edition of *50 Hikes in Ohio*, my mind kept returning to that special place and the trail that leads to it. So, at 10 a.m. on a hot day in mid-August 2006, with braces on both lower legs and 77 birthdays behind me, I hung a camera around my neck, put a hydration pack on my back, and, with two trekking poles, headed up the trail alone. Tucked in my pack were the necessities of the trail plus one of Manfrotto's Super Clamps to allow me to document the trip. At 11:47 a.m. I was standing on the platform, basking in the noonday sun, elated by my accomplishment. At 12:57 p.m., with photos of butterflies, flowers, scenery, and a self-portrait taken, I started my return trip. By 2:47 p.m. I was back at my car, very tired, but very pleased with my hike.

I have made that climb many times, but no two by the same route. In recent years, the folks from The Nature Conservancy and the Cincinnati Museum Center, who manage the area, have established a good, stable foot trail to the promontory, albeit still a difficult climb. It's one that should be taken by every Ohioan who wants to stand on the western edge of the Allegheny Escarpment, in the Outer Bluegrass Region of the state, at the center of the 13,000-acre Edge of Appalachia Preserve, the "crown jewel of Ohio's natural areas." Open to the public since 1967, Buzzardroost Rock

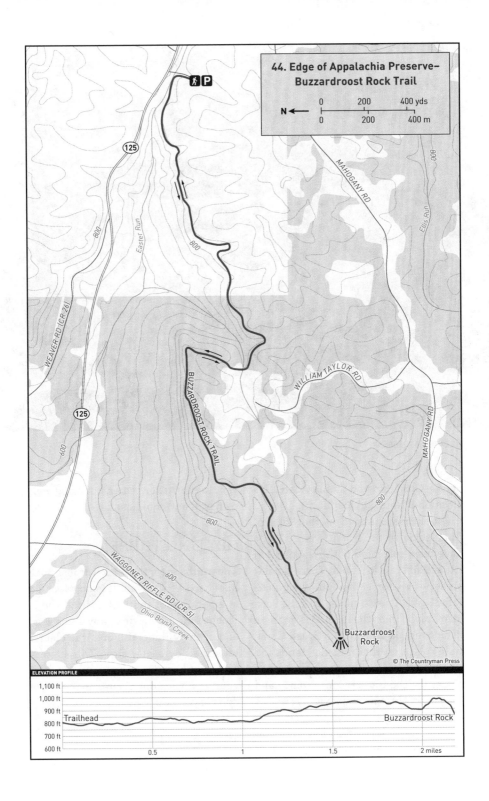

44. Edge of Appalachia Preserve–Buzzardroost Rock Trail

N

| 0 | 200 | 400 yds |
| 0 | 200 | 400 m |

MAHOGANY RD

Ellis Run

125

Easter Run

800

WEAVER RD (CR 26)

125

BUZZARDROOST ROCK TRAIL

WILLIAM TAYLOR RD

MAHOGANY RD

800

800

600

WAGGONER RIFFLE RD (CR 5)

600

Ohio Brush Creek

Buzzardroost
Rock

© The Countryman Press

ELEVATION PROFILE

| 1,100 ft |
| 1,000 ft |
| 900 ft |
| 800 ft | Trailhead | | | | Buzzardroost Rock |
| 700 ft |
| 600 ft |

| 0.5 | 1 | 1.5 | 2 miles |

BUZZARDROOST ROCK

honors Christian and Emma Goetz. It is a National Natural Landmark.

Much has changed at the Edge of Appalachia in the last 10 years. Trails have been relocated with new parking lots at a different locations. There is a new preserve visitor center on Waggoner-Riffle Road. A new trail, the 1.6-mile Portman Trail, climbs the hillside from there to an overlook above Ohio Brush Creek valley. Also on that hillside stands the beautiful Charles Eulett Center, with offices for The Nature Conservancy and Cincinnati Museum employees, as well as laboratory, education, and program facilities for the preserve. Should you care to add a float trip on Ohio Brush Creek to your itinerary while you are in Adams County, there is a boat launch ramp adja-cent to the visitor center, but bring your own boat and equipment.

GETTING THERE

The trailhead for the Buzzardroost Rock hike has been moved. It is now located at a parking lot south of OH 125 and is reached via a short driveway at the west end of the village of Lynx. It is clearly identified by a new sign. This is very rural southern Ohio, so be sure to stow your valuables out of site, or better yet don't leave valuables in your vehicle.

THE TRAIL

The newly rerouted Buzzardroost Rock trail enters the Christian and Emma

Goetz Preserve at an information kiosk on the west side of the lot. This is an earthen foot trail, and I hope that it will always remain so. To me, there is something special about a dirt path. At the onset of your hike you should know that you're embarking on a climb of about 400 feet before the trail descends to the promontory long known as Buzzardroost Rock. You will be ascending the front of the Appalachian escarpment to 1,040 feet above sea level first. At the overlook, you will be about 400 feet above Ohio Brush Creek and 900 feet above sea level. (Remember, the highest point in Ohio is Campbell Hill, on the outskirts of Bellefontaine, at 1,550 feet. The lowest is 455 feet, at the point where the Ohio River leaves the state.) The hike is 4.4 miles round trip. Along the way you will travel over calcareous soils derived from dolomites, calcareous shales, and limestone, where grow a number of species of plants more often seen in drier situations. Naturalists tend to refer to them as "prairie species."

The trail begins by crossing the distinctive calcareous Silurian-age Estill Shale barrens. Some of the hardiest of the prairie grasses and forbs hang on in this area, where true topsoil is scarce. The recently redesigned and upgraded trail crosses seven washes of various sizes on small bridges before reaching the ridge and a sign indicating a right turn. There, in the acid soil country of the Appalachian Plateau grow oaks,

pines, huckleberries, orchids, and more. The trail heads southwest along the edge of the escarpment, skirting a knob or two, then descends on a bit of boardwalk to Buzzardroost Rock. The works of man show up here in a polygon-shape railing. Drink in the view, take a few photos, enjoy a snack, and leave no trace of your visit to this very special spot.

Next, it's back up the ridge and down the slope to the parking lot. If time permits, why not explore one of the other trails in Richard and Lucille Durrell Edge of Appalachia Preserve before leaving "poor" but naturally very rich Adams County.

AUTHOR ATOP BUZZARDROOST ROCK

Edge of Appalachia Preserve– Lynx Prairie Preserve

DISTANCE: 1.3 mile (1.6 km)

HIKING TIME: 1 hour

MAXIMUM ELEVATION: 835

VERTICAL RISE: 250

MAPS: USGS 7.5' Lynx

ACCESSIBILITY: Rough terrain makes access by the physically challenged virtually impossible.

FACILITIES: None

My first visit to the prairie openings around the Adams County town of Lynx was in the late spring of 1949 on a college plant ecology field trip. My field notes refer to them as "cat" prairies, a term I have never heard anywhere else. Perhaps Professor Wolfe dubbed them that because of the nearby village of Lynx.

It took a long time for me to accept the fact that these small patches of grasses and forbs on the worn-out fields of Ohio's poorest county were, in fact, prairies. How could a cowboy on horseback come across one of these? There was hardly enough room for one horse, let alone "a thundering herd coming out of a cloud of dust." I had plunked down enough thin dimes for a Saturday afternoon serial at the local movie house to know what a prairie looked like. Tom Mix wouldn't be caught dead in an Adams County prairie.

In the nearly half-century since I first saw shooting star, Indian paintbrush, hoary puccoon, and yellow-star grass in bloom among the short, green shoots of little bluestem and sideoats grama on the "cat prairies" of southern Ohio, I have seen grasslands of all sizes on two continents. Yet nothing gives me quite the same thrill that I get when, spring, summer, or fall, I discover a flower that is an old friend or one I have never seen before in one of these prairies.

Essentially these grasslands are relics of an earlier time, when the climate of the interior part of North America was warmer and drier. The prairies spread eastward to wherever soil and exposure gave advantage to grasses and forbs over forest. Analysis of Ohio peat bogs shows that such a xerothermic period brought prairie species into western Ohio perhaps 3,000–5,000 years ago.

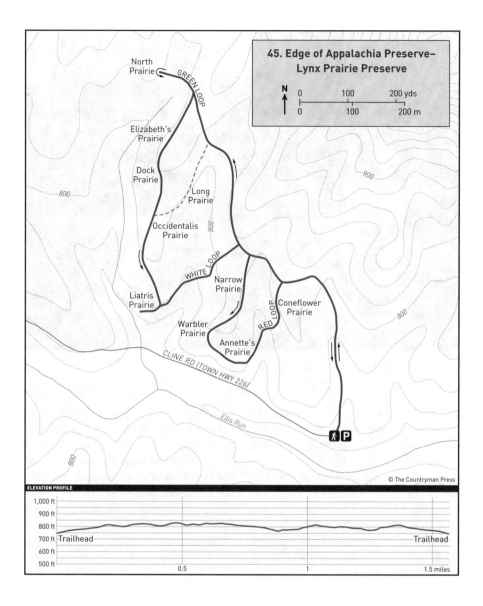

45. Edge of Appalachia Preserve–Lynx Prairie Preserve

North Prairie

GREEN LOOP

Elizabeth's Prairie

Dock Prairie

Long Prairie

Occidentalis Prairie

WHITE LOOP

Narrow Prairie

Liatris Prairie

Coneflower Prairie

RED LOOP

Warbler Prairie

Annette's Prairie

CLINE RD (TOWN HWY 226)

Ellis Run

ELEVATION PROFILE

A return to a cooler, moister climate resulted in re-expansion of forests into most of Ohio. Here, on the hillsides and cliff tops of this part of Ohio, where shallow soils overlay porous Silurian-age dolomite, conditions were not conducive to the growth of trees. But the long-lived, deep-rooted, fire- and drought-resistant perennial plants of the prairies could survive and grow, so the "cat prairies" remained.

There are other places in Ohio with outcrops or cliff tops where shallow soil exists over limestone or dolomite. Many, like Glen Helen and Stillwater Prairie Reserve, have small populations of some prairie plants. But here, where the glaciers never scraped the land flat,

RARE ORCHID, CRESTED-CORALROOT, AT LYNX PRAIRIE

the dolomites are exposed around the hillsides; thus prairie openings at essentially the same elevation strung around the hillsides south of Lynx.

In 1959, at the urging of the late Dr. E. Lucy Braun of the University of Cincinnati Department of Botany, the brand-new Ohio Chapter of The Nature Conservancy purchased the 53-acre tract now known as Lynx Prairie. It was soon transferred to the Cincinnati Museum of Natural History for care. Now, nearly four decades later, it is a unit of the extensive Edge of Appalachia Preserve, jointly owned and managed by the conservancy and the museum. At least 66 plant species considered to be threatened or endangered in Ohio are known to grow in Adams County, and the management of the prairie openings has helped spawn the young science of restoration management.

A walk on the trail through Lynx Prairie is very special. The hike will help those who love the out-of-doors learn about the incredible diversity of life that makes up this earth—not just the biodiversity of the tropical rainforests of the southern hemisphere that we hear so much about, but of special places close to home.

GETTING THERE

To reach Lynx Prairie Preserve travel either east from West Union or west from Portsmouth on SR 125 to the small Brush Creek Township village of Lynx. There, turn south on Tulip Road (CR 9) to Cline Road. (Township Highway 226). There, turn left (east) to the Lynx Prairie Preserve parking lot at the end of the road, a distance of less than a half mile.

THE TRAIL

A pileated woodpecker greeted me at 7:30 a.m. the last time I walked this trail. Every visit to this preserve has brought some special treat, and on that particular day I received my first of many treats just as I entered the preserve.

A sign marks the entrance to the preserve and the starting place for this hike. A 10-minute walk along a woodland leads to Coneflower Prairie. I suggest making a right turn onto the trail to explore the preserve in a clockwise direction. You are now on Red Loop. This hike uses the Red, Green, and Blue loops and they are so blazed. There are low signposts with blazes at all trail junctions.

Coneflower Prairie is known for its mid-summer display of purple coneflower. But like all of the prairie openings, it will have a variety of grassland forbs in bloom from early spring through late fall.

After leaving Coneflower Prairie, you will find a signpost marking a left turn for the red trail. Don't turn—this is your return route. Instead go straight ahead past another signpost, this one identifying White Trail. Proceed directly ahead (north) through the woodland for about 500 feet to a wet draw at the approach to a footbridge. This stream bottom is a

TIGER SWALLOWTAIL NECTARING ON SUNFLOWER AT LYNX PRAIRIE

BLUEHEARTS BLOOM AT LYNX PRAIRIE

good place to look for hog peanut, great bullrush, boneset, and sensitive fern in the summer. I've also been told that it is a good place to see the purple-fruited elderberry shrub in the fall.

It is from this bridge that one hot summer afternoon I saw six box turtles apparently cooling themselves in the stream. I've seen enough box turtles in this preserve to consider the species a common resident. Keep your eyes on the lookout and your ears tuned for the shuffling sound they make crawling through the woods when you are quietly walking these trails. (Oh yes! When you are driving in this part of Ohio and see a box turtle on the road, pull over and give it a helping hand, moving it to the side of road in the direction it seemed be heading. Too many turtles get smashed under car wheels.)

Beyond the bridge there is a signpost noting the juncture of White Loop Trail with Green Loop Trail. Continue forward on Green Loop Trail. Another sign roughly 250 feet ahead has Green Loop Trail turning left, but I urge you to desert the blazes and walk straight ahead on an unnamed trail, across a bridge and then up the hill (a total walking distance of about 250 feet) to North Prairie (or, as it was formerly called, Blueheart Prairie). This is the "cat prairie" that first got me hooked on Adams County botanizing and hiking. This is a preserve in the truest sense of the word, a place where plants seldom seen elsewhere in the state are protected in their native setting. Look for big bluestem, Indian grass, a prairie orchid, prairie dock, bluehearts, blazing star, and many more rare species.

Now it's "about face." Turn and go back down the hill, across the bridge, and then up the slope to the previous signpost. A right turn here leads to Elizabeth's Prairie. A special place almost any time of the year, it is named in honor of the late Elizabeth Brockslager, a Cincinnati naturalist and a friend and frequent field companion of University of Cincinnati Professor E. Lucy Braun. It was Dr. Braun who brought this unique habitat to the attention of scientists and did so much to assure its preservation. It was my special privilege to have known both Professor Braun and Elizabeth Brockslager, both very exceptional Ohioans, and I visited Lynx Prairie in their company. In the middle of Elizabeth's Prairie is Annette's Rock, a frequent resting place for Dr. Braun's sister, Annette. This is a block of Peebles dolomite like that which underlies all of these prairie openings and gives them their alkaline soil. This 350-foot-long prairie opening that backs up against the edge of the Appalachian forest is a great place to see butterflies of both forest and field aloft or nectaring. Birders, too, will not be disappointed by a visit to Lynx during avian breeding season. Among other species, the elusive prairie warbler is reported to be heard and seen in the preserve.

Continuing on Green trail, the flora to be seen indicates slightly drier soils with occasional seeps. Hence plants like little bluestem, side-oats, gramma grass, goldenrod, obedient plant, and the rare purple three-awn are found here. The broad-leaved composite prairie dock also does well here where there is a seep or a seasonal wet spot. But, if you really want to walk amidst tall prairie dock, turn left at the next signpost and follow Green Trail for a short way. A detour up this sometimes-muddy trail will make you think you've died and gone to prairie dock heaven.

Now it's back to the last signpost and a left turn onto White Trail. It will soon enter Occidentalis Prairie and introduce you to western sunflower, uncommon in Ohio. Because of the exposure to the open southern sky, many butterflies may be seen puddling, nectaring or breeding here.

Four hundred feet down slope through woods and a small prairie opening brings you to another signpost. White Trail, on which you are now hiking, makes a hard left at this point. However, I suggest that before you make that turn you take a short trail down the slope to the right to visit Liatris Prairie. Here in mid-summer you can face and photograph at eye level butterflies nectaring on sunflower blossoms. Or, if you lean over just a bit, you can find them through your viewfinder on prairie blazing star (*Liatris*).

Now, back on White Loop Trail you will soon enter a young red cedar/oak forest. In the springtime this is a good place to see rue-anemone, and in the summer the rare crested coral-root orchid can be found.

Another 600 feet of trail and a footbridge will take you to a signpost/junction. Turn right here, then less than 100 feet down trail turn right again on to Red Loop Trail. Narrow Prairie, which you will soon enter, features such prairie forbs as rough and scaly blazing stars, western sunflower, and rosinweed. In the spring, the blossoms of the redbud tree that ring this prairie are spectacular.

The prairie where the trail begins turning left, Warbler Prairie, needs no explanation. The uncommon prairie warbler has been seen and heard in this area, but I offer no promises.

In the woodland between prairies, pink lady's slipper orchid blooms near to blazing star, an indication of a change in substrate from alkaline to acid (i.e. from dolomite derived to shale derived).

Annette's Prairie, the southernmost, is known for its angle-pod, a milkweed vine, growing among the prairie grasses and the mountain mint. In the gravelly soil near the distant end of this prairie opening you may see the rare prickly foliaged rock sandwort, a rare small mustard, and the rare wedge-leaf whitlow-grass.

The large rock ledge seen as the trail goes north, before reaching Coneflower Prairie, is a good place to see just how thin the soil of the area is. This ledge is draped with columbine in the spring.

The name of Coneflower Prairie describes the flora of the next opening, a fitting end to a short (1.3 mile) but delightful and educational walk. A right turn at the next signpost will put you on the trail to the parking lot.

Over the past 65 years, I've spent many long days hiking these trails. During my visits at all times of the year I made many pleasing photographs, consuming many canisters of film from the "Great Yellow Father" (Eastman Kodak Company).

You have just walked through a living museum with treasures to be protected and enjoyed. Please collect only by way of camera and memories and leave only footprints!

GREEN MILKWEED

Edge of Appalachia Preserve–The Wilderness Trail

TOTAL DISTANCE: 2.5 miles (4 km)

HIKING TIME: 2 hours

MAXIMUM ELEVATION: 875 feet

VERTICAL RISE: 235 feet

MAPS: USGS 7.5′ Series Lynx; TNC/CMC Edge of Appalachia Preserve brochure

On the east side of Ohio Brush Creek, on the edge of the Appalachian Plateau, The Nature Conservancy and the Cincinnati Museum Center own and manage a magnificent 17,000-plus-acre natural area known as Edge of Appalachia Preserve. It is home to many rare species of plants and animals and some of the finest wilderness scenery in Ohio. Open to the public year-round, it includes a number of trails that lead to the best places to enjoy the unique flora of the cedar glades and prairie openings that are scattered throughout the preserve.

The Wilderness Trail is in an area of the preserve that has long been referred to as "The Wilderness." Use of the name dates back to a visit to the area in September 1961 by the curator emeritus of the Museum of Zoology at The Ohio State University, and nature writer for *The Columbus Dispatch*, in the company of E. Lucy Braun, a noted botanist. After his visit, the curator described the area as a "howling wilderness," and the name stuck.

The boundary of the advance of the Illinoian glacier lies 7 miles northwest of The Wilderness area. To the west, beyond the valley of Ohio Brush Creek, lie the rolling and fertile lands of the Outer Bluegrass Region of the Interior Low Plateau. To the east is the deeply dissected Mississippian-Pittsburgh Plateau of the Appalachian Plateau. The Wilderness lies in a transition zone between these topographies. The bedrock ranges from 450-million-year-old Ordovician to 325-million-year-old Mississippian. In between, massive Silurian-age dolomites are present, forming sharp cliffs and promontories. Soils range from very alkaline to quite acidic. Plants that do well on one or the other or both are found in the preserve.

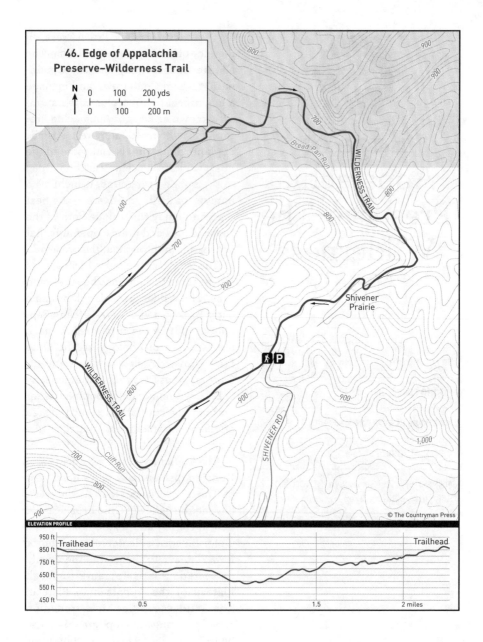

46. Edge of Appalachia
Preserve–Wilderness Trail

GETTING THERE

The village of Lynx and Edge of Appalachia Preserve are located on SR 125 in Adams County. Travel from central Ohio over US 23, US 52, and SR 125 requires a little more than two hours.

The trip on SR 125 from the eastern suburbs of Cincinnati takes slightly more than an hour. Finding the trailhead for The Wilderness Trail is a bit difficult. It is located almost at the end of Shivener Road, about .3 mile north of Lynx Road. Shivener Road runs north from Lynx

Road at the west end of the community. Lynx Road is the "main street" of Lynx and was once SR 125 before a bypass was constructed south of the village.

Follow Shivener Road north past several houses. After it makes a hard left turn it turns equally hard to the right and descends gently; look for a spot on the left that will hold several cars. A cedar post and barbed wire fence mark the lot. The entrance to the trail is to the left of this parking area. Do not go farther on the road, as there is a steep slope ahead.

THE TRAIL

Enter the woods through the opening in the fence located about 20 feet to the left of the parking lot. The trail is marked with 2-inch-by-6-inch yellow blazes painted on trees at slightly above head height. Sometimes they are difficult to see, but they are close enough together that you can usually spot the next one ahead while you stand beside one. Look for them as you walk, and if you fail to see one for more than the usual distance between them, retrace your steps to make certain you have not missed a change in the trail's direction.

With the exception of the cedar glades and prairie openings toward the end of your trek, this is a woodland trail. It is not heavily traveled and has nothing other than the natural surface. The trail is not without poison ivy, and though it has been many years since I have seen one, this is copperhead country—mind where you step. Staff and volunteers try to keep it open and clear of obstacles, but expect an occasional deadfall. If you would like to volunteer to help maintain this and other trails in Edge of Appala-

chia Preserve, call the preserve office at 937-544-2188.

The trail immediately begins dropping into a draw. Follow the blazes to an old road or logging skid on the right-hand slope. After dropping to the creek, the trail begins to climb the right side of the ravine. Occasional red cedar (*Juniperus virginiana*) trees in the deciduous forest indicate that this area was probably cleared early in the last century. These junipers were the first species to invade the area as it began to recover from clearing or pasturing. The hardwoods that followed grew at a faster rate and have now overtopped the evergreens. Because their canopies can no longer get enough light to produce food through their green foliage, they will die, with the needles turning brown. The smaller ones are useful as fenceposts. There is a growing cedar-products industry in the county, using the rot-resistant wood of these tree trunks for such things as birdhouses and feeders.

As you near the end of this ravine, you will see northern white cedar trees (*Thuja occidentalis*), also known as arborvitae, along with the red cedars. This species is considered a relic of a time in the immediate postglacial period when the climate of this part of the world was cooler. The trees still persist in Ohio, mostly in cool ravines with dolomite bedrock such as those found in Adams, Highland, and Greene Counties, in a few other areas of exposed calcareous bedrock, and in fens such as Cedar Bog in Champaign County. Their presence here indicates that you are reaching the top of the Peebles dolomite and will soon see an outcrop of this Silurian-age rock around the side of the hill. Redbud and chinquapin oak, species that also grow on calcium-rich soils, give further

PRAIRIE OPENING AT THE WILDERNESS

evidence of dolomite bedrock not too far beneath the surface. An occasional prairie forb, such as tall coreopsis (*Coreopsis tripteris*), appears along the trail, a vestige of the prairie vegetation that grew on this slope before junipers and hardwoods re-invaded.

The descending trail soon passes through a narrow dolomite cliff edge and past large slump blocks, utilizing an old logging skid. Watch for a double blaze, the traditional way of alerting the hiker to a turn in the trail. At that point, it goes to the right to travel on the level for nearly a half mile, paralleling the broad valley of Ohio Brush Creek. A stand of papaw trees indicates a seepage on the hillside; someone has put short pieces of railroad ties crosswise on the trail to keep feet dry. Tall tuliptrees (*Liriodendron tulipifera*) shade dying red cedars. At a point where, for the first time since entering the trail, you see open grassland to the left, the trail crosses a creek and then turns east to begin its return. Here you will see some yellow pieces of metal, like pieces of venetian blind slats, nailed to the trees alongside the painted blazes. These are markers for Edge of Appalachia Trail, which connects many areas of that preserve. It was laid out by the late Richard Durrell, the University of Cincinnati geology professor whose dream and perseverance brought "the Edge" into being.

The ravine the trail now enters is the site of a long-established trail in The Wilderness. The stream is Bread Pan Run, and it tumbles over some beautiful falls and through some small gorges as it drains the hills to the east. The yellow-blazed Wilderness Trail climbs the left side of the valley at an angle before joining an earlier trail blazed with orange metal markers. This is Knob Trail, a favorite of mine and of many other naturalists for decades. To the left on the orange-blazed trail is a high promontory known as The Knob; it's worth a side trip if you can still discern the trail.

Following the yellow paint blazes to the right, The Wilderness Trail winds its way up the ravine. As you rise in elevation, the dolomite that had been an outcrop on the hillside above on the left becomes the rock of the gorge through which the stream runs on the right. Arborvitae grows in this lush, cool environment, and the rare sullivantia (*Sullivantia sullivantii*) grows on the pockmarked face of the Peebles dolomite in the gorge. The distribution of this plant is very limited and spotty; it's found only south of and near the glacial border in Ohio, Indiana, and northern Kentucky. In springtime such wildflowers as large-flowered trillium (*Trillium grandiflorum*) and yellow lady's slipper (*Cypripedium calceolus*) can be found nearby. Soon the trail reaches two small bridges only a short distance apart. In May the columbine (*Aquilegia canadensis*) that clings to a large slump block to the left of the trail attracts ruby-throated

YELLOW LADY'S SLIPPER LOOKS DOWN ON THE WILDERNESS TRAIL

hummingbirds (*Archilochus colubris*) to sip its sweet nectar.

Now the trail ascends the creek valley along the right bank. The uncommon green violet (*Hybanthus concolor*) and four-leaved milkweed (*Asclepias quadrifolia*) grow along this trail. Two hundred feet up the ravine the trail climbs to the right on a switchback to emerge on a prairie opening known as Shivener, for the family who occupied this land for several generations. Interestingly, the late Charles Shivener recalled this hillside prairie at one time being a hillside corn patch. Abandoned crop fields on the thin soil over dolomite take only a few years to revert to prairie. By the same token, it does not take long for red cedar to invade the prairie, in due time to be followed by hardwoods. Maintaining the diversity of habitat that makes Edge of Appalachia Preserve so unique requires careful management. In the case of the prairie openings, this involves periodic prescribed burning and some removal of woody plants by hand.

The sights and sounds of Shivener Prairie through the seasons are something to behold. Big bluestem (*Andropogon gerardii*), sideoats grama grass (*Bouteloua curtipendula*), whorled rosinweed (*Silphium trifoliatum*), dense blazing star (*Liatris spicata*), hoary puccoon (*Lithospermum canescens*), false aloe (*Agave virginica*), Indian paint-

TINY SHRUB, THE RARE CAMBY'S MOUNTAIN LOVER

brush (*Castilleja spp.*), oxeye (*Heliopsis helianthoides*), Seneca snakeroot (*Polygala senega*), lyre-leaved sage (*Salvia lyrata*), and yellow star grass (*Hypoxis hirsuta*) are just a taste of what is in store for hikers as they pass through the prairie. In late April and May and then again in July and August, you might want to carry an SLR camera with a 90–105 millimeter macro lens to let you capture the blossoms and butterflies of this special natural garden. In spring the prairie warbler (*Dendroica discolor*) can be heard singing its scale-like song from the tops of red cedar trees.

When the trail is about to turn left and leave the prairie, there is a short dead-end trail to the left that leads to the best area for Indian paintbrush. If you are traveling the trail in May, don't miss this spot. I often have seen pipevine swallowtail (*Battus philenor*) butterflies nectaring on this striking prairie wildflower. Like the poinsettia (a member of the euphorbia family) of the holiday season, the Indian paintbrush (a member of the snapdragon family) owes its appearance of having a bright scarlet bloom not

to flower petals but to a splash of red on the tips of the bracts. When the butterfly seeks nectar from this plant, it must extend its proboscis deep into the top of the blossom to reach the nectaries on the inconspicuous flower hidden below.

Following the trail uphill means leaving the thin, dry alkaline soils of the prairie behind and entering the woodland with its acidic soils derived from the underlying Ohio black shale. It's a different world. Chinquapin oaks (*Quercus muehlenbergii*) are replaced by chestnut oaks (*Quercus montana*). Yellow lady's slippers give way to the pink (*Cypripedium acaule*) ones. The obligate calciphiles (plants that must have alkaline soils to grow) disappear. Virginia pines (*Pinus virginiana*) are the pioneer tree species now.

A short way up the slope, the trail turns sharply to the left to exit the woods onto the Shivener homestead grounds. The house and most outbuildings have been removed, but one building used for educational purposes and latrines remains. To reach your car, walk up the hill on the road to the parking area.

Fort Hill Earthworks and Nature Preserve— Fort and Gorge Trails

TOTAL DISTANCE: 1.4 and 3.1 miles (2.5 km and 5 km)

HIKING TIME: 4 hours

MAXIMUM ELEVATION: 1,290 feet

VERTICAL RISE: 470 feet

MAPS: USGS 7.5' Sinking Spring; Arc of Appalachia Fort Hill brochure

Fort Hill State Memorial, located off OH 41 in Highland County about a dozen miles south of Bainbridge, contains a prehistoric Native American hilltop enclosure that is one of the best preserved archaeological sites in Ohio. Equally important is the natural history of the area, with its rock outcrops and its great variety of plant and animal life. This tract of land is a piece of wilderness in the true sense of the word, an area not profoundly affected by human use. More than 10 miles of well-marked nature trails enable you to reach nearly all parts of the memorial. Deer Trail is the most rugged, taking you up and down the slopes, past most of the seven major plant communities identified there by the late E. Lucy Braun in her 1969 treatise, *An Ecological Survey of the Vegetation of Fort Hill State Memorial, Highland County, Ohio, and Annotated List of Vascular Plants.*

The presence of this ancient "fort" on this high hill in southwestern Ohio has been known by archaeologists for more than 150 years. John Locke wrote about it in 1838 in the *Second Annual Report on the Geological Survey of the State of Ohio.* The often-referenced *Ancient Monuments of the Mississippi Valley,* written by Squire and Davis in 1848, contained a detailed map of the 48-acre enclosure. No wonder, then, that when the opportunity arose in 1932 the state sought to protect it by purchasing a key 237-acre parcel. A plaque at the end of the parking lot provides some insight into how this site was acquired. It reads, "In memory of Morton Carlisle, 1869–1947, of Cincinnati, Ohio, whose vision, zeal, and generosity were largely responsible for the establishment of Fort Hill State Memorial." Individuals do make a difference. Additional purchases have enlarged it to 1,200 acres.

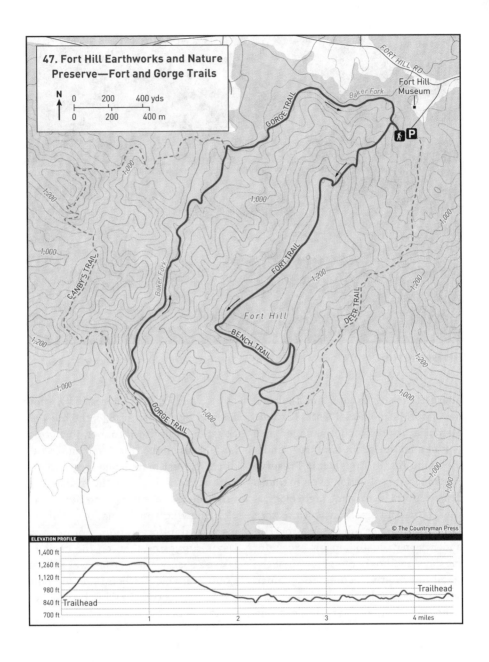

47. Fort Hill Earthworks and Nature Preserve—Fort and Gorge Trails

N

| 0 | 200 | 400 yds |
| 0 | 200 | 400 m |

Fort Hill Museum

GORGE TRAIL

Baker Fork

FORT HILL RD.

1,000

1,200

CANBY'S TRAIL

Baker Fork

FORT TRAIL

Fort Hill

BENCH TRAIL

DEER TRAIL

GORGE TRAIL

1,200

1,000

© The Countryman Press

ELEVATION PROFILE

1,400 ft				
1,260 ft				
1,120 ft				
980 ft				Trailhead
840 ft	Trailhead			
700 ft	1	2	3	4 miles

The Depression-era Civilian Conservation Corps did much of the development work to open the area to the public. A monument near the museum reads, "In memory of the boys who served in Company 1505 Civilian Conservation Corps, Fort Hill, 1933–34." According to the records compiled by the Civilian Conservation Corps Alumni Association, this was an African American company. They came by train to Peebles and were trucked to the worksite and camp at Fort Hill. The small museum at the site was built in 1968 to provide

THE RARE SULLIVANTIA

interpretation of the natural and cultural history of the memorial. Fort Hill State Memorial is now being managed as a unit of a not-for-profit land trust under the name Arc of Appalachia Preserve System. It is a collection of more than a dozen natural history and archeological sites, large and small, in southwestern Ohio. Few changes will occur at Fort Hill under the new custodianship except for the days and hours of operation of the small interpretive center. Some much needed changes have been made to the route and amenities (steps, bridges, and boardwalk) of the trail under the leadership of Bob Glotzhober, longtime though recently retired Ohio Historical Society naturalist. Thanks, Bob.

Though the builders of the earthwork have not been clearly identified, it is presumed that the work was done by the Native Americans of the Hopewell culture that inhabited Ohio between 300 B.C. and A.D. 600. Interestingly, when Locke visited here in 1838, the hill was covered with virgin timber, including large trees on the "fort" wall and in the ditch. He estimated one large chestnut on the wall and a 7-foot-diameter tuliptree in the ditch to be 600 years old. Allowing some time for abandonment and reforestation, Squire and Davis suggested that, on the basis of Locke's observation, the fort was at least 1,000 years old. Carbon-14 dating puts the Hopewell time in Ohio back about twice that far.

The unusual natural history of this tract of land has a number of causes. First, the geology here is uncommon: a hill of carboniferous shale with a sandstone cap and a dolomite base, which makes for acidic soils on the hillside and alkaline soils in the stream valley. Also, the area's proximity to the edge of the advancing glaciers seemingly left it rich in flora. More than 650 species of vascular plants have been found at Fort Hill. The size of the tract and the age of the trees apparently affect the number of bird species that use it for nesting—particularly the neotropical species that come north only to breed. Hiking at Fort Hill is like walking the pages of an ecology text.

This is not a hike for a hot and humid summer day, but rather a great one for spring or fall. The trails are open 8:00 a.m. to 8:00 p.m. daily, year-round. The museum was renovated in the mid-1990s as a part of the Ohio Historical Society's "Gateway Initiative." Picnic facilities, drinking water, and restrooms are available during the warm months of the year.

GETTING THERE

From Columbus, travel south on US 23. At Chillicothe, take US 50 west (right) through Bainbridge, after which you make a left turn onto OH 41 south. Turn right onto Fort Hill Road and travel to the memorial entrance. The best route from Cincinnati is US 32 east to OH 41. Turn left (north) onto OH 41 and travel to Fort Hill Road on the left, which leads to the memorial entrance.

THE TRAIL

This trail is for the hardy hiker. It has the greatest vertical rise of any hike in this book, 430 feet, and all of it occurs in the first half mile. This is a "semi-wilderness nature preserve." The hiker should carry a map and a good compass and know how to use both. There are places where the trail can be wet and very slippery, and some sections are quite primitive. A good hiking staff or a pair of trekking poles will serve you well. Extensive repair and upgrading was performed on Gorge Trail during 2005–2006. Allow at least 45 minutes per mile of trail. There is adequate, but limited, signing and blazing. Fort Trail has no paint blazes; the blazes on Gorge Trail are yellow. Buckeye Trail—marked with blue paint blazes—and North Country Trail and American Discovery Trail—identified with distinctive symbols—pass through this area, using mostly Deer Trail but overlapping Gorge Trail in two places. To avoid becoming lost, stay on the trails and read all posted maps and signs carefully. Enjoy.

This hike begins on Fort Trail, departing from a trailhead kiosk on the right side of the parking lot farthest from the entrance. You start with a turn to the right but quickly turn left to begin a 400-plus-foot ascent to the top of Fort Hill. Using switchbacks, the trail essentially goes directly up the hill. At one point it passes between the wind-thrown root balls of two large trees, exposing the shaley soil.

Fort Hill is very interesting geologically. The bedrock below the surface on the top of the hill is Berea sandstone of the Upper Devonian period. This is a gray compact rock composed of quartz grains firmly cemented by a small amount of clay. In most places in Ohio it is only 10 to 40 feet thick, but where it is still mined at South Amherst in Loraine County it's more than 200 feet thick. Because of its resistance to weathering, the slope of the hillside is steep at the level of the Berea rock. Directly below is the noncalcareous Bedford shale, also of the Devonian, and fairly resistant to weathering, especially when protected by the sandstone. The remainder of the hillside down to the parking lot is

MAIDENHAIR FERN FRONDS

underlined by Ohio black shale, perhaps as much as 300 feet thick. There is a bench on the hillside at the top of this carboniferous shale.

This bare-ground trail up the hillside can be slippery when wet. The northeast-facing slope hosts a typical mixed mesophytic forest. You will know when you are close to the top, as the trail passes through the fort wall, conveniently pointed out by a sign. An old sign at the top reads, VIEWPOINT OVERLOOKING BAKER FORK AND THE BEECH FLATS AREA NORTHWEST OF FORT HILL. You will want to rest and take in the view of the countryside to the north. From here, the trail goes south-southwest on the nearly level hilltop, paralleling the fort wall. The forest here is dominated by several

species of oak, hickories, sugar maple, and tuliptrees, with papaw prominent in the understory. The area has certainly been timbered at least once. The trees growing on the fort wall probably better reflect the pre-Columbian forest composition.

Somewhere on the top of the hill would be a good place to pause and contemplate what this area must have been like at the height of its use by Native Americans. Was it really a fort? Was there a village here? Was it only a place of worship or burial? Perhaps it was used for different purposes at different times of year or in different eras. Were there trees here then? How long did it take to construct the wall? Can you still hear the voices of the occupants here praying, mourning, gossiping, fighting, or just trying to keep warm on a cold winter's night? Let your imagination run wild.

After a half mile, Fort Trail turns left to travel around the hilltop and return to the parking lot via the incoming route. To continue this 4.5-mile hike, at the southwest corner of the hilltop go straight ahead down a rugged trail, passing through the fort wall. You will lose about 90 feet of elevation before reaching what looks like a service road where the trail makes a sharp left turn. Some old maps called this Bench Trail and, in fact, it does run on a natural bench atop Ohio black shale. The rare wild pink grows in this area. This trail continues southeast on the bench for about 1,500 feet, then it makes a wide left turn toward the north and travels another 500 feet. Here a trail joins from the right rear. This is the yellow-blazed Gorge Trail, and a service road. A 6-by-6 post identifies the trails with abbreviations and provides the distances to destinations such as picnic areas. Make a hard right turn and follow Gorge Trail downhill as it switches right, then left, before reaching another intersection. Deer Trail goes straight ahead on the same roadbed as Gorge Trail, and to the right to return to the parking lot. The latter is the last easy escape route if you want to cut short your hike. It's a slow, steady 1.25-mile drop from here to the parking area. In spring, the woodlands along this trail are full of Canada violets.

To enjoy the beauty that awaits you in Baker Fork Gorge choose the trail to the right, the combined Deer and Gorge Trails. The forest on this southwest-facing slope is chestnut oak. After a gentle downhill trek of less than a half mile, there is another intersection. The trail straight ahead is the combined Buckeye, American Discovery, and North Country Trail heading out of the Fort Hill property. The trail to the right, the one you want to take, is the combined Gorge Trail, Deer Trail, BT, ADT, and NCT. A signpost indicates that you have 3 miles to go on Gorge Trail before arriving back at the parking lot.

At this point, the trail has arrived at the bottom of the hillside underlain by Ohio black shale. Below you is the gorge of Baker Fork. It was created when the ponded waters of a former north-flowing stream, trapped by the advance from the north of the Illinoian ice sheet, found a new outlet to the sea by entrenching the massive Silurian-age Peebles dolomite bedrock.

A hard right turn is the beginning of a new adventure. The trail enters the ravine of Spring Creek, which it crosses on a short bridge. Look to the right to see a small natural rock bridge. A large beech that lost its top to a windstorm is a source of food for the local pileated woodpeckers: near the base you'll find a rectangular hole made by one of these denizens of the deep forest seeking carpenter ants. Across the creek is the first of many water-shaped dolomite cliffs of Baker Fork Gorge. In a very short time the trail reaches the main stem of Baker Fork. There it turns on itself to the right to climb a set of wooden steps. Next is a short but difficult section that clings to the hillside near the mouth of Sulfur Creek. Walking fern nearly covers a dolomite slump block. There is fragrant sumac in the shrub layer, and on the cliff face above the stream grows *Sullivantia sullivantii*, the rare member of the saxifrage family named after the Ohio botanist William Starling Sullivant of Columbus, who first collected it in the gorges of Highland County in 1839. Another set of stairs carries the hiker up a steep slope and away from the mouth of Sulfur Creek.

Where the trail drops to the floodplain, a post announces Deer Trail's departure to the left, along with its traveling companions, the Buckeye Trail, American Discovery Trail, and North Country Trail. These combined trails cross the creek, gain about 25 feet in elevation, then turn right to cross over Keyhole Bridge. If you look carefully, you can see the natural arch from Gorge Trail just after you pass the junction. Beyond there, the trail works its way up the hillside to a set of steps where a post announces that you have come 2 miles and have 2 miles yet to go—in short, the middle of Gorge Trail.

A 20-foot bridge carries the trail across the creek flowing from Beech Ravine. When I scouted the trail in August 2006, the hillside past there was full of mid-summer flowers, including both species of jewelweed blooming side by side. A wood frog crossing the trail in front of my feet made my day. The trail moves away from the stream and up the hillside, then returns to near the water's edge. A huge dolomite slump block lies along the creek and the trail slips between it and a rock wall. Just beyond where the trail crosses Shelter Creek on a short bridge, it hugs the side of a cliff before climbing 45 steps to a knob where you can take a dozen steps on a "wild" side trail to look directly down at Baker Fork. The floodplain widens out and sycamores, basswood, beech, and papaws reclaim the old streamside pasture.

A short way up the trail sits a wide-open cabin with benches inside where a hiker could retreat from a short rain shower or snack on an energy bar. Though the trail runs beside the cabin, it looks like most hikers actually include the cabin on the trail, going in one door and out the other. A 12-foot bridge carries the trail over Sunset Creek. Signs along the trail heading north from the cabin indicate that Deer Trail, BT, ADT, and NCT are coming in from the left to again join Gorge Trail. The distance to the area and trailhead is shown as 1 mile. The combined trails turn right and then cross a 12-foot bridge, heading east. The trail still clings to the hillside, now in an area of open woods. In one place a section of boardwalk traverses a seepage area. A 30-foot bridge with a single rail carries the trail over a deep ravine. Now dropping to run along the stream, the trail includes a section of about 30 feet that has recently been rerouted to avoid a wet area. Ahead are three sets of four steps with some boardwalk between them. The trail leaves the tall trees and crosses some A-frame bridges and a mowed area. On a post near the edge of the parking lot there is a Buckeye Trail blue blaze and the emblems for the ADT and NCT, and in the distance the trailhead kiosk where the trail began.

The Magnificent Chestnut

The American chestnut (*Castanea dentata*), a large, rough-barked tree that sometimes grew to 100 feet tall and 10 feet in diameter, was once a dominant tree of the mixed oak forest of the dry sandstone ridges and knobs of eastern Ohio, in the Allegheny Plateau. This magnificent nut-bearing tree is virtually gone from its original North American range, the victim of a blight caused by an imported fungus, *Cryphonectria parasitica*. Introduced on Chinese chestnut, it was first reported in New York in 1904. It spread so fast among native trees that had no resistance to the fungus that by the middle of the twentieth century the American chestnut was virtually gone. Many of the shelter houses built in the state parks and forests in southeastern Ohio by the Civilian Conservation Corps during the 1930s were made of chestnut planks cut from salvaged victims of the blight. The search for a blight-resistant American chestnut or hybrid American/Chinese or Japanese chestnut continues to this day. Look for chestnut stumps on your walks; you may be lucky enough to find one with a few live sprouts.

48

Glen Helen Nature Preserve

TOTAL DISTANCE: 3, 5, or 10 miles (4.8, 8, or 16 km)

HIKING TIME: 2 hours

MAXIMUM ELEVATION: 1,003 feet

VERTICAL RISE: 133 feet

MAPS: USGS 7.5' Clifton; USGS 7.5 Yellow Springs; GHA Glen Helen trail map

Antioch University's Glen Helen Nature Preserve has been described as one of Ohio's best-kept secrets. Its 26 miles of foot trails take the hiker past waterfalls, a national- and state-designated Scenic River, beautiful Silurian-age limestone and dolomite cliffs, a National Natural Landmark woods, a 75-year-old pine forest, and the bountiful spring from which the nearby village of Yellow Springs got its name. Numbered posts on many of the Glen's trails are keyed to *A Guide to the Historical Sites in Glen Helen*, generally available at the Glen Helen Building or at Trailside Museum. A map can be purchased at the museum, which also has the only restrooms and drinking water in the glen.

Glen Helen was given to Antioch College in 1929 by Hugh Taylor Birch, as a living memorial to his daughter, Helen Birch Bartlett. More land has since been added. Thanks to recent acquisitions by the Glen Helen Association (a "friends" group) of adjacent Girl Scout Camp Greene and the Barbara and David Case Woods property, the total acreage of Glen Helen is now near 1,080. Antioch College recently placed modern conservation easements on the entire preserve, giving it permanent protection. These easements are held by the local Tecumseh Land Trust. Glen Helen was also incorporated into the village of Yellow Springs, so in the event of an emergency a 911 call will elicit aid. Beginning in 1969, local Boy Scout Troop 78 managed Glen Helen Scout Hiking Trail in the preserve, one of the few such trails in the state located entirely off-road. Over the years, thousands of Scouts and their leaders walked the trail, earning an attractive commemorative patch and spending a day in the woods, many for the first time ever. Though that opportunity may no longer be available, the

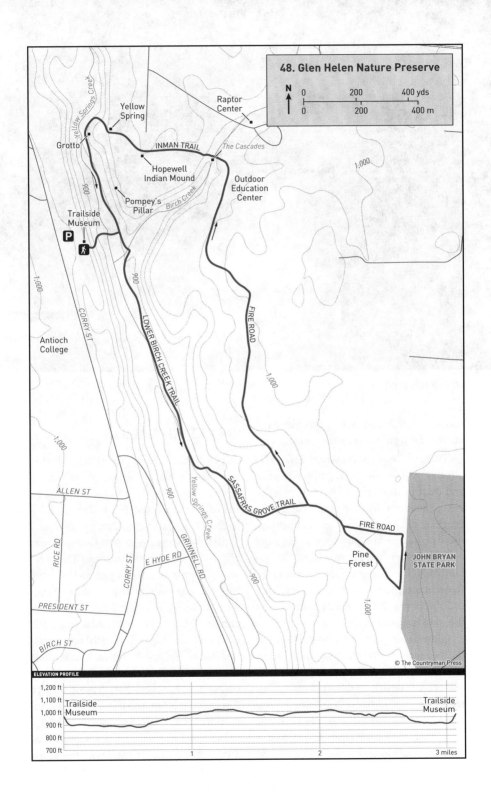

48. Glen Helen Nature Preserve

N

| 0 | 200 | 400 yds |
| 0 | 200 | 400 m |

Raptor Center

Yellow Spring

Grotto

INMAN TRAIL

The Cascades

Hopewell Indian Mound

Outdoor Education Center

Pompey's Pillar

Birch Creek

Trailside Museum

P

LOWER BIRCH CREEK TRAIL

Yellow Springs Creek

FIRE ROAD

Antioch College

CORRY ST

SASSAFRAS GROVE TRAIL

FIRE ROAD

ALLEN ST

RICE RD

CORRY ST

E HYDE RD

GRINNELL RD

Pine Forest

JOHN BRYAN STATE PARK

PRESIDENT ST

BIRCH ST

© The Countryman Press

ELEVATION PROFILE

1,200 ft			
1,100 ft	Trailside Museum		Trailside Museum
1,000 ft			
900 ft			
800 ft			
700 ft	1	2	3 miles

THE CASCADES AT GLEN HELEN

trails of Glen Helen are open to anyone during daylight hours year-round.

Trailside Museum is where folks hiking the trails of the glen generally park and begin their trek. To help defray the cost of keeping the area open to the public, there may be a small fee for parking. As the glen is not a park but a privately owned nature preserve, there are no facilities for camping or picnicking. Accommodations for both are available in John Bryan State Park, which adjoins the glen to the east.

Glen Helen is especially well known for its nearly continuous show of native wildflowers. Each season offers a new collage of nature. Hike and enjoy the trails of this natural treasure often. From 1973 to 1990, I was the director of Glen Helen and I never missed a chance to explore the natural world at my very doorstep. What a special privilege it was.

GETTING THERE

Begin hiking the trails at Glen Helen from Trailside Museum, off the main Glen Helen parking lot on Corry Street, in Yellow Springs. (The Vernet Ecological Center at 405 Corry Street and Trailside Museum at 505 Corry Street share the same parking area.) The sidewalk directly in front of you on the drive into the parking lot takes you to Trailside Museum. To reach Glen Helen from central Ohio, travel I-70 west to US 68, the 52A exit. Turn left (south) and travel 8 miles to Yellow Springs. Make a left turn at Corry Street, the northernmost traffic light in town, then drive .6 mile to the parking lot on the left. From the Cincinnati area, travel I-75 north to I-675, then take I-675 east toward Columbus. Turn right (east) at the Dayton–Yellow Springs Road exit and go 6 miles into Yellow Springs. The third traffic light after entering the village is at Corry Street. Turn right, go one block to cross US 68, then travel .6 mile farther on Corry Street to the parking lot on the left. You may be asked to pay a small parking fee. Unfortunately the trails are not handicapped accessible.

THE TRAIL

The trail begins on the Inman Terrace outside the museum, where a recently restored native stone stairway leads to a bridge across Yellow Springs Creek. Be cautious as you descend; the native stone steps are worn and have shifted over their 75 years of use. At the bottom of the steps a section of plastic boardwalk carries the trail to a span across the stream. The trail reaches a T 100 feet below. I suggest that you turn right and walk to the stepping-stone that will carry you across Birch Creek. Once on the far bank, turn right again and follow the trail paralleling the east bank of Yellow Springs Creek for a half mile. Along the way it will move close to or away from the stream, but it always stays within hearing distance of the babbling water.

After about 1,000 feet you will see a trail leading toward the water and a set of stepping-stones crossing the creek. These lead to the south end of Talus Trail. At the same point, a trail to the left goes away from the stream to Traveler's Spring. In April, detour up this trail to see marsh marigolds in bloom in that wet area. To continue the hike detailed here, keep on the trail headed south. Soon you will pass another trail leaving from the left that also goes to the spring. Ignore it and travel another 1,500 feet to where you pass two steel posts that for many years supported a swinging bridge. Just beyond there, the trail turns left and then quickly right before splitting. The right fork continues downstream and the left fork heads uphill obliquely.

Take the heavily used left fork as it scrambles over rocks and gullies, then winds its way uphill at a gentle gradient. After about 200 feet, the trail arrives at the northwest corner of a large conifer plantation known as Pine Forest. It's a bit of a misnomer, since it also includes Norway spruce trees. They were all planted in 1926 when this area of Glen Helen was part of John Bryan's Riverside Farm, which had just been given to the state. Hugh Taylor Birch worked a land swap to acquire it for the Glen. It's a place with a magical quality all its own. This is especially true of the white pine area directly up the trail into the plantation from the southwest corner. Experience the feeling for yourself by following the trail through the plantation to where it comes out on a fire lane road along the east boundary of the property.

Out of Pine Forest, turn left and follow the fire lane along the east and north edges of the conifers. Continue down the trail that you came out on, except this time make a right turn after 60 feet. Follow this lane—actually a segment of the old Yellow Springs–Clifton stagecoach road—for almost a mile as it twists and turns toward the Glen Helen Outdoor Education Center (OEC). This was pastureland when the glen was acquired. Here and there in the forest to either side of the road you will see dead or dying red-cedar trees. These were the first trees to invade the old fields after grazing was halted, but they are now overtopped by the hardwoods. You will also see Osage orange trees that were originally planted as living fences. Students at the OEC have adopted one as a climbing tree. Turn left after the fire lane passes a cable gate and an old stone bridge. This short trail leads to the bridge above the Cascades on Birch Creek. The view from below, looking upstream at the Cascades, is the most picturesque and best-known scene in Glen Helen. A photograph of the Cascades graced the cover of the second edition of this book.

The OEC lies to the right of the fire lane, opposite the entrance to the trail to the Cascades. It is the location of the glen's year-round school camp program and in summer hosts Ecocamp, a natural history-oriented camp for youngsters of all ages. At the Glen Helen Raptor Center, located at the OEC, ill, orphaned, and injured birds of prey are treated in an effort to return them to the Ohio sky. To visit the Raptor Center, go straight ahead on the fire lane instead of turning toward the Cascades Bridge.

Birch Creek marks the eastern edge of the 250-acre National Natural Landmark section of the glen. At the west end of the Cascades Bridge, enter the woods on the middle trail directly ahead. Soon you will pass Helen's Stone, which bears a poem written by the glen's namesake. Directly south of here, but not visible, is the site of an 1826 Owenite settlement. In quick succession, the trail passes a Hopewell Indian mound; a kiosk telling the story of a white oak that fell nearby; the site of the late-eighteenth-century Neff House resort hotel; the spot where in 1803 pioneer Lewis Davis built the first

THE YELLOW SPRING AT GLEN HELEN

SNOW TRILLIUM ABOVE CLIFFS AT GLEN HELEN

cabin in the area; and, last, the famous spring from which the village gets its name. Flowing year-round at 52 degrees and 70 gallons per minute, the spring is not really yellow but rust-colored from iron impurities in the bedrock through which the water travels before reaching the surface. Neither this nor any other spring in Glen Helen is approved as a source of public drinking water.

Beyond the human-landscaped spring is Bone Cave, a small cavern that can hold a dozen or more schoolchildren all scrunched together. The trail arcs downhill to the left. On the right are the ruins of a dam that at one time impounded Yellow Springs Creek. There was a dance hall overlooking the lake's upper end. Can you picture people traveling to Neff Park by interurban to fish, boat, ice-skate, promenade alongside the lake, or just dance the night away? Just beyond on the left is the Grotto, where the water from the springs falls into a man-made pool before running to the creek. The water deposits some dissolved limestone as it tumbles over the falls, causing the lip of the falls to build out like a tongue rather

than be eroded back as most falls are. Next is an area where you can see some of the 10,000 years of tufa deposits that have created the travertine mound on the slope below the spring.

A walk through the forest is a walk among giants, specifically the three or four giant bur oak trees that have been growing on this floodplain since the time when Native Americans were the area's only inhabitants. Pileated woodpeckers have nested in this area for many years. The spring flora in this rich river bottom is as good as it gets. Spicebush forms a solid shrub layer and such trees as wafer ash, blue ash, papaw, redbud, and bladdernut occupy the understory. On the hillside to the left a tall tower-like slump block called Pompey's Pillar has been creeping downhill away from the cliffs for centuries. From this point, a boardwalk will carry you across the frequently flooded valley floor to the bridge below Trailside and your climb to the parking lot. Stop to smell a crushed leaf of the fragrant sumacs outside of Trailside, and make sure your hiking shoes are clean before heading home.

49

Miami Whitewater Forest

DISTANCE: Three trails totaling 3.6 miles (5.8 km)

HIKING TIME: 3 hours

MAXIMUM ELEVATION: 715

VERTICAL RISE: 215

MAPS: USGS 7.5′ Harrison

ACCESSIBILITY: Access to any trail described here would be difficult to impossible for the physically challenged.

FACILITIES: Restrooms, drinking water, golf course, bridle trails, ball fields, bird museum, visitor center, boating, and fishing.

Miami Whitewater Forest, at 3,639 acres, is the largest of the regional natural area parks of the Hamilton County Park District. Land purchases for the park, the third in the system, began in 1948, and an 85-acre lake was completed on the site in 1971.

The topography of the area varies from flat, glacial outwash plain to very hilly. The Kansan and Illinoian glaciers reached into the area, but the principal visible effects came from the Wisconsinan Glacier, whose advance halted a few miles to the north. Meltwater from that ice sheet cut valleys and deposited outwash in them. The park, most of it upland, is situated between the valleys of the present-day Great Miami and Whitewater Rivers, hence its name.

Underlain by Ordovician limestone and shales, the soils support rich, mixed mesophytic woodlands. The park district manages the area to provide a great diversity of habitat and is presently working to establish a 100-acre wetland, a 750-acre prairie, and a wetland/prairie native plant seed nursery.

The avifauna of the area is rich and diverse. The park is considered one of Ohio's best areas for birds of prey.

Miami Whitewater Forest provides a wide variety of recreational opportunities for the residents of southwestern Ohio. Among these are three fine hiking trails: the 1.5 mile-long Badlands Trail of challenging difficulty, the 1.25-mile-long Oakleaf Trail of moderate difficulty, and the .6-mile-long easy hike on Tallgrass Prairie Trail. Singly or as a package, these trails provide fine hiking in a natural setting.

As with all parks in the Hamilton County Park District, visitors must either have an annual vehicle parking pass or purchase a daily permit to enter the area.

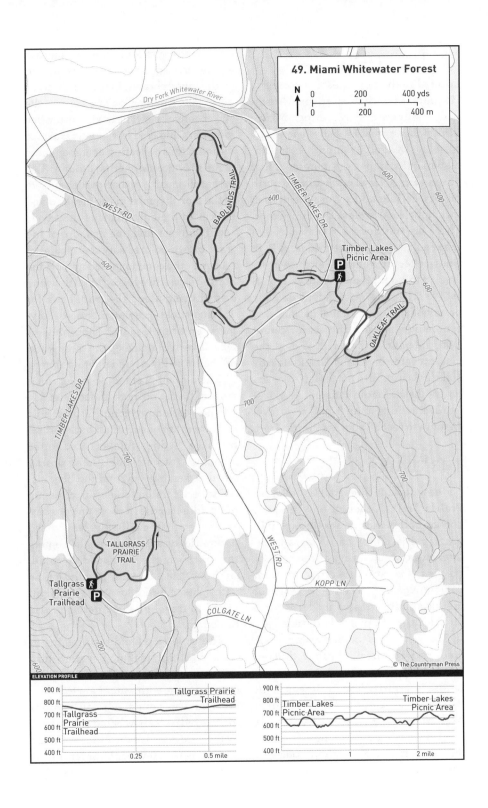

49. Miami Whitewater Forest

N

| 0 | 200 | 400 yds |
| 0 | 200 | 400 m |

Dry Fork Whitewater River

WEST RD

BADLANDS TRAIL

TIMBER LAKES DR.

600

600

600

Timber Lakes
Picnic Area

P

OAK LEAF TRAIL

600

700

TIMBER LAKES DR.

700

700

WEST RD

700

TALLGRASS
PRAIRIE
TRAIL

Tallgrass
Prairie
Trailhead

P

KOPP LN

COLGATE LN

600

700

© The Countryman Press

ELEVATION PROFILE

	Tallgrass Prairie
900 ft	Trailhead
800 ft	
700 ft	Tallgrass
600 ft	Prairie
500 ft	Trailhead
400 ft	

0.25   0.5 mile

	Timber Lakes
900 ft	Picnic Area
800 ft	Timber Lakes
700 ft	Picnic Area
600 ft	
500 ft	
400 ft	

1   2 mile

GETTING THERE

Located in the northwestern corner of Hamilton County in Harrison, Crosby, and Whitewater townships, Miami Whitewater Forest is easily reached by traveling west on I-74 from I-75 in Cincinnati or from the 1-275 outerbelt. Exit I-74 via Exit 3, Dry Fork Road. Go north on Dry Fork Road to West Road, then turn right (east) to cross Dry Fork Creek. There are entrances on both sides of the road just east of the bridge. A Park District Motor Vehicle Permit will be needed to enter Miami Whitewater Forest Park. The charge is $3 for a one-day permit or $10 for an annual permit. One can be purchased at the visitor center near the park entrance or, should the visitor center be closed, at the nearby golf clubhouse. Turn north (left) to reach the trailheads for the Badlands and Oakleaf Trails. Turn south (right) and travel 1.1 miles to reach Tallgrass Prairie Trail.

THE TRAIL

The easiest of the three trails is Tallgrass Prairie Trail. Although only a small portion of this trail passes through tallgrass prairie, it provides a pleasant and interesting walk during any season of the year. It is especially attractive from July through frost, when a procession of tallgrass prairie grasses and forbs come into bloom in the planted prairie area.

The trail passes through young woodland, mature forest, shrubby thicket, old field-type meadow, and planted tallgrass prairie. The trailhead sign illustrates some of the small creatures likely to inhabit this diverse habitat, but don't expect to see any of the marvelous miniature mammals of the woods and grasslands, for virtually all move about during the hours of darkness when park visitors have gone home. Focus instead on the invertebrates. In the sunny areas during the summer, look for some of the six species of swallowtail butterflies found in Ohio, and in the fall watch for the monarchs collecting nectar en route to their Mexican wintering ground. Also in the fall, look for golden garden spiders in the morning mist in the meadow and prairie. In the light shade of the woods see if you can find one or more of the three brown-colored satyr butterflies of the area—the common wood nymph, the northern pearly eye, or the little wood satyr flitting along the trail. Look for walking sticks, praying mantises, ladybugs, and much more. Thousands of Ohio invertebrates keep the same working hours as hikers and photographers. This is a good place to begin learning more of them and more about them.

The yearlong resident birds of this trail are those of suburban backyards—birds of hedge, thicket, and open meadow: towhee, goldfinch, downy woodpecker, blue jay, and the like. Listen for the familiar cheer-up, cheer-up of a cardinal and let it cheer up your day.

The trail immediately leaves the parking lot on a grassy path, then enters the woods on gravel, headed downhill. At about 75 feet from the parking lot the path splits to form a loop. Head straight ahead to travel in a counterclockwise direction.

The wide woodland trail begins to drop, eventually making a gentle S-turn as it crosses a draw and heads uphill on crushed stone with water bars to retard erosion. The young regrowth woods include red cedar now being overtopped by the hardwoods, indicating that cedar is an early field invader after farming is halted. Like much of southwestern Ohio, the shrub layer here contains the alien bush honeysuckle, and garlic-mustard is abundant in the herbaceous layer.

A trail sign announces your arrival at the planted tallgrass prairie for which the trail is named. The sign tells of the loss of Ohio's original prairie and of naturalists' attempts to reconstruct this once-important ecosystem. This prairie is said to contain at least 150 species of prairie grasses and forbs and a smaller number of the animals indigenous to the prairie.

Enter the magic of the prairie environment. It was early morning on a mid-August day when I explored this trail. The flowers were simply gorgeous: here and there a goldfinch bounced in and out to steal a seed for vegetarian energy. Dew was still on the purple coneflowers and, as the sun hit a tall blazing star, a tiger swallowtail was close behind. Cordgrass stood tall along the trail in the lower, swale-like area, but for most of the reach of the trail through the prairie, big bluestem was hanging over the path. At my feet, yellow partridge pea bloomed, and the drying pods of prairie false-indigo stood out across the landscape. The ambrosia-like aroma of milkweed blossoms was in the air. The 180 millimeter APO macro lens on my camera helped me capture on film close-up vignettes of the prairie plants and the incredible six-legged creatures with which they evolved. A slide of a tall coreopsis blossom examined later showed a crab spider virtually the same color as the flower petals lying in wait for an unsuspecting morsel. Even after frost, when snow has yet to bring the prairie plants to their knees, the seeds and stems against the sky fill a camera's frame or a mind's eye majestically.

It is difficult to move on from here.

Perhaps it's the ephemeral nature of the prairie that draws one back to it. The grasses change from just showing green above the soil in May to shoulder high in August seems like magic. Trees are visible year-round but the moment of the prairie seems fleeting; yet, like the trees, long-lived perennials carry on life beneath the surface of the earth six months of the year.

Continuing the counterclockwise loop, the trail heads downhill past some beautiful tall tuliptrees under which is a jumble of vines, including another alien, Japanese honeysuckle. Now on a crushed limestone surface, the trail reaches a bridge with king-post truss sides. Swinging left, it rises from the creek, passing nice shagbark hickories, oaks, and sugar maples before dropping again to a small creek. More tall timber appears as the trail continues to swing right, then passes an open area where there is a sign saying "wildlife management area."

More beautiful tuliptrees and then mixed hardwoods stand above red cedars as the trail drops to the same small creek. There is a small pond off to the right. The trail passes occasional meadow openings and stands of juniper, then turns left along the stream where jewelweed sparkles with dew in late summer. A narrower trail here, it turns left, crossing water bars as it drops to a raised boardwalk over a small draw. Moving uphill on a few wooden steps, the trail moves gently to the right and rises to the top of a low hill.

Now moving through young woodland that must have been pastureland not too long ago, the trail heads in a left arc toward its junction with the trail to the parking lot.

This short hike starts out very

TRAIL THROUGH ESTABLISHED PRAIRIE AT MIAMI WHITEWATER FOREST

ordinary but becomes very special at the farthest point from the trailhead. Enjoy it year-round, but especially in late July and August.

To reach Oakleaf Trail, travel north on Park Road, cross West Road, and continue on Park Road to its intersection with Timber Lakes Road. Leave Park Road on Timber Lakes Road, taking it to Timber Lakes picnic area. There is a restroom close by. The entrance to Oakleaf Trail is directly across from the restroom door. There is a sign describing the trail and an arrow pointing the way. The 1.25-mile-long trail is described as moderately difficult, requiring an hour to an hour-and-a-half to travel.

This foot trail drops quickly off the

understory, but toward the bottom of the slope a more natural layering of small trees, shrubs, and groundcover returns.

Where the trail reaches the lake area there is a sign that tests your knowledge about oak trees, with upside-down answers. As I read through the quiz, a male Carolina wren called its "teakettle, teakettle, teakettle" song loudly and clearly quite nearby.

There are two "timberlakes." The trail passes over the earthen dam that impounds the one to the right. The headwaters of the one to the left is the outlet stream that comes under the dike from the lake to the right. Above the sill pipe carrying water between the lakes grow spotted jewelweed and tall bellflower in late summer. The lakes appear fairly clean and not overgrown with the algae often seen on park and golf course lakes. Perhaps they get less light in this fairly deep ravine, but they do drain land outside of the park; it is hard to determine what nutrient load the runoff may bring to them.

At the end of the dike, turn right to travel counterclockwise around the loop trail. Soon an interpretive sign tells about the beech trees of the area, admonishing visitors to stroke but not to cut the grey bark of these lovely trees. A 4-foot-wide boardwalk carries the trail to the pond shore where a handrail is provided for safe travel. Quiet in August, this pond must resound with the "jug-a-rum" of bull frogs in late May and June.

At the end of the boardwalk the trail returns to the hillside on gravel. Soon a short bridge spans a small stream entering from the left. Beyond the bridge there is an interpretive sign touting the successful return (on their own) of pileated woodpeckers to the area. Watch

high ground, passing through tall hardwoods. On the day I walked it, a wood pewee was calling in the distance. The entry trail down the slope has been rerouted with switchbacks to correct an erosion problem. The crushed limestone trail is also provided with water bars to reduce erosion. At the onset of the trail there seems to be an absence of a good and listen for one of these crow-size, red-crested black-and-white woodpeckers of the deep forest. They are a joy to see in flight or to watch as they probe a standing dead tree for carpenter ants and other edibles.

Just before the pond turns into a creek the trail becomes a boardwalk for a short way, then turns to the left up the hill. Climbing perhaps 150 feet in elevation and traveling maybe 150 yards in distance, the trail has well-spaced ties to keep the gravel in place. Before reaching the top of the hill, the trail turns left, still moving through pleasant mixed mesophytic deciduous forest. Sugar maples make up much of the understory in these deep woods. The trail finally reaches the wide ridge top, with land falling off to both right and left. There is a large burl on an oak tree here, and a sign talks about the parasitic plant, squawroot, that is common under the oak trees in the area.

As the trail begins to drop, widely spaced water bars begin to show up on the trail. Where it turns left to return to the valley of the "timberlakes," an interpretive sign appears, carrying the story of the incredible nutrients that come from fallen trees. Soon you will head straight down the trail to the water's edge. Before reaching the shore, the trail turns to the left to curve its way back to where it splits at the east end of the dike. First, though, there is a trail to the lake's edge that every hiker will want to take before completing the loop. As I approached the lake, a wood duck lifted off the lake to my right.

Return to the main trail and drop down six railroad-tie steps to near lake level. Then climb the hillside to move upstream and rejoin the trail across the dike to the hill and parking lot.

With nothing more exciting than beautiful tall oaks, hickories, beech, and other hardwoods, this trail appears to be lightly used. It is a real jewel, however, to be revisited often.

The same parking lot serves Badlands Trail, the third and longest of the Miami Whitewater Forest trails. According to the trailhead sign, this trail was named for some unique geological formations that occur along it. Many theories have been proposed as to their origins, but most likely they are large sinkholes made from eroded limestone. Note the "slippery when wet" warning at the trailhead. This hike, the most "natural" and most challenging of the park's trails, is 1.7 miles long and may take up to two hours to negotiate.

Almost immediately after leaving the trailhead sign, the trail drops downhill under tall oaks, hickories, sugar maples, and ash trees on a gravel surface. When it reaches the split that creates the loop the surface becomes dirt, or often mud. An arrow on a Carsonite post points to the left. The clockwise trail begins by hugging the hillside on the left side of the valley. There appears to be no shrub or understory layer, perhaps due to a present or past deer overgrazing problem. The absence of any lily family members on the hillsides seems to further substantiate this theory.

There is no better way to describe this trail than as "badlands." It negotiates the most unusual natural landscape that I have ever traveled in Ohio—a collection of pockets and knolls, narrow ridges and gullies, that is hard to believe. You will negotiate short railroad-tie steps with handrails, longer rises with water bars, here and there a piece of boardwalk, a number of bridges, including one 25 feet long, and more.

You will witness vegetative cover from mature forest to lone, white oak "wolf trees" and areas covered with sassafras and dogwood, indicating acid substrate. The vegetation is, however, mostly red cedars growing on the thin soil derived from Ordovician bedrock.

Much of the time while negotiating this trail I had no idea where I was. After many twists and turns, ups and downs, and creek and gully crossings, I descended a slope with railroad-tie water bars, yet still so slippery that I held onto the papaw trees on the right before reaching the 18-foot bridge over a dry streambed.

After that, I climbed a steep hillside with 10 railroad ties serving as steps of a fashion. As the trail began to level out, suddenly I ended up back at the junction where I had entered the badlands. A turn to the left and I was back on crushed limestone, scurrying across the 30 railroad-tie water bars on the short trail back to the parking lot.

This is a rugged, walking-stick ramble in a class by itself. Don't try it alone, like I did, but do try it: you'll like it.

50

Shawnee State Forest

TOTAL DISTANCE: 6.5 miles (10.4 km)

HIKING TIME: 6 hours

MAXIMUM ELEVATION: 1,210 feet

VERTICAL RISE: 512 feet

MAPS: USGS 7.5' Pond Run; ODNR
Shawnee State Forest Backpack Trail
brochure

When I wrote *50 Hikes in Ohio*, in 1989, I spent nine days of rigorous hiking on the 50-mile Shawnee Backpack Trail. I slept at every campsite and made copious notes and many photographs of my trailside observations. When my manuscript was returned from my editor after her first reading, for reasons of total book length, most of the trail north of SR 125 had been deleted. I understood the need to shorten the chapter but I was a bit more than disappointed. I had been on the trail in the last week of April, that magic time when the vernal wildflowers are near their peak of bloom and the neotropical birds are moving through the yet-to-leaf-out trees. It was on this part of the trail that I made my most exciting observations. A male scarlet tanager sat on a branch close to the trail singing at the top of his voice; a zebra swallowtail nectared on long-spurred violets close to my feet on the uphill side of the path; a ruffed grouse brooded eggs on a nest almost at my elbow and a box turtle moved along the trail at about the same speed I was traveling. This part of the trail was the most difficult, with steep climbs, but my travels on it were three wonderful days that I will never forget.

Since that time, the Shawnee State Forest staff has developed a new trail in this part of the forest that offers the opportunity to explore this rugged land without a backpack. The 6.5-mile Day Hike Trail travels about the same distance as a day's walk between campsites on Backpack Trail, but it is a loop trail that begins and ends just across SR 125 from the State Park Nature Center at the spillway end of Turkey Creek Lake. It is, by far, the most challenging trail in this volume, as it accomplishes a vertical rise (and fall) of a little more than 500

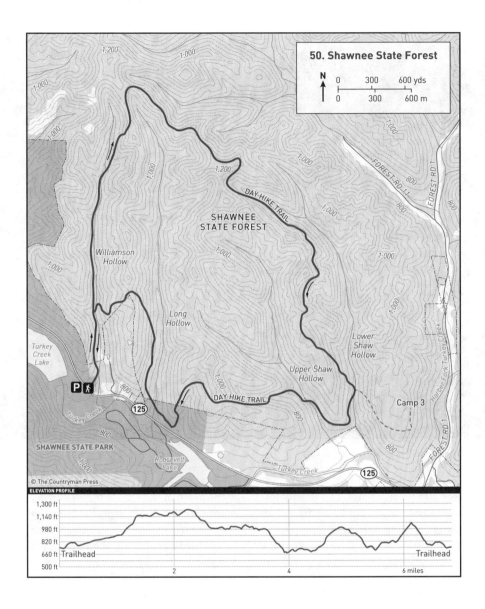

feet. There is no potable water available along the trail except near Backpack Trail Campsite #3, several hundred yards off the trail, so the hiker must carry drinking water. This is a trail to be taken by seasoned hikers in good physical condition who understand the challenge that it will present. But walking it will return rewards far beyond those of most of the other trails presented herein. Enjoy.

More than 63,000 acres, Shawnee State Forest is Ohio's largest state forest. Located mostly in Scioto County, in the Shawnee-Mississippian District of the Allegheny Plateau, it is the location of the most deeply dissected high-relief terrain in the state. Mississippian

SPRING COMES TO SHAWNEE STATE FOREST

Age siltstones, shales, and locally thick sandstones make up its bedrock, with the latter often seen as outcroppings on the hillsides. Mixed oak forests cover its ridges and south-facing slopes. Mixed mesophytic woods occupy the coves and northern exposures. It is the home to many rare wildflowers. The state endangered timber rattlesnake and the northern copperhead (both venomous) are found in the forest, especially in the vicinity of rock outcrops and shelters and rock-covered slopes. Nearly all of the fur-bearing quadrupeds of unglaciated Ohio, including black bear and bobcat, make their home here. Wild turkeys are common throughout.

Because of the extent of the un-fragmented forest, there is probably no better place in Ohio for the nesting of deep forest birds, including the neotropical songbirds that fly thousands of miles from Central and South America each spring to raise their young in eastern North America's deciduous forests. Insect larvae like loopers and inch worms, feeding on the tender young leaves of hardwoods, are food for vireos and warblers. Some of my best observations and photographs of Ohio's flora and fauna, butterflies especially, have been made in Shawnee State Forest, the "Little Smokies of Ohio."

This area's existence as public "natural resource lands" dates back to 1922, when 5,000 acres of cleared and fire-ravaged land were acquired. How it grew to what it is today is a long story, and worth reading in the state forest brochure. At the beginning of the twenty-first century, it includes an area designated as a state park within its borders, where there is a resort lodge, cabins, campground, golf course, marina, fishing lakes, nature center, and much more. In addition to harvesting timber on a selected rotational basis, the Division of Forestry maintains several hundred miles of bridle and hiking trails, a system of roads, and a wilderness and backcountry management area. Nearly all of the land is open to public hunting under the management of the Division of Wildlife.

GETTING THERE

To reach the Shawnee State Forest area, drive south from Central Ohio on US 23 to Portsmouth, then travel west on US 52 to Friendship. There, take SR 125 approximately 5.5 miles to the parking lot at the spillway end of Turkey Creek Lake on the left (south) side of the highway.

If you're up for more hiking while you in this special part of Ohio, consider walking the trails at The Nature Conservancy's Edge of Appalachia Preserve near the Adams County community of Lynx, about 12 miles west on SR 125. The Lynx and Buzzardroost Rock trails, along with a recently developed trail in The Wilderness unit of the more than 1,200-acre preserve, are described elsewhere in this volume. There are lodge

BLUETS AT SHAWNEE STATE FOREST

rooms, cabins, and a campground at Shawnee State Park, in addition to good motels and restaurants in Portsmouth along US 23 and US 52 in the town of West Union.

THE HIKE

To begin a day's adventure in Shawnee Forest, park your vehicle at the east end of the boat ramp parking area near the Turkey Creek Lake dam, adjacent to the Nature Center. The entrance to the trail is at a cable gate directly across SR 125 from the parking lot entrance drive. A single sign identifies the start of the trail. Blue paint blazes mark the trail; if you go a considerable distance without seeing a blaze, it's always a good plan to backtrack to the last paint blaze to make certain that you did not inadvertently miss a turn.

The trail leaves the highway on a grassy lane but soon turns into a woodland trail. A short way up the trail you will come to a side trail to the left marked with white blazes. This is the connecting trail that leads to the Backpack Trailhead. Ignore it and continue straight ahead into Williamson Hollow.

There will now be both blue and white blazes because this connecting trail utilizes the same tread as Day Hike Trail in connecting the Backpack Trail parking lot with Campsite #3. After a half mile of hiking, with the trail now following the right bank of the hollow, you will reach another junction with a white- and blue-blazed trail going to the right. This is the Backpack Trail connecting trail and also the returning trail of the Day Hike loop. I suggest traveling Day Hike Trail in a clockwise direction, thus taking the left fork to walk on the trail marked with blue blazes only. For the next mile, the trail goes nearly due north as it rises 1,200 feet at a fairly steady climb. It's a long, slow trek that will take close to an hour, but when the trail finally makes a hard turn to the right, you will be near the highest point on the hike.

The trail then follows the ridge in a southeasterly direction for about three quarters of a mile, then drops 200 feet down the right slope to catch the left side of another ridge at the 1,000-foot elevation level. After more walking near the ridge, you will turn due south and travel on the high land between Upper and Lower Shaw Hollows before dropping into the lower reaches of the latter.

Once at the lower elevation, you will encounter the white-blazed connecting trail exiting to the left that leads to Backpack Trail Campsite #3. The water cistern for that site is along this trail. If you plan to camp overnight in the forest, you must use a designated campsite and register for its use in advance. This campsite is the only one close to Day Hike Trail. To preregister, before you start your hike from the Day Hike trailhead drive to the Backpack Trail registration shelter located about three quarters of a mile farther west, at the intersection of SR 125 and the main park road that leads to the lodge and cabins. The last time I spent a night at Campsite #3, I watched a spectacular thunderstorm pass to the south. I was prepared to pull up stakes and evacuate my hillside site if lightning came too close, but I did not have to do so. If you do plan to camp, in order not to deplete the forest of firewood, I recommend that you carry a portable stove of some sort. In addition to a potable water source close by, there are latrines and a fire ring to contain your campfire at the site. In the springtime, you may drift off to sleep with whippoorwills calling

PAPAWS IN BLOOM ABOVE TRAIL AT SHAWNEE STATE FOREST

and awaken to the drumming of ruffed grouse or the gobbling of turkeys.

To complete the Day Hike loop, turn west at the trail junction (or return to it if you overnighted at Campsite #3) and follow the trail as it rises and then falls into Upper Shaw Hollow. Again, it is blazed with both blue and white. Then, heading west, the trail goes up a side ravine to eventually reach the 1,000-foot elevation, before turning south on the first leg of a long switchback that drops into Long Hollow. A steep 150-foot climb up the west slope of Long Hollow precedes a gentler 300-foot northward ascent to the high ground above Williamson Hollow and the outbound trail. From there, it's all downhill, as the trail drops 300 feet to the trail split. A left turn leads you out of the mouth of Williamson Hollow, past the Backpack side trail, with its white blazes, and exits right to the trailhead. Across the road is the Turkey Creek Nature Center/ Boat Ramp parking lot.

Index